Complete Norwegian

Teach Yourself®

Complete Norwegian

Margaretha Danbolt Simons

The publisher has used its best endeavours to ensure that the URLs for external websites referred to in this book are correct and active at the time of going to press. However, the publisher has no responsibility for the websites and can make no guarantee that a site will remain live or that the content is or will remain appropriate.

For UK order enquiries: please contact Bookpoint Ltd, 130 Milton Park, Abingdon, Oxon OX14 4SB. *Telephone:* +44 (0) 1235 827720. *Fax:* +44 (0) 1235 400454. Lines are open 09.00–18.00, Monday to Saturday, with a 24-hour message answering service. Details about our titles and how to order are available at www.teachyourself.co.uk

For USA order enquiries: please contact McGraw-Hill Customer Services, PO Box 545, Blacklick, OH 43004-0545, USA. *Telephone:* 1-800-722-4726. *Fax:* 1-614-755-5645.

For Canada order enquiries: please contact McGraw-Hill Ryerson Ltd, 300 Water St, Whitby, Ontario L1N 9B6, Canada. *Telephone:* 905 430 5000. *Fax:* 905 430 5020.

Long renowned as the authoritative source for self-guided learning – with more than 40 million copies sold worldwide – the *Teach Yourself* series includes over 300 titles in the fields of languages, crafts, hobbies, business, computing and education.

British Library Cataloguing in Publication Data: a catalogue record for this title is available from the British Library.

Library of Congress Catalog Card Number: on file.

First published in UK 1997 as *Teach Yourself Norwegian* by Hodder Arnold, 338 Euston Road, London, NW1 3BH.

First published in US 1997 as *Teach Yourself Norwegian* by Contemporary Books, a division of the McGraw-Hill Companies, 1 Prudential Plaza, 130 East Randolph Street, Chicago, IL 60601 USA.

This edition published 2010.

Typeset by MPS Limited, a Macmillan Company.

Printed in Great Britain for Hodder Arnold, a division of Hodder Headline, 338 Euston Road, London NW1 3BH by Cox & Wyman Ltd, Reading, Berkshire.

Hodder Headline's policy is to use papers that are natural, renewable and recyclable products and made from wood grown in sustainable forests. The logging and manufacturing processes are expected to conform to the environmental regulations of the country of origin.

Impression number	10 9 8 7 6 5 4 3 2 1
Year	2013 2012 2011 2010

Contents

Credits

Front cover: © Johner Images/Alamy

Back cover and pack: © Jakub Semeniuk/iStockphoto.com, © Royalty-Free/Corbis, © agencyby/iStockphoto.com, © Andy Cook/iStockphoto.com, © Christopher Ewing/iStockphoto.com, © zebicho – Fotolia.com, © Geoffrey Holman/iStockphoto.com, © Photodisc/Getty Images, © James C. Pruitt/iStockphoto.com, © Mohamed Saber – Fotolia.com

Pack: © Stockbyte/Getty Images

Acknowledgements

My greatest thanks are due to my editors at Hodder, Ginny Catmur and Laura Baxter, who patiently saw me through the whole process. I would also like to thank Karen Short from the University of Surrey for making my life so much easier and John Hart from Esher College for always being at hand to help me with English. A big 'thank you' goes to my son, Nick, for all his work keeping my computer going.

Thanks also to my friends in Norway, Kate Holen and Inger Marie Raastad, for their valuable help with local information. The enthusiasm of my family, William and Fiona, Steven and Pooh, Rebekka and Graeme and Nick and Rachel has been a great inspiration.

For Tom, Annie and Billy

Meet the author

My first teaching job was at a small school in a remote area of North Norway. From the start I knew that I was going to love teaching.

I have been living in England now for a very long time, where I teach Norwegian at many levels: at the University of Surrey (Norwegian ab initio on the MA in Translation Studies), at Adult Learning evening classes, and privately, and my love of teaching is as strong as ever. The courses I've written for the Teach Yourself series (**Complete Norwegian** and **Speak Norwegian**) naturally reflect the way I teach.

My students come from all walks of life, and all have reasons for wanting to learn Norwegian. My students are would-be or frequent travellers, people who want to live and work in Norway, spouses or grandparents and future translators. Many become close friends and keep in touch.

Every summer I stay in Norway for 2 to 3 months, immersing myself in Norwegian life and catching up on new trends, slang expressions and literature. This also gives me the opportunity to bring back new material for my classes.

Complete Norwegian, now in its 4th edition, progresses from simple greetings to more advanced topics. The essential grammar is clear and the cultural notes helpful. The book covers shopping and money, hotels and travel, accidents and parties as well as Norwegian festivals. The feed-back I get is very rewarding.

My students love the continuing story about the ups and downs of an English girl during her first year living in Norway. Her Norwegian boyfriend puts up with a lot!

Margaretha Danbolt Simons

Only got a minute?

You will soon notice that there are many words that are the same in English and Norwegian. Here are a few Norwegian words: 'restaurant', 'museum', 'park', 'bank', 'TV', 'arm', 'finger' and 'pub'. Recognize them?

There are many Norwegian words which aren't difficult to understand even though there is a slight difference in spelling: 'hotell', 'buss', 'universitet', 'fotball' and 'traktor'. So, as you can see, it isn't all completely new and different.

But be aware of what we call 'false friends'! An English lady was shocked to hear that her Norwegian gentleman friend was going to buy himself a dress! She didn't know that the word 'dress' means 'suit' in Norwegian. This course will help you to avoid such pitfalls.

When you look at a Norwegian text you will notice that there are some peculiar letters. There are three of them, and they look like this: **Æ**, **Ø** and **Å**.

They are situated at the end of the alphabet in that order, and they are all vowels.

How do they sound?

Æ is pronounced like the '*a*' in *cat*. Norwegian sheep say: **'Bææææ'** Try it!

Ø is pronounced similarly to the '*i*' in *first* or *bird*. The Norwegian word for *beer* is '**øl**'– a word which may be useful to know.

Å is pronounced as *aw*. Think of *awful* or *awesome* and you have got it.

So these are the three extra letters in the Norwegian Alphabet. On the other hand, some of the other letters are not really used at all.

Apart from in 'camping' and 'vitamin C', the letter **C** isn't used much at all. Where a 'c' is pronounced as 'k', it is written as 'k' and when it sounds like 's', that's how we write it.

There are no words with **Q** in Norwegian other than the name 'Quisling', now meaning *traitor*.

X and **Z** are only used in a few words of foreign origin.

5 Only got five minutes?

Norway is a beautiful country with stunning scenery. You may think I am biased, being Norwegian, but don't take my word for it – find out for yourself. The Northern Lights on clear frosty winter nights is a sight you will never forget. The midnight sun can be enjoyed north of the Arctic Circle in good summer weather. The further north you get, the longer the period when the sun never sets. But did you hear about the foreigner who, after witnessing the sun hovering over the horizon at midnight in northern Norway, exclaimed disappointedly: 'But where is the midnight sun? I can only see the ordinary sun!!'

When you are in Norway of course you will want to make contact with people, and so the first thing to learn is introductions. In Norway it is usual that one introduces oneself. You will also like to know where people come from, where they live and work and their nationality. You will want to give information about yourself as well. All this is covered in the first unit of the book.

The most common greeting in Norway is 'hei', meaning *hi* or *hello*. A more formal greeting is 'god dag' meaning *good day*.

Next you will want to introduce yourself. You could say *My name is ...*, which in Norwegian is a bit formal. More informal is 'Jeg heter ...', meaning *I am called ...*

You may want to point out that you are English: 'Jeg er engelsk', meaning *I am English*, also where you come from: 'Jeg kommer fra ...,' *I come from ...*, and where you live: 'Jeg bor i ...', *I live in/at ...*'.

Jeg heter ... *I am called ...*

Jeg er engelsk *I am English*

Jeg kommer fra England *I come from England*

Jeg bor i York *I live in York*

Perhaps you would like to get similar information from your new contact. For this you will need some question words. Almost all Norwegian question words start with 'hv', just as in English they start with *'wh'*: 'hva' means *what* and 'hvor' means *where*.

Asking questions is easy in Norwegian. Just rearrange the words and forget about the English *do*!

Hva heter du? *What are you called?*

Hvor kommer du fra? *Where do you come from?*

Hvor bor du? *Where do you live?*

A useful short cut is to return a question with: 'og du?' meaning *and you?*

Each unit in the book has a section called: **This is how we say it.** Here you will find many useful 'phrase book' expressions.

Norwegian: two languages

Norway, together with Denmark and Sweden, comprise the Scandinavian countries. Their languages are very similar, and Norwegians, Swedes and Danes can easily understand each other. There are in fact two languages spoken in Norway, **nynorsk** and **bokmål**. In this course we teach **bokmål**. It is spoken by about 85% of the population. **Nynorsk** means 'new Norwegian', and it is spoken by about 15% of the population. This language is really a collection of dialects and became an official language more than 100 years ago. Over the last 50 years **nynorsk** has declined, but all

Norwegians must learn both languages. The reason for there being two languages in Norway is historical.

For more than 400 years until 1814, Norway was part of Denmark. Norway and Denmark separated after the last Napoleonic war, when Denmark was on the losing side, and Norway was handed over to Sweden, which was on the winning team. Norway and Sweden formed a union, and Norway was now a nation more or less in its own right. In 1905, Norway finally obtained full independence.

During the years under Danish rule, Danish was the written language in both countries. After 1814 it became important for the Norwegians to have their own language.This happened in two ways. One was that more and more Norwegian spoken words were incorporated into written Danish, thus letting the language gradually develop. This language is called **Bokmål** meaning bookspeak, and it has diverged quite a lot from the original Danish.

The other way was to make a new language using the various dialects which had flourished in the valleys and the countryside. This language was at first called **Landsmål** meaning countryspeak, but was later renamed **Nynorsk**, meaning New Norwegian, and is the other official language in Norway.

After the Second World War almost 35% of Norwegians used **Nynorsk** as their main language, but this proporiton has been reduced to about 15%. The two languages have drifted towards each other over the years, but are still two separate languages, which all children must learn in school.

Where is **Nynorsk** in relation to Danish and Swedish? Taking similar words into consideration, we could place them in this order

Danish – Norwegian Bokmål – Nynorsk – Swedish

Worth noticing is that **Nynorsk** is the only language which operates with three genders. **Bokmål** has an optional feminine gender, but uses mainly two, common gender and neuter, in common with Danish and Swedish. In this book we use two genders, but the three-gender system is explained.

There are countless similar words in the Scandinavian languages, but beware of 'false friends'! A Swedish tourist to Norway asked the taxi driver to take him to **'et rolig sted'**. In Swedish this would mean a *fun, lively place*. He was surprised to find himself in a cemetery, as **'rolig'** in Norwegian means *quiet*.

The Dane told his Norwegian girlfriend that she was **'rar'**, meaning *nice* in Danish. She wasn't very pleased, as **'rar'** means *strange, peculiar* in Norwegian. **'å grine'** in Danish is *to laugh*, while in Norwegian it is *to cry*. Nevertheless, the Scandinavians are still good friends!

Finland and Iceland are Nordic countries, but they are not part of Scandinavia. The Icelandic language is in fact old Norse, which cannot be understood by Norwegians, Swedes or Danes unless they have studied it. Finnish is a language from a completely different language group.

The far north of Russia, Finland, Sweden and Norway is home to the Sami people. The Samis have a very different language, which is more related to Finnish. In the most northern county of Norway, Finnmark, there are Sami as well as Norwegian road signs, and you quickly realize that Sami and Norwegian have nothing in common!

Introduction

The aim of this course is to enable the student to speak and read everyday Norwegian, and to gain insight into the Norwegian culture and way of life.

Complete Norwegian is designed for the absolute beginner; no previous knowledge of any foreign language is required. Grammar is kept to a minimum; only what is necessary for this course is included, and grammatical terms are carefully explained.

Complete Norwegian is written in Bokmål. Bokmål is the standard Norwegian language, used by approximately 85–90% of Norwegians. It developed from the Dano-Norwegian, originating during the 400 or so years when Norway was part of Denmark, a union which ended in 1814. Nynorsk is the other official language of Norway and comprises a collection of Norwegian dialects. The remaining 10–15% of the population uses Nynorsk as their written language.

Norwegian is not a difficult language for an English-speaking person. Many words are similar. Pronunciation may at first seem a bit difficult, but there are some basic rules to follow. These are covered in the following section. The recording is a further help.

You will see in the list overleaf that each unit has several sections in it. To start you off, there is a list of what you will learn in the unit; then you can work through three dialogues or texts. These are followed by vocabulary boxes that list, in detail, the new words and phrases that have been introduced in the preceding dialogue or text. In this way, you can read through the dialogue or text, and/or listen to it on the recording at the same time, a few times so that you can get the gist of the situation. Then, to increase your vocabulary learning, you can look through the vocabulary box and make sure you understand all of it. It is helpful to say the words and phrases out loud, and to write them out so that you memorize them more easily. Finally, there are some **True or false?** phrases to make sure that you have really understood the dialogue/text.

Remember that the best way to learn a language is to listen and read a little and often and to increase your confidence gradually – this is far better than spending long infrequent sessions poring over the books!

The next section is called **This is how we say it,** and this gives you plenty of new phrases relating to the situations in the unit as a whole.

Language patterns and structures are the basis of the language and you need to master these so that you can express yourself freely in spoken and written Norwegian. It is not the most difficult language, but there are lots of turns of phrase and unexpected structures that are clearly and fully explained in this course. Make the most of the examples in this section because they will come in useful later when you are doing the practice section and the prompted speaking exercise at the very end of every unit.

Throughout the book there are sections giving you lots of useful information about the Norwegian way of life: just the sort of thing you will find most intriguing whenever you visit Norway, or if you get talking to a Norwegian abroad.

Finally, it is a good idea to do the exercise section soon after reading the language patterns sections so that the grammar is still fresh in your mind. However, remember to look back at previous units' language patterns sections to revise as you work through the course. At the back of the book there is a useful index to the grammar subjects. There are also lists of irregular nouns, irregular verbs and modal verbs as a useful reference once you are producing written Norwegian and you need to pay attention to the details.

All the answers to the exercises are listed in the back of the book, but make sure you complete each exercise, or even each unit of exercises, before looking up the answers.

Listen to the recording as much as you can. Even when you are not actually working with the book, remember to take the recording with you in case you have a few spare moments to listen to it – in the car, on a personal stereo on the train, while gardening or doing housework! It is a good idea to listen to the dialogues that you have worked on so that you refresh your memory of all the words and phrases used.

There are 16 units, each following the same pattern.

Every unit starts with an English summary of what you will learn.

Dialogue or text
There are three at the beginning of each unit. Use the recording to hear the correct pronunciation.

Vocabulary
After each dialogue or text there is a list of new words and expressions in the order in which they appear in the dialogue or text.

True or false
After each text there are some statements which may or may not be true. The aim of this exercise is for you to check whether you have understood the text.

This is how we say it
A repetition of useful expressions from the text and some extra ones which may come in useful.

Language and patterns
Notes on grammatical structures and how to use them.

Exercises

These are for you to practise what you have learnt. (Answers at the back.)

Do you understand?

In some units we give you another dialogue (sometimes, but not always, on the recording). This time your part is in English, so you have to translate.

Symbol and abbreviation

🔊 Material included on the recording.

lit. literally

Pronunciation

CD1, TR 1, 00:36

Norwegian is quite easy to pronounce, because it is usually spoken as it is written. There are some rules to follow, and some special sounds to get used to. When you have managed these, you will not find it difficult to pronounce Norwegian.

It is a good idea to listen to the recording and imitate the Norwegians you hear. If you live in the UK, you will be able to find Norwegian radio stations, but the reception is usually best late at night.

The most important thing to remember is that each letter is pronounced. An 'e' at the end of a word is always pronounced distinctly.

The Norwegian alphabet has 29 letters. There are three extra letters at the end of the alphabet used by English speakers. These are: Æ (as in cat), Ø (as in first) and Å (as in awful). The letters in brackets below indicate the pronunciation of the letter.

A	a	(ah)	K	k	(kaw)	U	u	(oo)
B	b	(beh)	L	l	(el)	V	v	(veh)
C	c	(seh)	M	m	(em)	W	w	(dobbeltveh)
D	d	(deh)	N	n	(en)	X	x	(eks)
E	e	(eh)	O	o	(o)	Y	y	(ee)
F	f	(ef)	P	p	(peh)	Z	z	(set)
G	g	(geh)	Q	q	(koo)	Æ	æ	(a)
H	h	(haw)	R	r	(air)	Ø	ø	(ir)
I	i	(ee)	S	s	(ess)	Å	å	(aw)
J	j	(jod)	T	t	(teh)			

Y is always a vowel in Norwegian and is pronounced more as in *typical* than *type*.

Vowels

🔊 CD1, TR 1, 02:32

There are nine vowels in Norwegian: **a, e, i, o, u, y, æ, ø, å.** The vowels are pure sounds as in French or Italian, and not diphthonged as in English.

The Norwegian vowels may be short or long. As a general rule vowels are long in open syllables, e.g. **si** (*say*), or if followed by a single consonant, e.g. **tak** (*roof*).

Vowels are short before a double consonant, e.g. **takk** (*thank you*).

hat	(*hatred*)	**hatt**	(*hat*)
dit	(*there*)	**ditt**	(*yours*)

Exceptions: Norwegian words cannot end in a double **m**, so there are some words which are pronounced with a short vowel even if there is only one consonant. For example:

rom	(*room*)
hjem	(*home*)

Also with a short vowel and single consonant are some common words:

han	(*he*)
hun	(*she*)
den	(*it*)

The vowels are divided into two groups:

a, o, u and **å** are hard vowels
e, i, y, æ and **ø** are soft vowels

This distinction is important for the pronunciation of words starting with **g** or **k**.

Norwegian vowel		Pronunciation	Example
a	long	like **a** in *father*	far (*father*)
a	short	"	hatt (*hat*)
e	long	like **ai** in *air*	sted (*place*)
e	short	like **e** in *bed*	gress (*grass*)
i	long	like **ea** in *eat*	min (*mine*)
i	short	like **i** in *kiss*	sild (*herring*)
o	long	like **o** in *moor*, but with tightly rounded lips	bok (*book*)
o	short	like **or** in *organ*	sokk (*sock*)
u	long	like **u** in *true*	hus (*house*)
u	short	like **u** in *full*	full (*full*)
y	long	**ee** with	by (*town*)
	short	rounded lips	kyss (*kiss*)
æ	long	like **a** in *cat*	være (*to be*)
	short		lærd (*learned*)
ø	long	like **ir** in *bird*	dør (*door*)
	short		først (*first*)
å	long	like **aw** in *awful*	år (*year*)
	short	like **o** in *not*	åtte (*eight*)

The pronunciation as described is only approximate. Listen carefully to the recording.

Pronunciation exercise

CD1, TR 1, 04:50

	Long vowels	Short vowels
a	Kari	Anne
e	Erik	Bente
i	Nina	Nils
o	Ole	Trond
u	Rut	Tulla
y	Yberg	Yngve
æ	Sæverud	Kjærstad
ø	Søren	Sølvi
å	Åse	Bård

Diphthongs

🔊 CD1, TR 2

There are three important diphthongs in Norwegian:

ei	as in the English *might*.	**vei**	(*road*)
		reise	(*travel*)
øy	no English equivalent.	**høy**	(*tall*)
	Don't say *Oi!*	**øye**	(*eye*)
	Say '**ø**' and then add the '**y**'.		
au	'**a**' as in *cat* followed by '**u**'.	**au!**	(*ouch!*)
		sau	(*sheep*)

Consonants

🔊 CD1, TR 2, 00:47

Norwegian consonant	Pronunciation	Example
b	like **b** in *bed*	**bok** (*book*)
c	only used in foreign words pronounced as s in front of soft vowels,	**centimeter**
	and as **k** in front of hard vowels	**camping**
d	like **d** in English	**dame** (*lady*)
f	like **f** in English	**fem** (*five*)
g	like **g** in *go* in front of hard vowels	**gate** (*street*)
	or consonants	**gris** (*pig*)
	like English **y** in front of soft vowels	**gi** (*give*)
h	like **h** in *hat*	**han** (*he*)
j	like **y** in *yes*	**ja** (*yes*)
k	like **k** in *kite* in front of hard	**Kari**
	vowels or consonants	**klær** (*clothes*)

	like **h** in *Hugh* in front of soft vowels	**kyss** (*kiss*)
l	like **l** in *life*	**liv** (*life*)
m	like **m** in ***miss***	**mor** (*mother*)
n	like **n** in ***not***	**ny** (*new*)
p	like **p** in ***pig***	**pen** (*pretty*)
q	like **q** in ***queen***. Only used in foreign words	**quiz**
r	in some parts of Norway the **r** is rolled	**reise** (*travel*)
s	like **s** in ***sense***	**se** (*see*)
	as **sh** in front of **l**	**slå** (*hit*)
t	like **t** in ***train***	**tog** (*train*)
v	like **v** in ***very***	**vil** (*will*)
w	as **v**. Only used in foreign words	**WC** (*toilet*)
x	as **s**. Only used in foreign words	**xylofon** (*xylophone*)
z	like **s**. Only used in foreign words	**zoo** (*zoo*)

Consonant combinations

CD1, TR 2, 02:14

ng	as in *ring*. The 'g' is not really sounded	**ring** (*ring*)
gn	as in *rain*, *slain*.	**regn** (*rain*)
sk	becomes **sh** before soft vowels	**skitt** (*dirt*)
skj	as **sh**	**skjorte** (*shirt*)
rs	often becomes **sh**	**norsk** (*Norwegian*)

Silent consonants

CD1, TR 2, 02:34

d	at the end of a word is almost always silent. Exceptions are: **ned** (*down*), **sted** (*place*).	
g	is silent in adjectives and adverbs ending in **-ig**	**deilig** (*delicious*) **ledig** (*free*)

h	is silent before j and **v**	**hjem** (*home*) **hva** (*what*)
t	is silent at the end of a definite neuter noun and at the end of **det** (*it*)	**huset** (*the house*)
v	is silent at the end of some words	**tolv** (*twelve*) **halv** (*half*)

Stress

CD1, TR 2, 03:20

In Norwegian the stress is normally on the first syllable. But there are many exceptions to this rule. This is particularly so with words of foreign origin. Words with German prefixes will usually have the stress on the second syllable:

betale (*pay*)
forklare (*explain*)

Words of Greek and Latin origin are stressed on the last syllable:

stasjon (*station*)
telefon (*telephone*)
universitet (*university*)

Accent

CD1, TR 2, 03:45

Peculiar to Norwegian and Swedish is the existence of two types of speech melody. This gives the languages that special singing sound. There are two 'tones': the single tone and the double tone.

The single tone is used for words with one syllable and for longer words ending in **-el**, **-en** and **-er**. It starts rather low and rises towards the end of the word:

pen (*pretty*)	**vakker** (*beautiful*)

The double tone is usually found in words with two or more syllables. It starts on a higher note than the single tone, dips about three tones and rises to a higher pitch than where it began:

pike (*girl*)	**deilig** (*delicious*)

Some pairs of words take on a different meaning by changing the tone:

Single tone	**Double tone**
hender (*hands*)	**hender** (*happens*)
ånden (*the spirit*)	**ånden** (*the breath*)

In essence, the single tone is a single increase in pitch in the course of a word. The double tone has a similar overall increase in pitch, but there is a slight fall initially before the increase takes place.

The Norwegian flag

1

Hei!

Hi!

In this unit you will learn

- ***How to greet people***
- ***How to introduce yourself***
- ***How to form simple statements and questions***
- ***How to form simple negative statements***

Dialogue 1

The main character in this book is Sue, who lives in London. She wants to go to Norway to work, so she has started going to a Norwegian class. Now she is in a café reading her **Complete Norwegian**. A boy stops at her table, looks at her book and says:

CD1, TR 3

Boy	Hei! Jeg er norsk!
Sue	Hei! Jeg er ikke norsk!

He sits down at her table.

Boy	Er du engelsk?
Sue	Ja, jeg er engelsk. Jeg bor i London. Hvor kommer du fra?
	(Contd)

Boy	Jeg kommer fra Norge. Jeg kommer fra Bergen, men jeg bor i London nå.
Sue	Hva heter du?
Boy	Jeg heter Arne. Hva heter du?
Sue	Jeg heter Sue.
Arne	Hei Sue!
Sue	Hei Arne!

Insight

We have used four verbs in this passage. They are in the present tense, which means the action they describe is happening now.

'er' *am/are/is*
'bor' *live/lives*
'kommer' *come/comes*
'heter' *am/are/is called*

You'll learn more about verbs in Language patterns 5 and 6.

QUICK VOCAB

bor (å bo) *live / lives*
du *you*
engelsk *English*
er (å være) *am / are / is*
fra *from*
hei! *hi!*
heter (å hete) *am called / are called / is called*
hva *what*
hvor *where*
i *in*
ikke *not*
ja *yes*
jeg *I*
kommer (å komme) *come / comes*
men *but*
Norge *Norway*
norsk *Norwegian*
nå *now*

True or false? 1

Say whether the following statements are true (T) or false (F).

(There will be a **True or false?** after each dialogue for you to test yourself.)

- **a** Sue er norsk.
- **b** Arne kommer fra Bergen.
- **c** Sue kommer ikke fra Norge.

Insight

An important expression is **'Jeg vil gjerne ...'** meaning *I would like to ...* You will be surprised how often this phrase is used! It will crop up a lot in this book.

Dialogue 2

Sue and Arne continue their conversation:

CD1, TR 4

Sue	Er du student i London?
Arne	Ja, jeg er student.
Sue	Jeg vil gjerne reise til Norge, og jeg lærer norsk.
Arne	Når vil du reise til Norge?
Sue	Jeg vil gjerne reise til Norge i sommer.
Arne	Vil du reise til Norge med fly?
Sue	Nei, jeg vil reise med motorsykkel.
Arne	Har du motorsykkel?
Sue	Ja, jeg har motorsykkel. Har du bil?
Arne	Nei, jeg har ikke bil. Jeg har sykkel.

Insight

If you are travelling by plane, you say: **'med fly'**, which really means *with plane*. In the same way, *by car* is **'med bil'**. It sounds a bit funny, but remember that one cannot always translate directly between languages.

QUICK VOCAB

bil (en) *car*
fly (et) *aeroplane*
har (å ha) *have / has*
i sommer *this summer*
lærer (å lære) *learn / learns*
med *with / by*
motorsykkel (en) *motorbike*
nei *no*
når *when*
og *and*
reise *travel*
student (en) *student*
sykkel (en) *bicycle*
til *to*
vil *will*
vil gjerne *would like to*

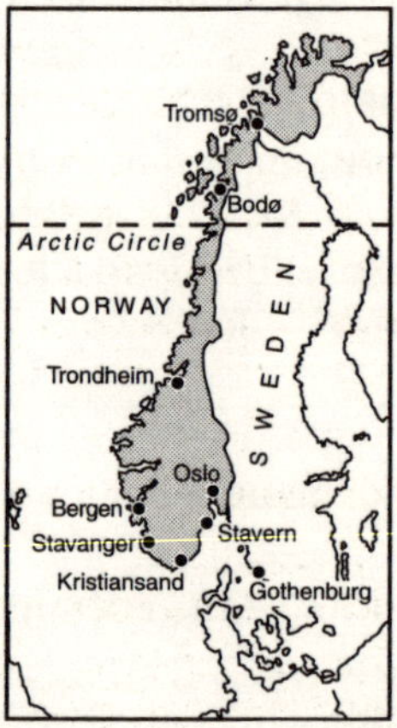

A useful expression
CD1, TR 4, 00:36

Jeg vil gjerne ... *I would like to ...*

True or false? 2

a Sue vil gjerne reise til Norge.
b Arne er ikke student.
c Sue kommer med fly til Norge.

Dialogue 3

Lørdag 1. april. *Saturday 1 April.* One month later. Sue and Arne meet in a pub. Arne tells Sue that he knows the couple sitting at another table.

CD1, TR 5

Sue	Hva heter han?
Arne	Han heter Odd. Han er norsk. Han kommer fra Oslo.
Sue	Er han student?
Arne	Ja, han er student.
Sue	Og hun, er hun engelsk?
Arne	Nei, hun er norsk. Hun heter Randi. Hun er au pair. Vil du ha et glass øl til?
Sue	Nei takk, jeg vil gjerne ha en kopp kaffe. Hva vil du ha?
Arne	Jeg vil ha et glass øl til.

Randi and Odd come over to them:

Odd	Hei, Arne! Hvordan har du det?
Arne	Fint, takk, – og du?
Odd	Bare bra. Hei!
Arne	Hun heter Sue. Sue lærer norsk. Hun vil gjerne reise til Norge.
Randi	Hei, Sue! Jeg heter Randi. Nå vil jeg gjerne ha et glass øl.
Sue	Hei, Randi! Fint å møte deg.
Odd	Jeg skal reise til Leeds nå. Jeg skal reise med tog. Ha det!
Arne	Fint å se deg! Ha det!

Insight

Did you notice that we don't say *of* in expressions of quantity?

'en kopp kaffe'	*a cup of coffee*
'et glass øl'	*a glass of beer*

QUICK VOCAB

au pair (en) *au pair*
bare *only / just*
bra *well / fine*
deg *you*
det *it*
en *a* (**en** words)
et *a* (**et** words)
fint *fine*
glass (et) *glass*
ha det! *bye bye!* (lit. *have it!*)
han *he*
hun *she*
hvordan *how*
kaffe (en) *coffee*
kopp (en) *cup*
møte *meet*
øl (et) *beer*
pub (en) *pub*
ser (å se) *see / sees*
skal *shall*
takk *thank you*
tog (et) *train*
å *to*

Some useful expressions
🔊 CD1, TR 5, 01:16

Jeg vil gjerne ha en kopp kaffe.	*I would like a cup of coffee.*
Jeg vil gjerne ha et glass øl.	*I would like a glass of beer.*
Jeg vil gjerne ha et glass øl til.	*I would like another glass of beer.*

True or false? 3

a Sue vil ha et glass øl.
b Odd skal reise til Leeds.
c Arne og Randi skal reise til Norge.

This is how we say it

🔊 CD1, TR 6

Expressions used in the dialogues:

Hva heter du?	*What is your name?/What are you called?*
Hvor kommer du fra?	*Where do you come from?*
Er du norsk?	*Are you Norwegian?*

Er du engelsk?	*Are you English?*
Jeg heter ...	*I am called ...*
Han heter Odd.	*He is called Odd.*
Hun heter Randi.	*She is called Randi.*
Jeg er student.	*I am a student.*
Han kommer fra Oslo.	*He comes from Oslo.*
Hei, Sue!	*Hi/hello, Sue!*
Ha det!	*'Have it'! Bye bye!*
Jeg vil gjerne reise til Norge.	*I would like to travel to Norway.*
Jeg vil gjerne ha en kopp kaffe.	*I would like a cup of coffee.*
Jeg vil gjerne ha en kopp kaffe til.	*I would like another cup of coffee.*

Insight

Norwegian is a 'gendered' language. And you actually have a choice! You can use three genders if you like: masculine, feminine and neuter; or stick with two: common gender and neuter. The two-gender system is slightly more conservative, and this book uses two genders. It is fully explained in Language patterns 2.

Language patterns

1 *En bil* a car, et tog a train

A noun is a word which means a thing, a person, animal or place. **Bil** (*car*), **student** (*student*), **katt** (*cat*) are examples of nouns.

Names of people or places, such as John, York, Norway are called proper nouns and are spelt with a capital letter in Norwegian as they are in English.

Norwegian nouns are either **en, ei** or **et** words. This is called the gender of the noun. In Norwegian every noun has a gender. This is masculine, feminine or neuter. The gender of a noun affects other words in connection with it. This means that each time you learn a new noun you should also try to remember the gender.

In the word lists you will find the gender **en, ei** or **et** in brackets after the noun. It is a good idea to try to memorize which gender word is needed with every new word you learn. This will save you a lot of time later when you become more confident using the language in spoken as well as written forms.

2 *En/(ei)/et* – English *'a'* or *'an'*

The indefinite article in English is *a* or *an*. In Norwegian, the indefinite articles are **en/(ei)/et**.

Here's a summary of the three genders in Norwegian:

en = *a/an*: masculine
(**ei** = *a/an*): feminine
et = *a/an*: neuter

All nouns belong to one of these categories.

Don't worry about the feminine gender because:

- most feminine nouns can be used as masculine
- there are not many feminine nouns
- in Norwegian literature, newspapers and formal speech, one seldom uses feminine gender.

For these reasons masculine and feminine nouns are grouped together and are called the common gender.

This leaves **en**-words and **et**-words.

In the **Vocabulary** at the back of the book, nouns will be listed like this:

bil (en) *car*
seng (en/ei) *bed*
tog (et) *train*

Unfortunately there are no simple rules to tell whether a noun is common or neuter gender. It is a good idea to try to learn the gender with the noun. You have already met these nouns. Now check their genders.

en bil *a car*
et tog *a train*
et fly *an aeroplane*
en motorsykkel *a motorbike*
en student *a student*
en sommer *a summer*

Note that there are no capital letters for seasons, months and days.

3 *Jeg har bil* – leaving out *'a'/'an'*

You might have noticed that it is not always necessary to use the word for *a* when stating certain situations, like: **jeg har bil**, and **jeg kommer med fly**.

The same applies for occupations. You usually say:

John er student.	*John is a student.*
Bente er au pair.	*Bente is an au pair.*
Hun er lærer.	*She is a teacher.*

4 *Jeg/du/han/hun/den/det* *I/you/he/she/it*

These words are called personal pronouns. These pronouns can be used to replace nouns.

John er engelsk.	*John is English.*
Han er engelsk.	*He is English.*
Bente kommer fra Norge.	*Bente comes from Norway.*
Hun kommer fra Norge.	*She comes from Norway.*

Den and **det** both mean *it*. **Den** is used to replace common gender words, whereas **det** is used to replace neuter words.

5 Verbs

A verb is a word which states what someone or something is doing. For example, **Kari reiser** (*Kari travels*) and **John går** (*John walks/goes*) are verb phrases.

Verbs are usually listed in what is called the infinitive. The infinitive of the verb expresses the meaning of the verb without being tied to who or what is doing the verb, or when it is taking place. In English a verb in the infinitive looks like this: *to travel*, *to go*.

With Norwegian verbs the infinitive is preceded by **å**, and usually ends in **e**. For example **å reise** (*to travel*). A few have no **e** ending as in **å gå** (*to walk/go*), **å se** (*to see*).

The shortest possible form of the verb is called the stem. You'll find the stem by removing the infinitive -e ending.

Infinitive:	**å reise** (to travel)	Stem: **reis**
Infinitive:	**å gå** (to walk/go)	Stem: **gå**

Endings are added for more identification; for example, to show if the action is taking place in the past, the present or the future.

6 Verbs in the present tense

Verbs are listed in the infinitive in reference sections such as a dictionary.

(å) reise *(to) travel*
(å) ha *(to) have*
(å) komme *(to) come*
(å) hete *(to) be called*
(å) bo *(to) live*

When you are deciding whether what is happening is taking place in the past, the present or the future, you are choosing what is called the 'tense'.

When you want to talk about what is happening to someone now, you use the present tense. To form the present tense you add an **r** to the infinitive.

Unlike in many other European languages it doesn't matter whether it is *I*, *you*, *he*, *she* or *it* who is carrying out the verb. You add an **r** to the infinitive regardless. It couldn't be simpler!

Infinitive	*I*	*you*	*he*	*she*	*it*
å reise	jeg reiser	du reiser	han reiser	hun reiser	den/det reiser
å ha	jeg har	du har	han har	hun har	den/det har
å komme	jeg kommer	du kommer	han kommer	hun kommer	den/det kommer
å hete	jeg heter	du heter	han heter	hun heter	den/det heter
å bo	jeg bor	du bor	han bor	hun bor	den/det bor

7 How to make sentences

Here are three basic sentences:

Statement:	**Han er norsk.**	*He is Norwegian.*
Negative:	**Han er ikke norsk.**	*He is not Norwegian.*
Question:	**Er han norsk?**	*Is he Norwegian?*

Han is the subject of these sentences, and **er** is the verb.

To form a question, you put the verb before the subject, as you can do in English! However, you can also use question words such as *what*, *where*, *who* or *how*. The word for *not* is **ikke**.

Question:	**Hva heter hun?**	*What is she called?*
Statement:	**Hun heter Kari.**	*She is called Kari.*
Negative:	**Hun heter ikke Kari.**	*She is not called Kari.*

When you use a question word, this comes first in the sentence.

Insight

So far we have used two of the modal ('helping') verbs, **'skal'** meaning *shall* and **'vil'** meaning *will*.

After a modal verb the main verb is always in the infinitive form. In Norwegian the infinitive is usually the same as the form for the present tense, but without the final 'r', whereas in English the infinitive is usually the same as the present tense. Look at this:

Jeg spiser. *I eat.*

I morgen skal jeg spise. *Tomorrow I shall eat.* (In Norwegian word order, 'Tomorrow shall I eat.')

So although in English the form after the modal verb is the same as after I in the present tense, this is not the case in Norwegian. This is easier to understand if we consider the verb *to be*, in which the infinitive and present tense after I are different:

Jeg er her. *I am here.*
Jeg skal være her i morgen. *I shall be here tomorrow.*

Remember: after a modal verb you need to use the infinitive, and in Norwegian the infinitive is not the same as the present tense, unlike English.

Exercises

1 Can you answer these questions? The first two – **a** and **b** – start **Jeg ...** . Look in the **Greetings** section overleaf for **c**.

a Hva heter du?
b Hvor kommer du fra?

c Hvordan har du det?
d Er du norsk?
e Hvor bor du?

2 How would you do the following? Look in the Greetings:
a Greet a friend.
b Say 'goodbye' to your elderly teacher.
c Say 'How do you do' to the Prime Minister.
d Say 'good night' to your family.
e Say 'bye bye' to a fellow student.

3 Answer these questions in the negative using **nei** and **ikke**:

CD1, TR 7

Example:	**Er Bente engelsk?**	**Nei, Bente er ikke engelsk.**
	Is Bente English?	*No, Bente is not English.*

a Er John norsk?
b Vil du ha en kopp kaffe?
c Kommer Bente fra York?
d Bor du i Wales?
e Har Bente bil?

4 Now can you change these statements into questions?

Example: Du er engelsk. Er du engelsk?

a John er norsk.
b Han kommer fra York.
c Du bor i London.
d Hun har bil.
e Bente lærer engelsk.

5 Make up questions for these answers, using the question words **hva**, **hvor** and **hvordan**.
a ____________________? Han heter John.
b ____________________? Jeg bor i London.

c ____________________? Takk, fint.
d ____________________? Han kommer fra York.
e ____________________? Han studerer norsk.

6 Fill in the gaps with a suitable verb to make a sentence:

Examples: John reiser med fly til Bergen. (*John travels by aeroplane to Bergen.*)
Han bor i London. (*He lives in London.*)

a Bente __________ med fly til Norge.
b John __________ i London.
c John __________ motorsykkel.
d Han __________ ikke bil.
e Kari __________ med tog til York.

7 Wordsearch: find the hidden Norwegian words in the grid below – they are either across or down. (There are seven of them.)

X	T	Z	A	J	Q	F	H	W	G	B
P	T	O	N	F	G	L	P	R	F	I
M	O	T	O	R	S	Y	K	K	E	L
M	G	H	R	L	D	Y	X	C	R	Q
X	G	M	S	Z	D	Z	Q	R	I	S
Q	Z	A	K	X	R	E	I	S	E	Z

If you get stuck, here are the English translations to help you: *aeroplane, travel, Norwegian, car, holiday, motorbike, train.*

Greetings

Norwegians like to shake hands, and invariably do so when they meet. Nowadays a peck on the cheek or a hug is common after having met a few times.

Hei is by far the most common greeting these days, and is used when one would say *hi* or *hello*.

Morn is another informal greeting.

More formal ways of greeting people:

god dag	*good day/hello/how do you do?*
god morgen	*good morning*
god kveld	*good evening*
god aften	*good evening*

Saying: Goodbye

ha det bra	*goodbye* (lit. *have it good*)
ha det godt	*goodbye* (lit. *have it good*)
ha det	*bye* (lit. *have it*)
morna	*bye bye*
adjø	*adieu/goodbye* (very formal)
på gjensyn	*looking forward to seeing you again*
god natt	*good night when going to bed*
god reise	*have a good trip/journey*

Asking: How are you?

hvordan har du det?	*how are you?*
hvordan går det?	*how goes it?*
takk, bare bra	*thank you, just fine*
takk, fint	*thank you, fine*
takk	*thank you*
mange takk	*many thanks*
tusen takk	*a thousand thanks*

Do you understand?

You meet a Norwegian student, and you want to practise your Norwegian. Give the Norwegian for the sentences in English:

CD1, TR 8

Du	(Say it in Norwegian!) *Are you Norwegian?*
Han	Ja, jeg er norsk. Men du er ikke norsk?
Du	*No, I am English. I am learning Norwegian.*
Han	Hva heter du?
Du	(Give your name.) *What are you called?*
Han	Jeg heter Per. Hvor kommer du fra?
Du	*I come from ________. And you?*
Han	Jeg kommer fra Nord-Norge.
Du	*Are you a student?*
Han	Ja, jeg er student. Jeg studerer medisin.
Du	*I shall travel to Norway in the summer.*
Han	Skal du reise med fly til Norge?
Du	*No, I have a motorbike.*

QV

medisin *medicine*
Nord-Norge *north Norway*
studerer (å studere) *study/studies*

The dialogues in this unit have given you about 60 words with which to start building up your vocabulary. So far we have avoided using genders, but read the Language patterns 1, 2 and 3 carefully, as genders will be used in Unit 2.

It is a good idea to make your own grammar summary as you go along.

Test yourself

Here are 10 multiple choice questions. You will find the answers in the key at the end of the book.

1 Hvor bor Sue?
  a I London. **b** I Bergen. **c** I York.

2 Hva lærer Sue?
  a Sue lærer engelsk. **b** Hun lærer ikke norsk.
  c Hun lærer norsk.

3 Har Arne bil?
  a Nei, han har motorsykkel. **b** Nei, han har sykkel.
  c Ja, han har bil.

4 Hvor vil Sue gjerne reise?
  a Hun vil gjerne reise til Wales. **b** Hun vil gjerne reise til USA.
  c Hun vil gjerne reise til Norge.

5 Skal Odd reise med bil til Leeds?
  a Odd skal reise med bil. **b** Odd skal reise med fly.
  c Odd skal reise med tog.

6 Er Odd au pair?
  a Odd er ikke au pair. **b** Sue er au pair.
  c Arne er au pair.

7 Vil Arne ha et glass øl?
  a Arne vil gjerne ha en kopp kaffe. **b** Arne vil ha et glass øl.
  c Arne vil ha en kopp te.

8 Hvor kommer Arne fra?
  a Han kommer fra Bergen. **b** Han kommer fra Bristol.
  c Han kommer fra Oslo.

9 Er Arne student i London?
  a Nei, han er ikke student. **b** Ja, han er student.
  c Nei, han er au pair.

10 Vil Sue reise med fly til Norge?
  a Sue vil reise med fly. **b** Sue vil reise med tog.
  c Sue vil reise med motorsykkel.

2

Jeg vil gjerne ...
I would like to ...

In this unit you will learn

- ***How to say what you do for a living***
- ***How to count to ten***
- ***How to get to Norway***
- ***The days of the week***

Insight

We shall be using the days of the week in this unit. Starting with 'mandag,' meaning: *Monday*, this is how they go: 'mandag', 'tirsdag', 'onsdag', 'torsdag', 'fredag', 'lørdag' and 'søndag'. They are not very different from their English counterparts, except perhaps 'onsdag', meaning: Wednesday, – named after the Norse god, Odin, and 'lørdag', meaning Saturday, which comes from the old Norse for washing – think of laundry. Not washing up or the house, mind you, but washing oneself before the holy day.

Sue and Arne start by telling each other what they do. Have a look at the vocabulary below the dialogue before you start.

Dialogue 1

Mandag 3. mai (*Monday 3 May*) Sue and Arne go for a walk and talk about what they do.

Sue	Jeg lærer norsk. Jeg vil gjerne bo i Norge.
Arne	Jeg er student. Jeg studerer. Jeg vil gjerne bli lærer. Jeg vil gjerne bli lærer på en stor skole i Norge.
Sue	Jeg vil gjerne bli hotell-direktør.
Arne	Jeg liker deg.
Sue	Jeg liker deg også.
Arne	Liker du å lære norsk?
Sue	Ja, jeg liker å lære norsk, men kurset er kjedelig. Læreren er kjedelig. Læreren er en kjedelig gammel dame.
Arne	Hvor er kurset?
Sue	Kurset er på en stor skole.
Arne	Når er kurset?
Sue	Kurset er hver mandag kveld.

CD1, TR 9

Insight

Arne is clearly a bit taken with Sue, and he says: **'jeg liker deg'** meaning: *I like you*. We know that *you* in English is **'du'** in Norwegian. So what is this **'deg'**? Have a look at this: **'du liker meg'**, meaning: *you like me*. You don't say: *you like I!* In English, as in Norwegian, there is a subject form and an object form of the pronouns. **'jeg'** and **'meg'** mean: *I* and *me*. But unlike in English, where both the subject form and object form for *you* are the same, there are two different words in Norwegian, **'du'** and **'deg'** – like in Old English *thou* and *thee*.

QUICK VOCAB

bli *become*
dame (en) *lady*
direktør (en) *manager/director*
ferie (en) *holiday*
gammel *old*
hotell (et) *hotel*
hver *each*
kjedelig *boring*
kurset (et kurs) *the course*
kveld (en) *evening*
liker (å like) *like/likes*
lærer (en) *teacher*
mai *May*
mandag *Monday*
også *also/as well*
på *on/at*
skole (en) *school*
stor *big*

True or false? 1

- **a** Arne er student i London.
- **b** Sue er en kjedelig gammel dame.
- **c** Arne liker ikke Sue.
- **d** Sue vil gjerne reise til Norge.

Dialogue 2

Sue and Arne continue their chat:

CD1, TR 10

Arne	Skal du på norsk-kurs i kveld?
Sue	Ja, men jeg vil heller gå på pub med deg!
Arne	Du kan møte meg etter kurset.
Sue	Det er så kjedelig!
Arne	Hvis du vil lære norsk, må du gå på kurset.
Sue	Du er hard!
Arne	Jeg møter deg etter kurset. Vi kan ta et glass øl sammen.
Sue	Jeg vil ha to eller tre glass!
Arne	Jeg vil gjerne være sammen med deg hele tiden. Jeg vil gjerne være sammen med deg i Norge.
Sue	Jeg vil gjerne være sammen med deg i Norge, men ikke hele tiden!

Insight

Adjectives give colour, shape, light and interest to nouns – life would be very dull without them! In the two dialogues you have just read, there are the adjectives **'kjedelig'** meaning *boring*, **'stor'** meaning *big*, and **'gammel'** meaning *old*.

Before starting the next dialogue it would be useful to know the numbers from 1 to 10:

1 **en**, *2* **to**, *3* **tre**, *4* **fire**, *5* **fem**, *6* **seks**, *7* **sju**, *8* **åtte**, *9* **ni** and *10* **ti.**

eller *or*
etter *after*
gå *go*
hard *hard*
hele *the whole*
heller *rather*
hvis *if*
i kveld *this evening*
kan *can*
meg *me*
må *must*
pub (en) *pub*
sammen *together*
så *so/then*
ta *take*
tiden (en tid) *the time*
to *two*
tre *three*
vi *we*
være *be*

QUICK VOCAB

True or false? 2

a Arne vil ikke møte Sue etter kurset.
b Arne vil gjerne være sammen med Sue hele tiden.
c Sue må lære norsk.
d Norsk-kurset er kjedelig.

Dialogue 3

Tirsdag 3. juni (*Tuesday 3 June*) Arne's term is almost over, and he is going home to Bergen. Sue will go to Norway on holiday. They plan to have some days together in Oslo. Listen to how Sue and Arne say 'Oslo'. Both versions ('Oshlo' and 'Oslo') are correct.

CD1, TR 11

Arne Når skal vi reise til Oslo?
Sue Jeg vil gjerne reise i juli.
Arne Det er fint. Jeg vil også reise i juli. Skal vi reise med fly?
Sue Nei, jeg vil reise med ferge. Jeg har motorsykkel. Du kan reise med fly, og jeg kan møte deg i Oslo.
Arne Jeg har en tante i Oslo. Vi kan bo hos henne. Har du pass?
Sue Fint! Ja, jeg har pass. Jeg skal bestille billett i morgen. Jeg vil gjerne ta ferge til Gøteborg i Sverige og kjøre på Europavei 6 som går videre til Oslo. Jeg vil gjerne se Sverige også.

(Contd)

Arne	Har du et kart?
Sue	Ja, jeg har et godt kart over Sverige og et bedre kart over Norge. Hvis jeg reiser på tirsdag, kommer jeg til Gøteborg onsdag. Jeg kan være i Oslo sent torsdag kveld.
Arne	Vi kan bo hos min tante fredag, lørdag og søndag og reise til Bergen på mandag. Jeg gleder meg til å være i Norge med deg!
Sue	Og jeg gleder meg til å reise på ferie til Norge!

Insight

Did you understand their travel plans? Luckily Arne has this accommodating aunt in Oslo …

Did you spot: **'et kart over …'**? In English we say: *a map of …* Direct translation isn't always possible, as you will often see.

QUICK VOCAB

bedre *better*
bestille *book*
billett (en) *ticket*
dager (en dag) *days*
Europa *Europe*
fem *five*
ferge (en) *ferry*
fire *four*
fredag *Friday*
gjerne *gladly*
godt (god) *good*
Gøteborg *Gothenburg*
henne *her*
hos *at the house of*
i morgen *tomorrow*
juli *July*
kart (et) *map*
kjøre *drive*
lørdag *Saturday*
min *my*
onsdag *Wednesday*
over *over/of*
pass (et) *passport*
seks *six*
sent *late*
som *which/that*
Sverige *Sweden*
søndag *Sunday*
tante (en) *aunt*
tirsdag *Tuesday*
torsdag *Thursday*
vei (en) *road*
videre *further*

A useful expression

CD1, TR 11, 01:40

Jeg gleder meg til å ...	*I am looking forward to ...*

True or false? 3

a Sue vil reise med fly til Norge.
b E6 går til Oslo.
c Arne har en tante i Oslo.
d Sue har et godt kart.

This is how we say it

CD1, TR 12

Jeg er lærer	*I am a teacher*
Jeg er hotell-direktør	*I am a hotel manager*
Jeg er student	*I am a student*

Do you remember from Unit 1 about using the indefinite article (*a/an*)? It is not necessary to use *a/an* when stating your job or profession; you simply say: *I am hotel manager*, *I am student*.

Hva gjør du?	*What do you do?*
Hva studerer du?	*What are you studying?*

Don't forget:

Jeg vil gjerne ...	*I would like to ...*
Jeg vil gjerne ha en kopp kaffe.	*I would like to have a cup of coffee.*
Jeg vil gjerne reise til Norge.	*I would like to travel to Norway.*
Jeg gleder meg til å ...	*I am looking forward to ...*
Jeg gleder meg til å reise til USA.	*I am looking forward to travelling to the USA.*
Jeg gleder meg til sommeren.	*I am looking forward to the summer.*

Jeg vil heller ...	*I would rather ...*
Jeg vil heller ha et glass øl.	*I would rather have a glass of beer.*
Jeg vil heller reise til USA.	*I would rather travel to the USA.*

Note that you don't use *of* in these phrases:

En kopp kaffe	*A cup of coffee*
Et glass øl	*A glass of beer*

▶ Here is a little poem about a lazy person's week:

På mandag gjør jeg ingenting	*(on Monday I do nothing)*
På tirsdag har jeg gode stunder	*(on Tuesday I have good times)*
På onsdag ser jeg meg omkring	*(on Wednesday I look around)*
På torsdag går jeg rundt og grunner	*(on Thursday I go round pondering)*
På fredag gjør jeg hva jeg vil	*(on Friday I do what I like)*
På lørdag stunder helgen til ...	*(on Saturday the weekend starts ...)*

Insight

This anonymous little poem has some rather difficult words. Don't worry if you find it a bit hard. When you come back to it later, it will be much easier!

The phrases in **This is how we say it** are very useful. It is a good idea to read them out aloud.

Language patterns

1 Nouns

Norwegian (as well as Danish and Swedish) is unusual in that the definite article, i.e. *the*, joins on to the end of the noun, **-en** at the end of **en**-words (common gender nouns), and **-et** at the end of **et**-words (neuter gender nouns).

en kopp (*a cup*) → **koppen** (*the cup*)
et glass (*a glass*) → **glasset** (*the glass*)

If the noun ends with an **-e**, you add an **-n** for **en**-words and **-t** for **et**-words. (For feminine nouns, the pattern would be: **ei hytte** (*a cottage*) → **hytta** (*the cottage*).)

2 How to describe the noun

Adjectives tell us more about the noun, such as its colour, size or appearance:

gul *yellow*	**liten** *small*
mørk *dark*	**pen** *pretty*
stor *big*	**stygg** *ugly*

QV

An adjective can also describe how one feels about things, such as **en god kopp kaffe** (*a good cup of coffee*), **et kjedelig kurs** (*a boring course*) or **en sint student** (*a cross student*).

3 Adjectives and nouns (part 1)

In Norwegian the adjective takes various endings according to the gender of the noun. This may seem complicated at first, especially as there is no such thing in English. But there is a pattern to follow, and it will all fall into place! There are a number of different situations to cover, so we will deal with this a bit at a time. For now have a look at these and memorize them.

en kopp	*a cup*
en stor kopp	*a big cup*
et glass	*a glass*
et stort glass	*a big glass*

So far we have only looked at indefinite singular nouns (*a* rather than *the*, and only one rather than more than one). In this situation:

- if the noun is an **en**-word, there is nothing added to the adjective
- if the noun is an **et**-word, a **-t** is added to the adjective

4 Nationalities and adjectives ending in *-ig*

The following groups of adjectives take no ending for **et**-words.

a Nationalities

en norsk student	*a Norwegian student*
et norsk kart	*a Norwegian map*

b Adjectives ending in **-ig**

en kjedelig dame	*a boring lady*
et kjedelig kurs	*a boring course*

5 'we/you/they'

In Unit 1 you looked at the personal pronouns in the singular:

jeg	*I*
du	*you*
han	*he*
hun	*she*
den/det	*it*

The plurals of the personal pronouns are:

vi	*we*
dere	*you (more than one)*
de	*they*

6 More about verbs: the future

In Unit 1 you saw that verbs are listed in the infinitive: **å reise** *to travel*. You have also seen verbs with the added **-r** in the present tense (what happens *now*). For example: **studenten reiser, han kommer, Bente går.**

But when do you use the infinitive as it stands, apart from when listing the verbs?

Make a note of these *helping verbs* (modal verbs):

vil	*will*	**kan**	*can*
skal	*shall*	**må**	*must/have to*

Things that will happen in the future are expressed by using one of these, most usually **skal** or **vil**, together with the infinitive of the verb. This is the same as in English:

Jeg skal reise i morgen.	*I shall travel tomorrow.*
John vil komme på fredag.	*John will come on Friday.*

7 *Å være* *to be*

In Norwegian this important verb is much easier than in English:

jeg er	*I am*
du er	*you are*
han/hun/den/det er	*he/she/it is*
vi er	*we are*
dere er	*you are*
de er	*they are*

8 Time expressions

It is difficult to make any rules about time expressions. They are just expressions that you should try to remember. Here are a few:

i kveld	*this evening*
i juli	*in July*

i sommer	*this summer*
i dag	*today*
i morgen	*tomorrow*
på torsdag	*on Thursday*

Insight

At the start of this course there seems to be quite a lot of grammar to get through. This is because so much has to be explained so that you can make sense of it all. You will find that as you progress through the book, there is actually less grammar.

Don't get into a panic if you don't remember it all! Keep doing the exercises – the key to the exercises is at the back of the book, – but don't look there *straight away!*

Exercises

1 Complete the following sentences following the guidance of the pictures below.

a Jeg vil gjerne reise ___________________.
b Jeg vil gjerne kjøre ___________________.
c Jeg vil gjerne lære ___________________.
d Jeg vil gjerne ha ___________________.

a

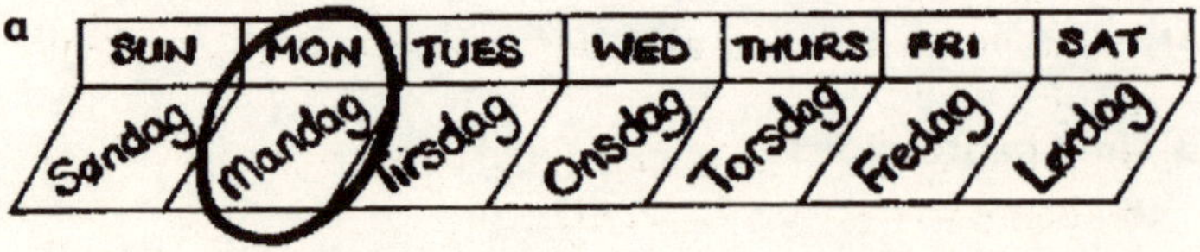

b

c

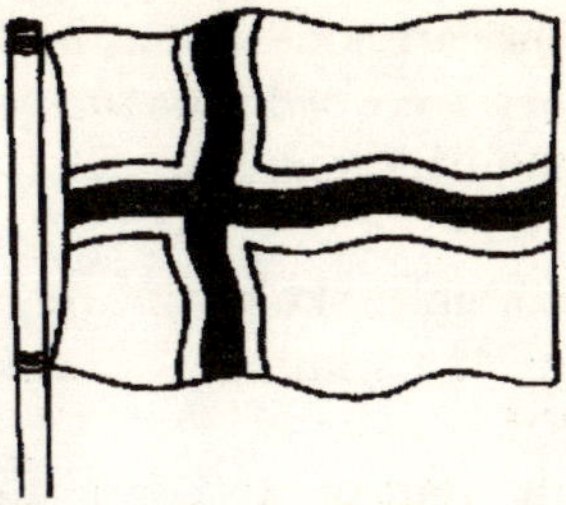

d

2 This is a list of nouns with their indefinite articles – *a/an*. Can you change the nouns to the definite article forms – *the* – using **en** or **et**?

Example: en lærer lærerer
et kurs kurset

a en skole
b en student
c et hotell
d en dame
e en ferge
f et kart
g en vei
h et pass

3 Fill in the gaps with verbs in the infinitive. Remember that there are no **-r** endings, as this is what is going to happen (future).

a John vil __________ med ferge til Sverige.
b Bente vil __________ et glass øl.
c Kari vil gjerne __________ en kopp kaffe.
d John vil __________ norsk.
e John skal __________ på motorsykkel i Norge.
f Han skal __________ billetter i morgen.

4 Here are some nouns in the definite singular. (That means that they are words like *the boy*.) What are they in the indefinite singular? (e.g. *a boy*)

Example:	skolen	en skole
	kurset	et kurs

a studenten
b direktøren
c damen
d hotellet
e læreren
f kvelden
g glasset
h koppen

5 Fill in the gaps with the correct forms of adjectives for **et**-words. Is there a **-t** or not?

Example: en god reise	et godt kart
a en stor motorsykkel	et __________ fly
b en gammel ferge	et __________ pass
c en kjedelig dame	et __________ kurs
d en engelsk pub	et __________ tog

6 Fill in the gaps in these statements (read **Dagene i uken,** and **Numbers,** which follow the exercises):

CD1, TR 13

a I dag er det mandag. I morgen er det ___.
b I dag er det torsdag. I morgen er det ___.
c To og tre er ___.
d Tre og sju er ___.
e Fire og fem er ___.
f Sju og tre er ___.

7 And now complete these phrases:

a Jeg vil gjerne ha (1) ___ kopp kaffe.

b John vil gjerne ha (5) ___ glass øl.

c Hun vil ikke ha (1) ___ glass øl.

8 Wordsearch: find the hidden Norwegian words. (There are 11 of them.)

M	W	Q	F	M	E	D	Z	J
Ø	W	Q	D	P	X	R	W	E
T	K	J	E	D	E	L	I	G
E	K	O	X	A	E	Æ	B	G
Z	N	H	H	M	C	R	Z	Q
H	A	N	X	E	W	E	Q	Z
U	U	Q	A	P	P	R	P	G
N	X	S	T	O	R	Z	O	G

If you get really stuck, here are the English translations to help you out: *meet, I, with, boring, they, he, she, big, and, teacher* and *lady*.

Dagene i uken *The days of the week*

CD1, TR 14

søndag	*Sunday*	**torsdag**	*Thursday*
mandag	*Monday*	**fredag**	*Friday*
tirsdag	*Tuesday*	**lørdag**	*Saturday*
onsdag	*Wednesday*		

Note that in Norwegian you do not use capital letters for the days of the week.

Some speakers don't pronounce the 'g' at the ends of words for the days.

Numbers

You will hear many people say **syv** instead of **sju** (7), especially older people. **Sju** has been the official number for many years, but old habits die hard.

The reason for this change is that **syv** sounded more old-fashioned and Danish. Norway was a Danish province for more than 400 years, and Danish was then the official language in Norway. **Sju** has a more Norwegian flavour!

Vi teller til ti *We count to ten*
CD1, TR 14, 00:17

0	**null**	**6**	**seks**
1	**en/ett**	**7**	**sju**
2	**to**	**8**	**åtte**
3	**tre**	**9**	**ni**
4	**fire**	**10**	**ti**
5	**fem**		

How do you get to Norway?

It is easy to travel to Norway by plane. Many flights arrive from Europe, the USA and other continents every day and there are several international airports. It is only two hours from London to Oslo by air.

If you want to travel by car, there are several ferry-crossings from ports in Denmark to Norway, and the road connections between Norway and Sweden are excellent.

But if you want to go to Norway by car ferry, you have a problem. There is no longer a car ferry link between England and Norway/Sweden. Either you have to cross from Harwich to Esbjerg in Denmark and take another ferry from north Denmark or from Copenhagen, or you can try to cross via a container ship with limited, though excellent, passenger accommodation.

Bergen, the second biggest city in Norway, is the gateway to the fjord country, with deep fjords, and high, snowcapped mountains, while Oslo, at the east side of Norway, has a completely different geography and atmosphere.

Do you understand?

You happen to sit next to a friendly-looking girl. She is reading a Norwegian newspaper. You start talking to her in Norwegian.

CD1, TR 15

Du	(Say it in Norwegian!) *Hi! Are you Norwegian?*
Hun	Ja, jeg er norsk. Men du er ikke norsk!
Du	*No, I am English.* (Translate!) *I'm learning Norwegian.*
Hun	Går du på norsk-kurs?
Du	*Yes, I go to a Norwegian class, but it is boring!*
Hun	Hvorfor er det kjedelig?
Du	*Because the teacher is a boring old lady.*
Hun	Jeg går på engelsk-kurs, men jeg har en hyggelig lærer. Hva heter du?
Du	(your name) *And you?*
Hun	Jeg heter Kari.
Du	*Hi, Kari! Nice to meet you. Would you like a cup of coffee?*
Kari	Nei takk. Nå må jeg gå. Jeg skal gå på kino og se en god film med min engelsk-lærer! På gjensyn!
Du	*Bye bye.*

film (en) *film*
fordi *because*
god *good*
hvorfor *why*
hyggelig *pleasant/nice*
kino (en) *cinema*
møte *meet*
på gjensyn! *hope to see you again!*

Test yourself

Your multiple-choice questions:

1 Hva vil Arne gjerne bli?
  a Hotell-direktør. **b** Student. **c** Lærer.
2 Er Sue på norsk-kurs?
  a Sue er på norsk-kurs. **b** Sue er ikke på norsk-kurs.
  c Sue er i Norge.
3 Når er norsk-kurset?
  a Hver mandag kveld. **b** Hver tirsdag kveld.
  c Hver lørdag kveld.
4 Hvor er kurset?
  a I en pub. **b** På en stor skole. **c** På toget til Leeds.
5 En kjedelig gammel dame, – er det Sue?
  a Det er Sue. **b** Det er læreren. **c** Det er Randi.
6 Arne vil reise på ferie med Sue. Hvor?
  a Til Blackpool. **b** Til Sverige. **c** Til Norge.
7 Hvor bor Arnes tante?
  a Hun bor i Bergen. **b** I Oslo. **c** I London.
8 Vil Arne være sammen med Sue hele tiden?
  a Ja. **b** Nei. **c** Nei, bare på fredag.
9 Hvordan skal Sue reise til Norge?
  a Med tog. **b** Med fly. **c** Med motorsykkel.
10 Sue har et godt kart. Kartet er over?
  a England. **b** Norge. **c** Wales.

3

På vei til Norge

On the way to Norway

In this unit you will learn

- ***How to say what you would like to eat***
- ***What sort of food you are likely to get in Norway***
- ***How to get to grips with Norwegian driving regulations***
- ***How to say 'Cheers!'***

Insight

In Unit 3 we'll focus on food and drink, likes and dislikes. There may be situations where it would sound rude to say that you don't like the food. But you could always claim you are allergic to it! **'Jeg er allergisk.'**

Dialogue 1

CD1, TR 16

We meet Sue on the ferry

Onsdag 4. juli (*Wednesday 4 July*) Sue is on her way to Norway. She wants to see a little of Sweden as well, and takes the overnight ferry to Gothenburg in Sweden. She will then travel to Oslo, the capital of Norway, on her motorbike. In this unit she is on the ferry.

Read the following passage through a few times, and remember to do the **True or false?** exercise which follows the vocabulary.

Sue er på vei til Norge. Arne reiser med fly, men Sue reiser med ferge. Hun skal kjøre motorsykkel.

Fergen til Gøteborg i Sverige tar tjuetre timer. Det er en stor ferge med plass til mange passasjerer, biler, lastebiler og busser.

Det er to restauranter, en kafeteria og mange barer ombord.

Det er to køyer i den lille lugaren. Det er en dame i lugaren. Det er en kjedelig gammel dame i lugaren! Det er norsk-læreren.

Læreren	God dag, Sue. Vi skal reise sammen. Skal vi spise middag sammen?
Sue	Jeg er sulten og tørst. Vi kan spise sammen.

De går til restauranten.

Insight

'Indefinite plural' is the term used to explain some or many of a noun. There were many passengers, cars, lorries and buses on the ferry. Did you notice the plural ending **er**?

en passasjer – **passasjerer**
en bil – **biler**
en lastebil – **lastebiler**
en buss – **busser**

QUICK VOCAB

barer (en bar) *bars*
biler (en bil) *cars*
busser (en buss) *buses*
de *they*
kafeteria (en) *cafeteria*
køyer (en køye) *bunks*
lastebiler (en lastebil) *lorries*
lille (liten) *small*

lugaren (en lugar) *cabin*
mange *many*
middag (en) *dinner*
ombord *on board*
passasjerer (en passasjer) *passengers*
plass *space/room*
restauranter (en restaurant) *restaurants*
spise *eat*
sulten *hungry*
timer (en time) *hours*
tjuetre *twenty-three*
tørst *thirsty*

True or false? 1

a Sue reiser med et stort fly til Norge.
b Det er plass til lastebiler og busser på fergen.
c Det er to køyer i lugaren.
d Sue er sulten og vil gjerne spise middag.

Dialogue 2

I restauranten (*In the restaurant*)

CD1, TR 17

Lærer Jeg liker å spise på fergen. Dette er en god restaurant. Her kan vi spise koldtbord. Det er typisk skandinavisk.
Sue Det er mye god mat her. Jeg liker fisk og reker.
Lærer Jeg liker ikke reker, men jeg liker kjøtt og salater. Her kan du spise så meget du vil. Vi kan ta dette bordet.
Sue Skal vi ta en flaske vin? Rødvin eller hvitvin?
Lærer Nei, jeg drikker ikke vin. Jeg drikker ikke alkohol.
Sue Men jeg vil gjerne ha et glass vin. Jeg liker rødvin best.
Lærer Du må huske at det er strengt forbudt å drikke alkohol når du kjører i Norge. Og du må ikke glemme å kjøre på høyre side av veien. Du må alltid ha lys på.

(Contd)

Sue	Selv om det er sol?
Lærer	Ja, du må alltid ha lys på. Du må passe på fartsgrensen, og husk å ha sertifikatet med deg!
Sue	Er det mer jeg må huske? Eller er dette nok? Men glem det nå! Jeg vil spise og drikke godt! Skål!

Insight

Did you notice Sue saying: **'Jeg liker fisk og reker'** – *I like fish and prawns*? The teacher answered: **'Jeg liker ikke reker'** – *I don't like prawns*. In Norwegian negative statements we don't use the verb *do*, as we do in English. We simply say *I like not*.

QUICK VOCAB

alkohol *alcohol*
alltid *always*
at *that*
av *of*
best *best*
bord (et) *table*
dette *this*
drikke *drink*
fartsgrense (en) *speed limit*
fisk (en) *fish*
flaske (en) *bottle*
forbudt *forbidden*
glemme *forget*
godt *well*
her *here*
huske *remember*
hvitvin *white wine*
høyre *right*
kjøtt (et) *meat*
koldtbord (et) *cold table/buffet*
lys (et) *light*
mat (en) *food*
meget *much*
mer *more*
mye *much*
nok *enough*
passe *mind/look after*
reker (en reke) *prawns*
rødvin *red wine*
salater (en salat) *salads*
selv om *even if*
sertifikat (et) *driving licence*
side (en) *side*
skandinavisk *Scandinavian*
skål! *cheers!*
sol (en) *sun/sunshine*
strengt *strictly*
typisk *typical*
vin (en) *wine*

A useful expression
Det er sol. *It is sunny.*

True or false? 2

- **a** Sue liker reker og fisk.
- **b** Sue liker rødvin best.
- **c** I Norge må du alltid ha lys på når du kjører.
- **d** Sue må ikke glemme å kjøre på høyre side av veien.

Dialogue 3

Torsdag 5. juli (*Thursday 5 July*) The next day Sue gets up early before the teacher awakes and goes to the restaurant for breakfast. It hasn't opened yet, so Sue waits outside. A young man is also there. He smiles at Sue, and they start talking. He tells her that his name is Jan.

CD1, TR 18

Jan Jeg er norsk. Jeg heter Jan. Er du engelsk?
Sue Ja, jeg er engelsk, men jeg snakker litt norsk. Jeg skal på en lang ferie. Jeg skal møte min venn i Oslo.
Jan Jeg skal tilbake til Oslo. Jeg bor i Oslo.
Sue Jeg vil ikke spise frokost med norsk-læreren min!
Jan Skal vi spise frokost sammen? Jeg er veldig sulten.
Sue Jeg vil gjerne spise med deg.
Jan Vi betaler når vi går inn og så kan vi spise så mye vi vil.
Sue Jeg vil gjerne ha et kokt egg og ristet brød med marmelade.
Jan Jeg tror ikke jeg vil ha egg. Jeg vil heller ha sild, og rundstykker med pølse og ost. Jeg vil ha mange kopper kaffe og et stort glass melk.
Sue Tror du jeg kan få en kopp god engelsk te?
Jan Nei, det tror jeg ikke!

Insight

Jan has a healthy appetite! You may find it strange to eat herrings and salami for breakfast, but this is common in Scandinavia. A reminder: **'en kopp kaffe'** – *a cup of coffee*, **'et glass melk'** – *a glass of milk*.

QUICK VOCAB

betaler (å betale) *pay/pays*
brød (et) *bread/loaf*
egg (et) *egg*
frokost (en) *breakfast*
få *get/receive*
inn *in to*
kokt *boiled*
lang *long*
litt *a little*
marmelade (en) *marmalade*
melk (en) *milk*
ost (en) *cheese*
pølse (en) *sausage*
ristet *toasted*
rundstykker (et rundstykke) *bread rolls*
sild (en) *herring*
snakker (å snakke) *talk/talks, speak/speaks*
te (en) *tea*
tilbake *back*
tror (å tro) *believe/believes*
veldig *very*
venn (en) *friend*

True or false? 3

a Sue møter Jan på fergen.
b Sue vil spise frokost med norsk-læreren.
c Jan vil gjerne ha et kokt egg til frokost.
d Sue vil heller ha sild.

As you have seen, there are many new words in this unit. It is a good idea to make your own vocabulary list, perhaps listing nouns with genders (**en ferge** = *a ferry*) (**et bord** = *a table*), and verbs in the infinitive (**å spise** = *to eat*), and in the present tense (**jeg/du/vi spiser** = *I/you/we eat*) to give you some examples.

This is how we say it

CD1, TR 19

▶ Here are some expressions for likes and dislikes, and also how to ask for something:

Jeg liker sild og poteter.	*I like sild and potatoes.*
Jeg liker hvitvin.	*I like white wine.*
Jeg liker akevitt bedre.	*I like aquavit better.*
Jeg vil gjerne ha en stor porsjon med reker.	*I would like a big portion of prawns.*

- **Kan jeg få ...** means *may I have* and is a perfectly polite way of asking for something.

Kan jeg få et glass vann?	*May I have a glass of water?*

Do you remember?

et glass vann	*a glass of water*
Jeg tror ikke jeg vil ha ...	*I don't think I will have ...*
Jeg liker ikke ...	*I don't like ...*
Jeg vil heller ha ...	*I would rather have ...*

Language patterns

1 Word order

The person or thing carrying out the action of the verb in a sentence is called the subject of the sentence. Usually the subject comes first in a sentence: **De reiser til Norge.** *They travel to Norway.*

But, if the sentence starts with one of the little words like **nå** or **så**, or an expression like **i morgen** or **i sommer**, or with a *dependent clause*, the subject and the verb change places.

a De reiser til Norge.	*They travel to Norway.*

If you start that sentence with **nå**, the subject and verb change places:

Nå reiser de til Norge.	*Now they travel to Norway.*
b De reiser til Norge i sommer.	*They travel to Norway this summer.*

If you start with **i sommer**, the subject and verb change places:

I sommer reiser de til Norge.	*This summer they travel to Norway.*

c **De skal spise når de kommer.** *They'll eat when they come/arrive.*

If you start with the *dependent* or *subordinate clause*, the subject and verb change place in the main clause:

Når de kommer, skal de spise. *When they come/arrive, they'll eat.*

Look out for word order in the dialogues!

2 Nouns (plural)

In the dialogues at the beginning of this unit, there are many examples of plural nouns – when there is more than one of something.

en bil	*a car*	**biler**	*cars*
en buss	*a bus*	**busser**	*buses*
et hotell	*a hotel*	**hoteller**	*hotels*

The plural of indefinite nouns is formed by adding **-er** at the end of the noun. If the word already ends with an **-e**, you just add **-r**.

Short (one syllable) **et**-words take no ending in the plural (with one or two exceptions):

et bord	*a table*	**bord**	*tables*
et kurs	*a course*	**kurs**	*courses*

This form of plural can be called the indefinite plural.

3 Adjective + noun (part 2)

In Unit 2, you saw how the ending of the adjective depends on whether it is accompanying an **en**-word or an **et**-word. In Norwegian, the adjective must be watched! The ending also depends on whether the noun is singular or plural (one or many) and whether it is indefinite (*a/an*) or definite (*the*).

Take a noun:	en bil	*a car*
Add an adjective:	en stor bil	*a big car*

Indefinite singular

en bil	*a car*
en stor bil	*a big car*
et kart	*a map*
et stort kart	*a big map*

Definite singular

bilen	*the car*
<u>den</u> store bilen	*the big car*
kartet	*the map*
<u>det</u> store kartet	*the big map*

Indefinite plural

mange biler	*many cars*
mange store biler	*many big cars*
mange kart	*many maps*
mange store kart	*many big maps*

Look carefully at the endings of the adjectives.

The definite singular is the really difficult one. Here you have the plural ending of the adjective, and in addition to the definite ending for the noun, you have a definite article as well! Note that in the definite singular you must use a separate definite article only when you have an adjective with the noun: The definite article **den/det** (*the*) is only used when there is an adjective before the noun.

The adjective takes the plural form, and you still have the definite ending of the noun. Remember these examples that illustrate this ruling:

Bente drikker vinen.	*Bente drinks the wine.*
Bente drikker den gode vinen.	*Bente drinks the good wine.*

The combination of adjective and noun is tricky to start with. Don't worry, it will soon make sense! Most people cope with it, but it does need some practice.

4 *Liten small*

One useful, but very irregular, adjective is **liten** (*small*).

en liten **bil**	**den** lille **bilen**	**mange** små **biler**
et lite **glass**	**det** lille **glasset**	**mange** små **glass**

Insight

It is a good idea to write out adjective/noun combinations on paper or your computer and take a good long look at them! In Unit 4 the final part will be revealed.

Exercises

1 Write out the following nouns in the indefinite form as in the list below, in the definite singular (*the*) and the indefinite plural:

Example: en bil, **bilen, mange biler**

a en kopp
b et glass
c en ferge
d et bord
e en time
f en middag

2 Now do the same, this time adding an adjective:

Examples: en stor bil, **den store bilen,** mange store biler
et stort hotell, **det store hotellet,** mange store hoteller

a en tørst student
b en sulten dame
c et norsk pass

d et engelsk sertifikat
e en liten bil
f et lite glass

3 Replace the verbs in the present tense in brackets below with a *helping verb* + the correct infinitive:

CD1, TR 20

Example: John **drikker** et glass øl. John **vil drikke** et glass øl.

a Bente (**spiser**) ___ reker.
b Studenten (**lærer**) ___ norsk.
c Han (**reiser**) ___ til Oslo.
d Hun (**kjører**) ___ fra Sverige til Norge.

4 Word order: Are the following phrases statements (S) or questions (Q)? (Question marks have been left out.)
a Fergen tar mange passasjerer.
b Hva heter han.
c Er hun norsk.
d Bente er au pair.
e Er John student.
f Kommer Bente fra York.

5 Make the following statements negative by using **ikke** (remember this is like English – see **Language patterns** 7 in Unit 1):

Examples: John er norsk.	John er **ikke** norsk.
Kari vil ha et glass øl.	Kari vil **ikke** ha et glass øl.

a Bente kommer fra Bergen.
b Fergen har mange passasjerer.
c Studenten lærer engelsk.
d Kari er sulten.
e Hun spiser en god middag.

6 Wordsearch: Find the hidden Norwegian words – they can be up, down or across! (There are ten words.)

D	W	R	E	K	E	R	Q	F	I	S	K
L	X	C	P	J	Q	P	K	A	F	F	E
I	E	B	R	Ø	D	O	O	Q	X	Z	W
S	A	L	A	T	D	R	Ø	D	V	I	N
M	R	G	R	T	D	Z	L	E	Q	I	N
M	M	A	R	M	E	L	A	D	E	E	M

If you get stuck, here are the English translations of the ten words: *prawns, coffee, salad, beer, marmalade, meat, fish, bread, herring* and *red wine.*

Regulations for driving in Norway

Du må alltid ha med deg sertifikat (et førerkort).	*You must always bring your driving licence with you.*
Du må alltid kjøre med lys på.	*You must always drive with headlights on.*
Du må kjøre på høyre side.	*Drive on the right (side).*
Du må passe på fartsgrensen.	*Keep to the speed limit.*
Du må ikke drikke alkohol.	*Don't drink!*

Skål *Cheers*

To say **skål** in Norway is an old custom.

- You lift your glass to someone in your party, saying that person's name.

- You then say **skål!** and, looking each other in the eye, you both sip your drinks.
- Keep eye-contact until your glass is resting on the table.

In earlier days, when people were more formal, and would say **De** rather than **du**, as well as using surnames, saying **skål** was a way of agreeing to drop formalities and be on first-name terms. It is also a lovely – and acceptable – way of conveying feelings. Try it! It is good fun.

On family occasions, big and small, on all formal occasions and on Norway's national day, 17 May (**syttende mai**), there will be several times when somebody will say:

Skål!
Skål for Norge!

Skål for brudeparet! *Cheers for the wedding couple!*
Skål for Kari!

and so on.

Then all will lift their glasses and drink together.

Koldtbord *Cold buffet*

Koldtbord is an institution in Scandinavia. Many of the dishes are the same across Scandinavia, but each country also has its own specialities.

At a Norwegian **koldtbord**, whether on a passenger ferry, in a restaurant or at a party, many of these dishes will be found:

røkelaks	smoked salmon
gravlaks	cured salmon
kokt laks	poached salmon

sild	pickled herring in many variations: **tomatsild, dillsild, sursild** (herring and raw onions in a sweet and sour brine)
reker	prawns, usually in their shells and always very fresh
roastbiff	cold, thinly sliced, rare fillet of beef
italiensk salat	Italian salad (much like coleslaw, but with chopped ham)

plus a variety of salads, hard-boiled eggs with fillings, cold chicken and so on.

To drink with this, one should really have a good glass of beer and a good measure of **akevitt**, the excellent and well-matured potato brandy known in English as *aquavit*.

There will also be:

ost	*cheese*
frukt	*fruit*

and some desserts, usually:

karamellpudding	*creme caramel*
gelé	*jelly*
sjokoladepudding	*chocolate mousse*
vaniljesaus	*custard*

Insight

Confusing for English travellers is 'biff' meaning *steak* and 'stek' meaning *roast*.

Try roast reindeer, and dishes made from stockfish, fish which has been hung to dry on wooden racks in the north of Norway, and has a strong 'fishy' taste.

Do you understand?

You are on the coach to the airport, and you find yourself next to a girl who is reading a Norwegian book. You want to practise your Norwegian so you start talking to her:

CD1, TR 21

Du	(Translate!) *Where are you going?*
Hun	Jeg skal reise med fly til Norge.
Du	*Are you Norwegian?*
Hun	Ja, jeg kommer fra Trondheim.
Du	*Where is Trondheim?*
Hun	Trondheim er en stor by nord for Oslo. Jeg skal reise med tog fra Oslo til Trondheim. Det tar åtte timer.
Du	*I'm going to Oslo too. I shall be in Oslo from Tuesday to Saturday.*
Hun	Hvor skal du reise på lørdag?
Du	*I shall travel over the mountain to Bergen. Next Wednesday I shall travel to America.*
Hun	Hva heter du?
Du	(Say your name.) *And you?*
Hun	Jeg heter Hilde. Jeg skal møte min tante på flyplassen.

Amerika *America*
by (en) *town/city*
fjell (et) *mountain*
flyplass (en) *airport*
neste *next*
nord *north*

QV

Test yourself

Which response is correct?

1 Hvor går fergen?
  a Fergen går til Newcastle. **b** Fergen går til Gøteborg.
  c Fergen går til Oslo.

2 Sue reiser med Arne.

a Ja, hun reiser med Arne.

b Nei, hun reiser ikke med Arne.

c Hun reiser med Odd.

3 Hva liker Sue å spise?

a Fisk og reker. **b** Sild. **c** Rundstykker med pølse.

4 Hva vil Sue drikke til middag?

a Et stort glass melk. **b** En kopp kaffe. **c** Et glass vin.

5 Spiser Sue frokost med norsklæreren?

a Ja, hun spiser frokost med norsklærern.

b Nei, hun spiser frokost med Arne.

c Nei, hun spiser frokost med Jan.

6 Vil Jan ha kokt egg til frokost?

a Nei, han vil ikke ha egg. **b** Ja, han vil ha egg.

c Han vil ikke spise frokost.

7 Hva vil Sue drikke til frokost?

a Et stort glass melk. **b** En stor kopp kaffe.

c En god kopp engelsk te.

8 Hva må du huske når du kjører i Norge?

a Du må passe på fartsgrensen.

b Du må glemme sertifikatet.

c Du må ikke ha lys på.

9 Kan du drikke alkohol og kjøre i Norge?

a Ja. **b** Nei. **c** Du kan drikke en flaske vin.

10 Er Sue norsklærer?

a Nei, Sue er ikke norsklærer. **b** Ja, Sue er norsklærer.

c Sue er engelsklærer.

4

Sightseeing i Oslo

Sightseeing in Oslo

In this unit you will learn

- ***What to see first in Oslo***
- ***How to express left and right, and understand directions***
- ***How to get around in Oslo***
- ***How to show your feelings about the sights***

Insight

Arne and Sue are sightseeing in Oslo. They then go by tram to the Sculpture Park, which is the most visited tourist attraction in Oslo. Have a look at the vocabulary list before you start.

Dialogue 1

Søndag 7. juli. (*Sunday 7 July*) Sue got herself to Oslo without mishap, and now she and Arne are staying with Arne's aunt. Today they are sightseeing in Oslo.

Sue og Arne er i Oslo. De ser seg om. De går i mange lange gater til de kommer til Aker Brygge. Her drikker de øl og spiser reker på en ute-restaurant. Solen skinner og sjøen er blå.

CD1, TR 22

Arne Ser du de to brune tårnene der borte? De likner to store brune geitoster. Det er Rådhuset.

Sue Jeg liker ikke norsk geitost! Er det en festning som ligger der borte?

Arne Ja, det er den gamle festningen som heter Akershus.

Sue Bor Norges konge på Akershus?

Arne Nei, kongen og dronningen bor på Slottet. Det er der de arbeider også.

Sue Jeg vil gjerne se Slottet.

Arne Ja, og så kan vi ta trikken til Frognerparken. Men først vil jeg ha et glass øl til.

Etterpå går de til Slottet. Det er ikke langt. Slottet er en stor gul bygning som ligger i en vakker grønn park.

Sue Slottet er et veldig stort hus. Kongen har god plass!

Insight

There is only one palace in Norway and it is called 'Slottet,' meaning The Palace. In Britain there are so many palaces that they all need to have names!

QUICK VOCAB

arbeider (å arbeide) *work/works*
blå *blue*
borte *away*
brune (brun) *brown*
brygge (en) *quay*
bygning (en) *building*
der *there*
dronningen (en dronning) *the queen*
etterpå *afterwards*
festning (en) *castle*
først *first*
gater (en gate) *streets*
geitoster (en geitost) *goats' cheeses*
grønn *green*
gul *yellow*
her *here*
hus (et) *house*
konge (en) *king*
langt *far*
ligger (å ligge) *lie/lies*
likner (å likne) *look/looks like*
park (en) *park*
Rådhuset (et rådhus) *the City Hall*
ser seg om *look/looks around*

sjøen (en sjø) *the sea*
skinner (å skinne) *shine/shines*
Slottet (et slott) *the palace*
trikken (en trikk) *the tram*
tårnene (et tårn) *the towers*
ute *outside*
vakker *beautiful*

As you should now be growing confident with the use of the indefinite and definite articles, and with the verb forms, the word lists from here won't repeat the noun in its singular form given in brackets if the main entry is in the plural, nor the infinitive form after the verb part. For nouns listed in the definite form, the indefinite form will be shown if it is not obtained by removing **-en** or **-et** from the definite. It's a good idea to learn the singular and plural forms of a noun at the same time, and the verb infinitives.

True or false? 1

a Sue og Arne drikker kaffe på en ute-restaurant.
b Norges konge bor på Akershus festning.
c Dronningen bor på Rådhuset.
d Solen skinner.

Dialogue 2

Sue and Arne are on the tram to Frogner Park.

Sue og Arne tar trikken til Frognerparken.

CD1, TR 23

Sue Jeg liker å kjøre med trikken. Oslo er en pen by.
Arne Ja, når det er sol! Oslo er bedre om sommeren.
Sue Du kan se mye av Oslo fra trikken.
Arne Ja. Nå kan du se Slottet til høyre. Parken er åpen for alle.
Sue Hva heter kongen og dronningen?
Arne De heter Harald og Sonja.
Sue Hva er den store bygningen til venstre?
Arne Det er den amerikanske ambassaden.
Sue Hvor er den britiske ambassaden?

(Contd)

Arne	Du kan ikke se den fra trikken.
Sue	Jeg vil gjerne se Akershus festning.
Arne	Vi kan gå dit i morgen.
Sue	Det er godt vi har mange dager. Det er mye å se i Oslo.
Arne	Ja, det er det. Men se! Der er Frognerparken. Vi skal gå av trikken her.

QUICK VOCAB

alle *everybody/all*
ambassaden (en ambassade) *the embassy*
amerikanske (amerikansk) *American*
bedre *better*
britiske (britisk) *British*
den *it*
dit *there*
gå av *get off*
om sommeren *in the summer*
pen *pretty/handsome*
venstre *left*
åpen *open*

True or false? 2

- **a** Norges konge heter Harald.
- **b** Den amerikanske ambassaden er til høyre.
- **c** Sue liker å kjøre med trikken.
- **d** Sue og Arne tar trikken til Akershus festning.

Dialogue 3

I Frognerparken (*In Frogner Park*)

CD1, TR 24

Sue	Hvem har laget alle disse skulpturene?
Arne	Det er Gustav Vigeland. Han har laget alle skulpturene, fontenene, portene og den store monolitten.
Sue	Jeg synes skulpturene er litt store og tykke.
Arne	Ja, den piken der likner på deg!
Sue	Og den lille sinte gutten likner på deg! Han er søt.
Arne	Jeg liker bronse-skulpturene her på broen. Men vi må se de store granitt-skulpturene rundt monolitten også.
Sue	Frognerparken er veldig fin, synes jeg. Men dette er nok! Jeg er sulten igjen og veldig tørst.

Arne	Jeg er ikke sulten. Men se, der er Randi og Odd! Hei!!
Odd	Hei Sue og Arne!
Sue	Jeg vil ikke se skulpturer. Jeg vil heller ha en kopp kaffe og litt mat!
Randi	Jeg også. Men Odd vil bare ha litt vann!
Sue	Arne er ikke sulten. Skal du og jeg gå på en kafé, Randi? Vi kan sikkert gå fra guttene.
Randi	Fint! Ha det, Odd og Arne

Insight

What a lot of new words! Of course some of the words from the **Frognerparken** dialogue are quite similar to their English counterparts. Read the dialogues once more and don't forget to listen to the recording.

QUICK VOCAB

broen (en) *the bridge*
bronse *bronze*
disse *these*
fontenene (en fontene) *the fountains*
granitt (en) *granite*
gutten (en) *the boy*
hvem *who*
igjen *again*
kafé (en) *café*
laget (å lage) *made*
monolitten (en) *the monolith*
piken (en pike) *the girl*
portene (en port) *the gates*
rundt *around*
sikkert *surely*
sinte (sint) *cross*
skulpturene (en skulptur) *the sculptures*
synes (å synes) *think(s)/to be of the opinion of*
søt *sweet*
tykke (tykk) *thick/fat*
vann (et) *water*

True or false? 3

a Gustav Vigeland har laget alle skulpturene i Frognerparken.
b Arne synes at Sue likner den lille sinte gutten.
c Sue er sulten igjen.
d Sue og Randi går til en kafé.

This is how we say it

◀) CD1, TR 25

Here is a list of useful expressions, of questions and answers, from this unit:

▶ **Hvor ligger Slottet?**	*Where is* (lit. *lies) the Palace?*
Slottet er til høyre.	*The Palace is to the right.*
Slottet ligger til høyre.	*The Palace is/lies to the right.*
▶ **Hvor er Akershus festning?**	*Where is Akershus castle?*
Akershus ligger til venstre.	*Akershus is/lies to the left.*
Du ser Akershus til venstre.	*You see Akershus on the left.*
▶ **Hvor er Rådhuset?**	*Where is the City Hall?*
Til venstre ser du Rådhuset.	*To the left is (you see) the City Hall.*
Du ser Rådhuset til venstre.	*You see the City Hall to the left.*
▶ **Kan du se Frognerparken?**	*Can you see Frogner Park?*
Den er der borte.	*It is over there.*
Du ser den der borte.	*You see it over there.*
▶ **Hvor er fontenen?**	*Where is the fountain?*
Den er der borte til venstre.	*It is over there to the left.*
Du ser den der borte til venstre.	*You see it over there to the left.*

And some opinions you might have or overhear!

▶ **Jeg liker den lille skulpturen.**	*I like the small statue/sculpture.*
Jeg synes at den pene piken er best.	*I think that the pretty girl is the best.*
Jeg vil gjerne se Holmenkollbakken.	*I would like to see the Holmenkoll ski-jump.*
Jeg liker å reise med trikken.	*I like to go/travel by tram.*

▶ **Jeg liker ikke den store granitt-skulpturen.**	*I don't like the big granite sculpture.*
Jeg synes ikke at Oslo er en pen by.	*I don't think Oslo is a beautiful city.*
Jeg synes ikke at kaffen er god.	*I don't think the coffee is good.*
▶ **Jeg synes at det er kjedelig å ta trikken.**	*I think it is boring to go by tram.*
Jeg synes at Frognerparken er kjedelig!	*I think Frogner Park is boring!*
Jeg vil heller reise til Amerika!	*I would rather go to America!*

Insight

We have now come to the final form for the nouns, what we call 'definite plural'. In English we say this as *the streets*, the cars and so on. In Norwegian the definite plural ending for nouns is **'-ene'**, so we have **'gatene'** meaning *the streets*, and **'bilene'** meaning *the cars*. Did you notice this in the dialogues?

Language patterns

1 Nouns: definite plural

In Unit 3 you looked at nouns in the indefinite and the definite singular, and in the indefinite plural. Here is a quick reminder:

Indefinite singular:	en bil	*a car*	(any one car)
Definite singular:	bilen	*the car*	(one particular car)
Indefinite plural:	biler	*cars*	(cars in general – more than one)

The final form of the noun is the definite plural:

Definite plural:	bilene	*the cars*	(some particular cars – more than one)

Bilene er store.	*The cars are big.*

The definite plural is formed by adding **-ene** to the noun. This rule covers both **-en** and **-et** words.

et kart	*a map*
kartet	*the map*
kart	*maps*
kartene	*the maps*

(Did you remember that short **-et** words have no added ending in the indefinite plural? e.g. **et kart, mange kart**)

2 Adjective and noun (part 3)

This is the final part about the adjective and noun combination. Here's the definite plural: **bilene** (*the cars*).

Bilene er der.	*The cars are there.*
De store bilene er der.	*The big cars are there.*

In the definite plural – just as in the definite singular – there is a definite article as well as the definite ending when the noun is preceded by an adjective.

Bilene.	***The*** *cars.*
De **store bil**ene.	***The*** *big cars.*

There will be many exercises for you to practise, as well as reminders.

Study this pattern:

Singular		*Plural*	
Indefinite	*Definite*	*Indefinite*	*Definite*
en bil	bilen	biler	bilene
en stor bil	den store bilen	store biler	de store bilene
et kart	kartet	kart	kartene
et stort kart	det store kartet	store kart	de store kartene

Do you remember this awkward adjective mentioned in Unit 3?
Liten (*small*)

en liten bil	**den lille bilen**
et lite kart	**det lille kartet**
små biler	**de små bilene**
små kart	**de små kartene**

The definite article

- In Norwegian (as in Swedish and Danish), there is no separate definite article unless there is an adjective in front of the noun.

bilen	***the*** *car*	**bil**ene	***the*** *cars*
den **store bil**en	***the*** *big car*	de **store bil**ene	***the*** *big cars*

- When an adjective precedes the noun, you must have a definite article as well as the definite ending of the noun.

  Note the adjective endings:

en stor **bil**	**den** store **bilen**	store **biler**	**de** store **bilene**
et stort **kart**	**det** store **kartet**	store **kart**	**de** store **kartene**

Insight

If you find this a bit tricky, don't worry! It will quickly fall into place. Go back to Units 2 and 3, Adjective and noun, Parts 1 and 2.

3 Adjectives

Here is a table showing the adjectives you have had so far. The first column has adjectives in the form used with **-en** words in the indefinite singular, e.g. **en stor bil**. The second column has adjectives as used with **-et** words in the indefinite singular: e.g. **et stort glass**. The third column has adjectives as used in the definite singular and both definite and indefinite plural for all nouns: e.g.

den store bilen	**store biler**	**de store bilene**
det store glasset	**store glass**	**de store glassene**

Indefinite Singular **-en**	*Indefinite Singular* **-et**	*Definite Singular + Indefinite and Definite Plural*	
brun	brunt	brune	*brown*
fin	fint	fine	*fine*
god	godt	gode	*good*
gul	gult	gule	*yellow*
hard	hardt	harde	*hard*
lang	langt	lange	*long*
pen	pent	pene	*pretty*
sint	sint	sinte	*cross*
søt	søtt	søte	*sweet*
tørst	tørst	tørste	*thirsty*

a Nationalities do not take a **-t** for **-et** words:

amerikansk	**amerikansk**	**amerikanske**	*American*
engelsk	**engelsk**	**engelske**	*English*
norsk	**norsk**	**norske**	*Norwegian*
skandinavisk	**skandinavisk**	**skandinaviske**	*Scandinavian*

b Adjectives ending with **-ig** do not take a **-t** for **-et** words:

hyggelig	**hyggelig**	**hyggelige**	*nice/pleasant*
kjedelig	**kjedelig**	**kjedelige**	*boring*

c Most adjectives with a double consonant drop one before the **-t**:

grønn	**grønt**	**grønne**	*green*
tykk	**tykt**	**tykke**	*thick/fat*

d Adjectives ending in **-el**, **-en** and **-er** are slightly irregular in the definite singular and the plural:

gammel	**gammelt**	**gamle**	*old*
sulten	**sultent**	**sultne**	*hungry*
vakker	**vakkert**	**vakre**	*beautiful*

e Some adjectives are just irregular:

blå	**blått**	**blå**	*blue*

Here are examples from each group:

	en gul bil	den gule bilen	gule biler	de gule bilene
	et brunt hus (*house*)	det brune huset	brune hus	de brune husene
a	en engelsk gutt (*boy*)	den engelske gutten	engelske gutter	de engelske guttene
	et norsk kart	det norske kartet	norske kart	de norske kartene
b	en hyggelig pike (*girl*)	den hyggelige piken	hyggelige piker	de hyggelige pikene
	et kjedelig kurs	det kjedelige kurset	kjedelige kurs	de kjedelige kursene
c	en grønn kopp	den grønne koppen	grønne kopper	de grønne koppene
	et grønt glass	det grønne glasset	grønne glass	de grønne glassene
d	en sulten dame	den sultne damen	sultne damer	de sultne damene
	et gammelt fly	det gamle flyet	gamle fly	de gamle flyene
e	en blå trikk	den blå trikken	blå trikker	de blå trikkene
	et blått tog (*train*)	det blå toget	blå tog	de blå togene

Keep this list handy when you do exercises involving adjectives. You will discover more as you progress on the course.

Insight

It would be a good idea to put a bookmark or a little sticker here. You will find these lists useful!

4 Relative pronouns ('who/which/that')

The relative pronoun is very easy in Norwegian. It is quite simply **som**, regardless of whether it is referring to people, animals or objects. **Som** = *who/which/that*.

Jeg ser en student. Han heter Per.	*I see a student. He is called Per.*
Jeg ser en student som heter Per.	*I see a student who is called Per.*
De tar trikken. Den går til Slottet.	*They take the tram. It goes to the Palace.*
De tar trikken som går til Slottet	*They take the tram that goes to the Palace.*
Trikken som går til Frognerparken, er stor.	*The tram which goes to Frogner Park is big.*

5 *Her – hit* = here; *der – dit* = there

There are two words meaning *here* and two words meaning *there*. You use **her** and **der** when there is no movement: when someone or something is simply at a place:

Jeg er her.	*I am here.*
John sitter der.	*John sits there.*

You use **hit** and **dit** when there is movement:

Han reiser dit.	*He travels there.*
Bente kommer hit.	*Bente comes here.*

Exercises

1 Fill the three remaining columns with the correct forms of the nouns. The first has been done for you.

	Indefinite Singular	Definite Singular	Indefinite Plural	Definite Plural
a	en buss	bussen	busser	bussene
b	en trikk	________	________	________
c	et fly	________	________	________
d	et tog	________	________	________
e	en lastebil	________	________	________
f	en ferge	________	________	________

2 Do the same again, but this time with an adjective:

	Indefinite Singular	Definite Singular	Indefinite Plural	Definite Plural
a	en stor buss	den store bussen	store busser	de store bussene
b	en gul trikk	________	________	________
c	et stort fly	________	________	________
d	et fint tog	________	________	________
e	en grønn lastebil	________	________	________
f	en god ferge	________	________	________

3 Fill the gaps to create a pattern as in Exercise 1 above:

a	en dame	________	damer	________
b	________	studenten	studenter	________
c	en skole	________	________	________
d	________	________	________	husene
e	et kurs	________	________	________
f	________	________	kopper	________
g	________	flasken	________	________

4 Link the two sentences with **som**:

Example: Jeg ser en student. Han heter John.
Jeg ser en student som heter John.

a Det er et stort hus. Det ligger i en grønn park.
b De tar trikken. Den går til Frognerparken.
c Solen skinner på sjøen. Den er blå.
d Bente spiser mange reker. De er gode.

5 Don't forget word order!

🔊 **CD1, TR 26**

De tar trikken til Frognerparken etterpå.		*They take the tram to Frogner Park afterwards.*
Etterpå tar de trikken til Frognerparken.	→	The sentence starts with an adverb.
Du kan se Slottet til høyre.		*You can see the Palace to the right.*
Til høyre kan du se Slottet.	→	The sentence starts with a preposition phrase.

Start these sentences with **nå** and adjust the word order:

a Vi kommer til Frognerparken.
b Vi skal spise reker.
c John og Bente går til Aker Brygge.

Start these sentences with **til venstre**:

d Du kan se den britiske ambassaden.
e Vi ser Slottet.
f John ser en restaurant.

6 Fill the gaps with the correct word for *here* and *there*:
a John går ___.
b Frognerparken ligger ___.
c Bente sitter ___.
d Trikken kjører ___.

7 Use the table of adjectives in **Language patterns 3** and fill in the gaps:

a Jeg har en ___ bil.
b Den ___ fergen går til Sverige.
c Kari spiser mange ___ reker og drikker en ___ kopp kaffe.
d De ___ husene ligger i den ___ gaten.

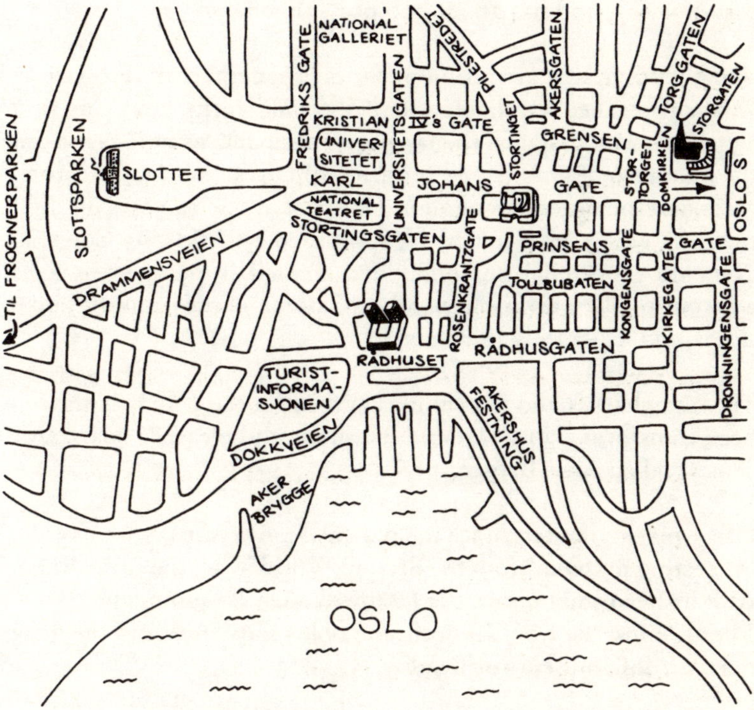

8 Look at the map of Oslo above. You are at Aker Brygge looking towards Rådhuset. Answer the questions:
a Er Akershus til høyre eller venstre for Rådhuset?
b Er Frognerparken på høyre eller venstre side av kartet?
c Er Slottet i en liten park?

9 Answer the following questions about Oslo using complete sentences:
a Hvor bor kongen og dronningen?
b Er Slottet en liten grønn bygning?
c Er trikkene i Oslo gule eller blå?

What to see in Oslo

Oslo is the capital of Norway (look at the town centre map **on the previous page**). It is situated at the end of the Oslo fjord in south-east Norway, and has about 500,000 inhabitants.

The biggest tourist attraction by far is **Frognerparken** (Frogner Park), also called **Vigelandparken** (Vigeland Park), after Gustav Vigeland, who designed the lay-out of the park, as well as making the hundreds of granite and bronze sculptures, the wrought-iron gates and the massive monolith. He spent about 40 years on this, and was given a free hand, sponsored by Oslo City Council. The park is open day and night, and, as well as the sights, it is a favourite place for picnics and sunbathing in the summer, and skiing and ice-skating in winter.

The old wharves and warehouses in front of the City Hall have been transformed into restaurants, shops and pleasure boat berths. This is called **Aker Brygge**.

Other places of interest are the old castle, **Akershus**, with its interesting museum from the Second World War, the cathedral with its beautiful murals, the Holmenkollen ski-jump, and the Viking ships, the Kon-Tiki raft, the polar ship *Fram* and the huge open-air folk museum at Bygdøy.

And not to be missed is the Edvard Munch museum! Some people think that Edvard Munch's paintings are the most interesting things to be seen in Oslo.

Public transport

Getting around by public transport is a cheap and worthwhile way of sightseeing. You can buy your ticket from the tram or bus driver, and the price is the same for any distance travelled. It is a good idea to buy a **flexi** card from any kiosk. You get four, or eight, journeys on one card. On entering the tram, you insert the card into a franking machine, and you can then travel and change tram/bus/underground train as much as you like for an hour, as long as you get on your last vehicle within the time printed on your card by the machine.

By far the cheapest way to see Oslo, if you intend going to some of the museums, is to buy an ***Oslo card***. For a very modest sum you can travel freely on public transport, including the fjord ferries, and have free entrance to museums and other attractions for one day. Start early as there is a lot you can do in one day in Oslo!

Do you understand?

You are in front of the Palace and you speak to an elderly lady:

CD1, TR 27

Du	*Is this the Palace?* (Say it in Norwegian!)
Damen	Ja, dette er Slottet. Synes du det er en pen bygning?
Du	*It is a fine building. Is the King here now?*
Damen	Nei, kong Harald og dronning Sonja er i London. Men du er ikke norsk! Hvor kommer du fra?
Du	*I come from …*
Damen	Du snakker godt norsk! Liker du å være i Norge?
Du	*Yes, I like Norwegian food. What is the long street there called?*
Damen	Den heter Karl Johans gate. Den er Oslos hovedgate.
Du	*I would like to go to Frogner Park.*
Damen	Du kan ta den trikken der til Frognerparken. Den går forbi den amerikanske ambassaden.
Du	*Thank you. I think that Oslo is a beautiful city.*
Damen	Ja, når solen skinner! Har du et kart over Oslo?
Du	*Yes, I have a good map. Here it is.*
Damen	Her er Slottet. Trikken stopper der.
Du	*Thank you. I'm going now. Goodbye.*
Damen	Adjø, og på gjensyn!

QV

forbi *past*
hovedgate (en) *main street*
stopper (å stoppe) *stop/stops*

Test yourself

This time the questions are different. You have to choose the correct Norwegian adjective/noun combination to translate the English phrase.

1 a big car
  a en stor bil. **b** et stor bil. **c** en stort bil.
2 the long street
  a den lang gaten. **b** den lange gaten.
  c den lange gatene.
3 the fat girl
  a en tykke pike. **b** den tykke piken. **c** de tykk pikene.
4 the cross boy
  a en sinte gutt. **b** de sinte gutten. **c** den sinte gutten.
5 a big building
  a en store bygning. **b** en stor bygning.
  c et stort bygning
6 the green park
  a den grønn park. **b** den grønn parken.
  c den grønne parken
7 a big palace
  a et stort slott. **b** et stort slottet. **c** et stort slottene.
8 a yellow tram
  a et gul trikk. **b** en gul trikk. **c** den gul trikk.
9 the long streets
  a de lang gater. **b** de lange gatene. **c** de lang gatene.
10 the big fountain
  a den store fontenen. **b** det store fontenen.
  c de stor fontenen.

5

Sue går til byen

Sue goes into town

In this unit you will learn

- ***How to ask for postcards and stamps***
- ***How to ask for directions***
- ***How to understand Norwegian money***
- ***How to count from ten upwards***

Insight

Buying postcards and stamps, going to the Tourist Information, to a bank and also asking for directions, are all part of travelling. Sue is doing all these things. It is now necessary to be familiar with numbers from 10 onwards. You will find them in this unit.

Dialogue 1

Sue and Randi went off without the boys, and Arne and Sue have now had their first quarrel. Arne has gone off somewhere, and Sue finds a kiosk to buy postcards and stamps. It is raining and she is in a bad mood.

Sue er i dårlig humør. Og nå regner det. Hun går til en kiosk og snakker til damen bak disken.

CD1, TR 28

Sue	God dag. Jeg vil gjerne kjøpe noen kort.
Damen bak disken	Kortene er der borte ved døren. Du kan se hvilke du vil ha.

Sue går til døren. Der er det et stort stativ med mange kort. Sue finner åtte pene kort. Hun går til disken.

Sue	Jeg vil gjerne kjøpe disse kortene.
Damen	De store kortene koster ti kroner hver og de små koster seks kroner. Det er fem store kort og tre små.
Sue	Hvor kan jeg kjøpe frimerker?
Damen	Vi selger frimerker også. Hvor skal du sende kortene?
Sue	Jeg skal sende sju kort til England og ett til Sverige.
Damen	Her er frimerkene. Det blir hundreogtrettiåtte kroner.
Sue	Her er to hundre kroner.
Damen	Takk. Og her har du sekstito kroner tilbake.
Sue	Mange takk. Hvor finner jeg turistinformasjonen?
Damen	Vet du hvor Aker Brygge er? Gå ned den gaten der til du nesten er på Aker Brygge. Du vil se en stor gul bygning på høyre side. Det er turistinformasjonen.
Sue	Mener du den gaten til høyre?
Damen	Ja, det er ikke langt.
Sue	Tusen takk! Ha det!
Damen	På gjensyn!

Insight

Did you look up the numbers? The Norwegian monetary system is also explained at the end of this unit. The **krone** is divided into **100 øre**. The **øre** isn't worth much these days. The only **øre**-coin in use is the **50 øre** coin, which is worth roughly *5 pence* or *7 cents*.

bak *behind*
disken (en) *the counter*
døren (en) *the door*
dårlig *bad*
finner (å finne) *find/finds*
frimerker (et frimerke) *stamps*
humør (et) *humour/mood*
hundre (et) *hundred*
hundreogtrettiåtte *a hundred and thirty-eight*
hvilke *which (plural)*
kiosk (en) *kiosk*
kjøpe (å kjøpe) *buy*
kort (et) *postcard(s)*
koster (å koste) *cost/costs*
kroner (en krone) *the Norwegian monetary unit*
mener (å mene) *mean/means*
ned *down*
nesten *almost*
noen *some*
post (en) *post*
regner (å regne) *rains*
selger (å selge) *sell/sells*
sende *send*
små (liten) *small*
stativ (et) *stand*
turistinformasjonen *the tourist information office*
ved *by*
vet (å vite) *know/knows*

QUICK VOCAB

True or false? 1

a Sue er i godt humør.
b Arne kjøper kort og frimerker.
c Turistinformasjonen er en stor grønn bygning.
d Turistinformasjonen er på venstre side.

Dialogue 2

Sue finds the Tourist Information Office and speaks to a helpful man:

CD1, TR 29

Mannen	Hei! Kan jeg hjelpe deg?
Sue	Ja, takk. Jeg er engelsk, men jeg snakker litt norsk. Hva kan jeg gjøre i Oslo?
Mannen	Her har du en brosjyre. Her kan du finne alt. Liker du pop-konserter? Liker du å se en god film? Du kan se hvilke filmer som går denne uken. Du finner alt her.
Sue	Er det mange museer i Oslo?
Mannen	Ja, det er mange fine museer. Her er åpningstider for museer og utstillinger.
Sue	Hvor er Sentralbanestasjonen?
Mannen	Gå til Nationaltheatret. Der finner du en trikk til Oslo S. Men du kan også gå dit. Det er ikke langt. Oslo S er i den andre enden av Karl Johans gate.
Sue	Unnskyld, kan du forklare det en gang til?
Mannen	Ja, gjerne det. Gå til Nationaltheatret. Da ser du Karl Johans gate. Du har Slottet til venstre. Gå til høyre. Gå hele Karl Johans gate. Da kommer du til Sentralbanestasjonen.
Sue	Nå vet jeg hvor jeg skal gå. Er det langt?
Mannen	Nei, kanskje tjue minutter. Her har du et godt kart over Oslo og her er en Oslo-guide.
Sue	Takk for hjelpen! Morna!
Mannen	Ingen årsak. Kom tilbake hvis du vil vite mer. Morna!

Mannen smiler til Sue. Hun går ut. Det regner.

Insight

You have come across **'hvilke'**, meaning **which** in the plural. **'Hvilke'** has three versions, as you will come across later; **'hvilken'** meaning *which* in connection with common gender nouns, **'hvilket'** with neuter nouns and, as here, **'hvilke'** with plurals. Examples:

hvilken bil er din?	*which car is yours?* ('en bil')
hvilket hus bor du i?	*which house do you live in?* ('et hus')
hvilke kort vil du ha?	*which cards will you have?*

QUICK VOCAB

alt *all/everything*
andre *other*
brosjyre (en) *brochure*
denne *this*
enden (en) *the end*
for *for*
forklare (å forklare) *explain*
gjøre *do*
hjelpe *help*
hjelpen (en) *the help*
ingen *no*
kanskje *perhaps*
mannen (en) *the man*
minutter (et minutt) *minutes*
museer (et museum) *museums*
Nationaltheatret *the National Theatre* (also a bus/train and tram stop)
pop-konserter (en pop-konsert) *pop concerts*
smiler (å smile) *smile/smiles*
Sentralbanestasjonen *the Central Railway Station*
tjue *twenty*
uken (en uke) *the week*
unnskyld *excuse me*
ut *out*
utstillinger (en utstilling) *exhibitions*
åpningstider (en åpningstid) *opening times*

Some useful expressions
CD1, TR 29, 02:10

En gang til	*Once more*
Ingen årsak	*No reason/that's all right/don't mention it*

True or false? 2

a Sue vil gjerne vite hvor Sentralbanestasjonen er.
b Sue kan ikke ta en trikk til Oslo S.
c Det er kanskje 20 minutter å gå til Oslo S.
d Mannen har ikke et kart over Oslo.

Dialogue 3

Sue needs some Norwegian money. She goes to the nearest bank.

Sue trenger norske penger. Hun finner en bank.

CD1, TR 30

Damen i kassen	Hei! Kan jeg hjelpe deg?
Sue	Jeg vil gjerne veksle noen reisesjekker.
Damen	Har du pass?
Sue	Ja, her er det. Og her er reisesjekkene. De er begge på £100. Og så har jeg £20 som jeg gjerne vil veksle i norske penger.
Damen	Hva slags sedler vil du ha?
Sue	Jeg vil gjerne ha en tusen-kroneseddel og resten av pengene i hundre-kronesedler og i mynter.
Damen	Vil du skrive navnet ditt på disse sjekkene og på dette papiret her?
Damen	Takk. Her har du pengene dine og dette er kvitteringen.
Sue	Takk for hjelpen. Ha det!
Damen	Ha en hyggelig dag. Ha det godt!

Sue går ut av banken. Det regner og regner.

Suddenly she hears:

Jan	Hei Sue! Husker du meg? Fra fergen?
Sue	Hei Jan! Hyggelig å se deg! Hvordan har du det?

Jan Fint! Er du alene i byen?
Sue Ja, Arne er i dårlig humør. Jeg også! Det er altfor mange skulpturer i Frognerparken! De er altfor like hverandre. Det er ikke lett å huske dem!
Jan Ja, det er sant. Kom med meg til en kafé! Vi kan spise noe godt og snakke sammen.
Sue Det vil jeg gjerne!

Insight

Of course there are 'hole in the wall' cash dispensers/ATMs with easily understood instructions in the main European languages. They can be found outside all banks and many supermarkets and are clearly labelled 'Minibank'.

QUICK VOCAB

alene *alone*
altfor *much too*
bank (en) *bank*
begge *both*
dine *your/yours* (plural)
ditt *your/yours* (singular for **et** words)
hva slags *what kind of/what sort of*
hverandre *each other*
kassen (en) *the till/cashdesk*
kvitteringen (en) *the receipt*
lett *easy*
lik *like*
mynter (en mynt) *coins*
navnet (et) *the name*
noe *something*
papiret (et) *the paper*
penger *money*
reisesjekker (en reisesjekk) *traveller's cheques*
rest (en) *remainder/rest*
sant *true*
sedler (en seddel) *notes/banknotes*
sitt *his/her own*

skrive (å skrive) *write*
trenger (å trenge) *need/needs*
tusen (et) *thousand*
veksle (å veksle) *change/exchange*

True or false? 3

a Sue trenger ikke å veksle noen reisesjekker.
b Hun vil gjerne ha en tjue-kroneseddel.
c Sue møter Odd.
d Sue er i dårlig humør.

This is how we say it

Some useful expressions from this unit:

▶ **Jeg vil gjerne kjøpe**	*I would like to buy*
Kan jeg få...?	*May I have ...?*
▶ **Kan du si meg hvor ... er?**	*Can you tell me where ... is?*
Hvor er ...?	*Where is ...?*
Vet du hvor ... er?	*Do you know where ... is?*
Hvor finner jeg ...?	*Where will I find ...?*
▶ **Mener du den gaten der?**	*Do you mean that street there?*
Vil du si det en gang til?	*Would you say it once more?*
Vil du forklare det en gang til?	*Would you explain it once more?*
▶ **Du må gå ned den gaten der.**	*You must go down that street there.*
Gå til venstre bort denne gaten her.	*Go/turn left along this street here.*
Ta den trikken du ser der borte.	*Take the tram you see over there.*

▶ **Kortene koster tjueseks kroner.**	*The cards cost 26 kroner.*
Frimerkene koster atten kroner.	*The stamps cost 18 kroner.*
▶ **Jeg har ingen norske penger.**	*I have no Norwegian money.*
Jeg trenger norske penger.	*I need some Norwegian money.*
Jeg vil gjerne veksle noen reisesjekker.	*I would like to cash some traveller's cheques.*
▶ **Hvor er banken?**	*Where is the bank?*
Hvor er Slottet?	*Where is the Palace?*
Hvor finner jeg en kiosk?	*Where do I find a kiosk?*
Hvor finner jeg et toalett?	*Where do I find a toilet?*
▶ **Unnskyld!**	*Excuse me/sorry!*
▶ **Takk.**	*Thank you.*
Takk for hjelpen.	*Thank you for the (your) help.*
Ingen årsak.	*No reason/'don't mention it'.*

Insight

It's very useful to be able to ask directions and understand the answers. Don't worry about asking a second time! **'Unnskyld, vil du si det en gang til?'** meaning: *Sorry, will you say it once more?* is a phrase which could come in handy.

Language patterns

1 Demonstratives: 'this/these, that/those'

These words are used in the same way as in English:

denne = *this*	den = *that*
dette = *this*	det = *that*
disse = *these*	de = *those*

The only things to remember are:

Denne is used with **en**-words and **dette** with **et**-words.
Den is used with **en**-words and **det** with **et**-words.

Jeg kjører i denne bilen.	*I drive in this car.*
Hun bor i dette huset.	*She lives in this house.*
Studentene spiser disse rekene.	*The students eat these prawns.*
John går ned den gaten.	*John goes down that street.*
Han ser på det kartet.	*He looks at that map.*
Trikken kjører i de gatene.	*The tram drives in those streets.*

Her is often used with **denne, dette, disse.**
Der is often used with **den, det, de.**

This strengthens the demonstrative:

Jeg kjører i denne bilen her.	*I drive in this car here.*
Hun bor i dette huset her.	*She lives in this house here.*
Studentene spiser disse rekene her.	*The students eat these prawns here.*
John går ned den gaten der.	*John goes down that street there.*
Han ser på det kartet der.	*He looks at that map there.*
Trikken kjører i de gatene der.	*The tram drives in those streets there.*

As you see, **den, det,** and **de** have more than one meaning. They are demonstratives as well as definite articles used with adjectives + nouns. Notice the noun still has the end-article.

2 Imperatives

Imperatives are verbs giving orders or commands, and generally tell someone what to do. The version of the verb used to do this is the shortest form. You might remember from Unit 1 (**Language patterns 5**) that this is called the 'stem'. The stem is the version of a verb used to give commands.

In English the imperative looks like this: *sit!*, *go!*, *drive!*
In Norwegian: **sitt! gå! kjør!**
(The verbs listed as infinitives are: **å sitte, å gå, å kjøre.**)

3 Nouns

As you no doubt remember, the four forms of the noun are:

en bil	**bilen**	**biler**	**bilene**
et hus	**huset**	**hus**	**husene**

This applies if the nouns follow a regular pattern.
Unfortunately some nouns don't follow the normal rule:

en seddel	**seddelen**	**sedler**	**sedlene**	(*banknote*)
en lærer	**læreren**	**lærere**	**lærerne**	(*teacher*)
et teater	**teateret**	**teatre**	**teatrene**	(*theatre*)
en mann	**mannen**	**menn**	**mennene**	(*man*)

There is a complete list of the irregular nouns used in this book in the Grammar section at the back.

4 *Og, men, fordi* – *'and, but, because'*: Three examples of conjunctions

Words which are helpful when you want to join sentences together are called conjunctions.

De store kortene koster åtte kroner.	*The big cards cost eight kroner.*
De små kortene koster fem kroner.	*The small cards cost five kroner.*
De store kortene koster åtte kroner og **de små kortene koster fem kroner.**	*The big cards cost eight kroner **and** the small cards cost five kroner.*
Hilde har bil.	*Hilde has a car.*
Erik har ikke bil.	*Erik doesn't have a car.*

Hilde har bil, men **Erik har ikke bil.**	*Hilde has a car,* ***but*** *Erik doesn't have a car.*
Han drikker øl.	*He drinks beer.*
Han er tørst.	*He is thirsty.*
Han drikker øl fordi **han er tørst.**	*He drinks beer* ***because*** *he is thirsty.*

There is more about conjunctions in Unit 13.

5 *Johns motorsykkel* John's motorbike

Indicating who or what owns something is very simple in Norwegian. You just add an -s to the owner – as in English, but without the apostrophe.

Johns motorsykkel	*John's motorbike*
Bentes ferie	*Bente's holiday*
Oslos hovedgate	*Oslo's main street*
Bentes tante	*Bente's aunt*

Other aspects of the genitive are covered fully in Unit 16.

Exercises

1 Insert a demonstrative to complete these sentences:

a Hvor er banken? Banken ligger i ___ gaten der.
b Hva heter ___ gaten der?
c Vil du ha ___ kortet her?
d Nei, takk. Jeg vil heller ha ___ kortene der.
e Jeg liker ikke ___ skulpturene der.
f Jeg vil gjerne kjøpe ___ kartet her.

2 Insert a verb in the imperative that matches the infinitive given in brackets:

a ___ dit! (å **kjøre**)
b ___ på den stolen der! (å **sitte**)
c ___ til kiosken! (å **gå**)
d ___ melk og kaffe! (å **kjøpe**)

3 Don't forget the nouns! Nouns in the indefinite and definite, singular and plural have this pattern:

en bil	bilen	biler	bilene
et hus	huset	hus	husene

Fill in the missing words:

a	en ferie	___	ferier	___
b	___	byen	byer	___
c	en vei	___	___	veiene
d	___	___	hoteller	___
e	___	parken	___	___
f	et kort	___	___	___
g	___	frimerket	___	___

4 Fill in the gaps. The adjective is in the brackets. You must find the correct form. Look at the table in Unit 4 (**Language patterns** 4).

CD1, TR 31

a en (**stor**) ___ bil
b den (**kjedelig**) ___ læreren
c de (**gammel**) ___ damene
d det (**blå**) ___ huset
e mange (**norsk**) ___ studenter
f de (**grønn**) ___ parkene
g det (**pen**) ___ kortet

5 Look at the map of Oslo in Unit 4, Exercise 8. Find your way:
a fra Oslo S til Nationalgalleriet (*the National Gallery*)
b fra Nationalteatret til Akershus
c og så til Slottet

6 Translate this passage – remember to use the **Vocabulary** at the back of the book, if you get stuck.

Bente er i dårlig humør. Det er dårlig vær (*weather*). Det er ikke pent vær. Det er ikke sol. Det regner. John er i Oslo alene.

Han er i godt humør. Han kjøper mange pene kort og noen frimerker. Så går han til turistinformasjonen og til en bank. Han har ingen penger, og han vil gjerne veksle noen reisesjekker.

Insight

Are you doing the exercises? Believe me, you will progress much quicker if you do! Get on with them, not forgetting the very last one in each unit: Test yourself.

You will find the key to the exercises towards the back of the book, but don't look at the answers before you have completed them!

Newsagents and kiosks

Newsagents and kiosks in Norway display a big, multi-coloured 'N' on a blue board. This stands for the name Narvesen. Here you can buy books, magazines, postcards, hot-dogs, sweets and so on. You can also buy stamps for letters and cards to send all over the world, so it is not necessary to find a post office unless you want to send parcels.

NARVESEN

Numbers

Vi teller videre fra ti *We count up from ten*

CD1, TR 32

In Unit 2 you discovered that 7 = **sju** has the older version **syv**, which is still used by a lot of people. 20 = **tjue** and 30 = **tretti** also have an old form: **tyve** = 20 and **tredve** = 30. If you use **tyve** and **tredve**, you also have to count in the old-fashioned way, which many people still do. See forms in brackets.

11	elleve	30	tretti (tredve)
12	tolv	31	trettien (en og tredve)
13	tretten	32	trettito (to og tredve)
14	fjorten	40	førti
15	femten	50	femti
16	seksten	60	seksti
17	sytten	70	sytti
18	atten	80	åtti
19	nitten	90	nitti
20	tjue (tyve)	100	hundre
21	tjueen (en og tyve)	200	to hundre
22	tjueto (to og tyve)	1000	tusen
23	tjuetre (tre og tyve)		

In this book you'll find the modern way of counting.

The Norwegian money system

The system is not complicated. Ten kroner is roughly equivalent to one British pound. At the time this book was revised, the pound was weak, and £1 was roughly kr 9.

The krone is divided into 100 øre. There used to be various copper coins, but at the time of writing the smallest unit is 50 øre.

The coins are 50 øre, 1 krone, 5 kroner, 10 kroner and 20 kroner. The notes are 50 kroner, 100 kroner, 500 kroner and 1000 kroner. Prices are usually written like this: kr 45,50.

In banks and in lists of monetary currency, the krone is written like this: **NOK** = Norwegian krone.

The decimal point is always a comma, not a point. This is the same for distances and weights and so on.

1 kilometer (km) = 1000 meter (m) 1,6 km = 1 mile (roughly)
1 Norwegian mile (**mil**) = 10 km **1 kilo (kg) = 1000 gram (g)**
0,450 **kg** = 450 g = 1 lb (roughly)

Do you understand?

You are standing on a street corner looking around. You are lost. A young man speaks to you:

Mannen	Kan du si meg hvor Rådhusgaten er?
Du	*I don't know. I come from England.*
Mannen	Jeg kommer fra Bodø. Jeg vet ikke hvor jeg er.
Du	*I have a map. We can look at it.*
Mannen	Jeg heter Martin. Hva heter du?
Du	(your name)
Martin	Du snakker godt norsk! Er du student?
Du	*Yes, I'm studying in England. Are you a student?*
Martin	Nei, jeg kjører en stor lastebil. Men nå er jeg på ferie. Skal du være i Oslo lenge?
Du	*No, I shall travel to Bergen on Monday.*
Martin	Skal du reise med tog?
Du	*No, I shall travel by plane.*
Martin	Nå skal vi finne Rådhusgaten.
Du	*I will go with you.*
Martin	Det er fint. Vil du ha en kopp kaffe? Jeg vil gjerne snakke engelsk.

Du	*I would like a cup of coffee, but I would rather talk Norwegian!*
Martin	Liker du å være i Norge?
Du	*Yes, but I would rather travel to America!*

lenge *a long time*
se på *look at*
si *say, tell*

Test yourself

Choose the correct number.

1 sekstiåtte
a 65. **b** 68. **c** 78.

2 trehundreog fem
a 305. **b** 304. **c** 315.

3 sjuhundreog trettitre
a 703. **b** 730. **c** 733.

4 sytten
a 7. **b** 70. **c** 17.

5 tjuefire
a 24. **b** 25. **c** 26.

6 nittito
a 91. **b** 92. **c** 99.

7 firehundreog femtifire
a 404. **b** 444. **c** 454.

8 åttehundreog åttiåtte
a 888. **b** 818. **c** 808.

9 førtini
a 59. **b** 49. **c** 94.

10 elleve
a 11. **b** 21. **c** 12.

6

Hallo!

Hello!

In this unit you will learn

- ***How to use the telephone***
- ***How to use numbers***
- ***How to make appointments***
- ***How to say 'Please'***

Insight

It's just as well you practised the Norwegian numbers in Unit 5! Telephone numbers in Norway always have eight digits and are normally said in twos: 22 65 88 04 = **tjueto – sekstifem – åttiåtte – null – fire**. You'll learn more information about using the phone towards the end of this unit.

Dialogue 1

Sue and Arne quarrel. Sue goes off with Jan, and Arne phones home.

Det er fint vær igjen, men både Sue og Arne er i dårlig humør. De er ikke venner og de vil ikke være sammen. Sue vil gjerne se Kon-Tiki og vikingskipene, og etterpå reiser hun med Jan til en liten by som heter Stavern.

Arne vil reise til Bergen, og han ringer hjem.

CD1, TR 33

Tom	Hallo!
Arne	Hei, lillebror! Hvordan har du det?
Tom	Ikke så verst. Når kommer du hjem?
Arne	Kanskje i morgen. Er mor hjemme?
Tom	Ja, jeg skal hente henne. Mor!!! Arne er på telefonen!!
Mor	Hallo, Arne, så godt å høre fra deg. Er du ikke snart på* vei hjem?
Arne	Jo, jeg kommer i morgen hvis jeg får plass på toget.
Mor	Kommer Sue?
Arne	Nei, jeg kommer alene. Vi bare krangler. Vi kranglet i hele går.
Mor	Det skal bli godt å se deg. Du må bestille plass på toget. Togene er fulle nå i ferien.
Arne	Jeg skal ringe til Oslo S. Hils far og de andre. Ha det, mor! Jeg gleder meg til å komme hjem.
Mor	Ha det godt, gutten min.

*Arne's mother says '… på snart …' This is very colloquial!

Insight

Did you notice Arne saying: **'hils far …'**? This is the imperative of the verb **'å hilse'** meaning *to greet*, and is the form of the verb used for instructions or giving orders. In English we would probably say *Give my love to Dad*, or *Say hello to Dad* rather than *Greet Dad!* You cannot always translate word for word between different languages.

QUICK VOCAB

andre *others*
både *both*
far (en) *father*
fulle (full) *full*
hente *fetch*
hils (å hilse) *greet*
hjem *home* (also **et hjem** *a home*)
hjemme *at home*
høre (å høre) *hear*
i hele går *all yesterday*
ikke så verst *not too bad*
jo *yes*
Kon-Tiki *the Kon-Tiki raft*
krangler (å krangle) *quarrel/ quarrels*

kranglet *quarrelled*
lillebror (en) *little brother*
mor (en/ei) *mother*
nummeret (et) *the number*
ringer (å ringe) *ring/rings*
slår (å slå) *knock/knocks, tap/taps, dial/dials*
snart *soon*
telefonen (en) *the telephone*
verst *worse*
vi *we*
vikingskipene (et) *the Viking ships*
vær (et) *weather*

Some useful expressions
CD1, TR 33, 01:14

Jeg gleder meg til å ... *I am looking forward to ...*
Ikke så verst ... *Not too bad ...*

True or false? 1

a Både Sue og Arne er i godt humør.
b Sue ringer til Bergen.
c Arne snakker med Tom og far.

Dialogue 2

Arne phones the Norwegian State Railway booking office.

CD1, TR 34

Damen	22 17 14 00. Vær så god?
Arne	Hei! Jeg vil gjerne bestille billett på toget til Bergen i morgen.
Damen	Nå skal jeg se. Et øyeblikk. De to første togene er fulle, men du kan få plass på toget som går klokken 14.55, altså fem minutter på tre. Dette er en 'grønn avgang', så reisen blir billigere.
Arne	Det var heldig! Er det en vindusplass ledig?
Damen	Nå skal jeg se etter. Det er ikke mange plasser igjen. Jo, du kan få en vindusplass. Skal du ha returbillett?
Arne	Nei, men jeg vil gjerne ha plassbillett.

Damen	Du må hente billetten i dag. Jeg kan holde den til klokken to.
Arne	Jeg kommer med en gang. Takk for hjelpen. Ha det!
Damen	Ha det bra.

Insight

Try to learn the useful expressions! As mentioned in the previous 'Insight', you cannot always translate word for word. There isn't a single word meaning 'please' in Norwegian. **'Vær så god'** is the phrase for *May I help you?* **'Med en gang'**, word for word, would be a meaningless phrase: with one time. What it really means is *at once*.

QUICK VOCAB

altså *which means*
avgang (en) *departure*
billigere *cheaper*
heldig *lucky*
holde *keep/hold*
igjen *left/again*
klokken *at … o'clock*
ledig *free*
med en gang *at once*
plassbillett (en) *seat reservation*
returbillett (en) *return ticket*
se etter *check, look for*
var (å være) *was/were*
vindusplass (en) *windowseat*
vær så god *can/may I help you?*

Useful expressions
CD1, TR 34, 01:05

Vær så god	*May I help you? (Be so good)*
Et øyeblikk	*One moment/please wait a moment*
Med en gang	*At once*

True or false? 2

a Arne vil bestille plass på toget til Bergen.
b Sue skal ikke reise til Bergen.
c Toget går fem minutter over tre.
d Arne bestiller returbillett.

Dialogue 3

Arne collects his rail ticket and phones his aunt Maiken.

Arne hentet billetten sin på Oslo S. Nå vil han ringe til tante Maiken, og han slår nummeret hennes, 22 27 95 44, og tanten svarer:

CD1, TR 35

Tante Maiken	Tjueto tjuesju nittifem førtifire, vær så god?
Arne	Hallo, tante Maiken! Nå er jeg på Oslo S. Jeg har kjøpt billett til Bergensbanen i morgen. Jeg reiser klokken fem på tre.
Tante Maiken	Jeg er glad for at du reiser til mor og far. Det blir fint for deg å komme hjem til familien din. Men jeg får ikke se deg mye før du reiser. Nå skal jeg på en konsert med en venn og i morgen har jeg bestilt time hos tannlegen og frisøren.
Arne	Jeg blir i Oslo i kveld, men jeg kommer tilbake for å pakke.
Tante Maiken	Har du hørt fra Sue?
Arne	Nei, men hun har adressen min. Hun skal ringe til meg om noen uker. Hun er veldig vanskelig. Jeg forstår henne ikke. Hun sa at hun ville være i Oslo et par dager til. Men plutselig tok hun teltet sitt og motorsykkelen sin og reiste.
Tante Maiken	Jeg liker Sue. Men det er viktig at dere er fra hverandre en stund. Og du kan være litt vanskelig, du også!
Arne	Tante Maiken, da!
Tante Maiken	Du er en veldig hyggelig gutt, Arne. Det har vært noen hyggelige dager siden du kom og jeg vil veldig gjerne ha deg her hos meg noen dager til. Ha det! Ser deg senere!
Arne	Jeg blir sen. Ikke vent på meg. Ser deg til frokost i morgen. Hei, hei!

Insight

In Unit 2 we had **'å bestille billett'** meaning *to book a ticket*. If you want to book a seat or place on a train, coach or plane, you would say: **'jeg vil gjerne bestille plass på …'**. In this dialogue you came across **'å bestille time'** meaning *to book an appointment*. **'en time'** really means *an hour*. This is a fixed expression, regardless of whether your appointment is for 10 minutes or all day!

QUICK VOCAB

adressen (en adresse) *the address*
Bergensbanen *the Oslo – Bergen railway*
bestilt (å bestille) *ordered*
dere *you* (plural)
et par *a couple of/pair of*
familien (en familie) *the family*
for å *in order to*
forstår (å forstå) *understand/understands*
frisøren (en) *the hairdresser*
før *before*
glad for at *pleased/happy that*
hennes *her/hers*
hentet (å hente) *collected/fetched*
hos *with*
hørt (å høre) *heard*
kjøpt (å kjøpe) *bought*
kom (å komme) *came*
om *in*
pakke *pack*
plutselig *suddenly*
reiste (å reise) *went/travelled*
sa (å si) *said*
sen *late*
senere *later*
siden *since*
sin *his/her/their own*
stund (en) *while*
svarer (å svare) *answer/answers*

tannlegen (en tannlege) *the dentist*
telt (et) *tent*
tok (å ta) *took*
uker (en uke) *weeks*
vanskelig *difficult*
vent (å vente) *wait* (imperative)
viktig *important*
ville (å ville) *wanted*
vært (å være) *been*

Some useful expressions
CD1, TR 35, 01:34

Å bestille time	*to make an appointment*
Om noen uker	*in a few weeks*

True or false? 3

a Sue og tante Maiken skal reise til Bergen.
b Arne har billett til fergen til England.
c Sue vil bestille time hos frisøren.
d Arnes familie bor i Bergen.

This is how we say it

There is no single word meaning 'please' in Norwegian:

▶ **Ja takk.**	*Yes, please.*
Nei takk.	*No, thank you.*
Vær så snill å …	*Please (asking someone to do something for you, be so good as to …)*
Vil du være så snill å…?	*Please (will you be so good as to …?)*

▶ **Jeg er glad for å ...**	*I am pleased to ...*
Jeg er glad for at ...	*I am pleased that ...*
▶ **Jeg er glad i ...**	*I love/like very much ...*
Vær så god	*Here you are/may I help you? (when you hand someone something, and when you answer the phone)*
▶ **Vil du ha et glass øl?**	*Would you like a glass of beer?*
Her er et glass øl, vær så god.	*Here is a glass of beer (for you).*
Vær så snill å gi meg et glass øl til!	*Please give me another glass of beer!*
Vil du være så snill å gi meg et glass øl til?	*Please give me another glass of beer?*

This expression is important enough to need repeating:

▶ **Jeg gleder meg til ...**	*I am looking forward to ...*
Jeg gleder meg til ferien.	*I am looking forward to the holiday.*
Jeg gleder meg til å se deg!	*I am looking forward to seeing you!*
Jeg gleder meg til å reise fra Norge!	*I am looking forward to travelling from Norway!*
▶ **Hvor er det en telefon?**	*Where is there a telephone?*
Hvor er det en telefonkiosk?	*Where is there a telephone booth?*
Hvor er det en telefonkatalog?	*Where is there a telephone directory?*
Kan jeg få snakke med ...?	*Please may I speak to ...?*
Et øyeblikk.	*Just a moment.*
Jeg vil gjerne bestille time.	*I would like to make an appointment.*

Insight

You now see what I mean about the lack of that very useful word: *please*. But we always get round the problem somehow!

'Jeg er glad i ...' is much stronger than *I am fond of*, and really means *I love/I like very much*.

Language patterns

1 Questions

You have seen earlier that questions are simply made by changing the word order, or by using a question word, such as **hva** and **hvor**, and ending with a question mark.

Heter han John?	*Is he called John?*
Hvor bor du?	*Where do you live?*

It is very common in Norway to use the negative when asking questions:

Heter han ikke John?	*Isn't he called John?*
Bor du ikke i Taunton?	*Don't you live in Taunton?*

There are two words for *yes*: **ja** and **jo**.
If you answer *yes* to a question, you say **ja**.
If you answer *yes* to a 'negative' question, you say **jo**.
Jo is also a slightly doubtful *yes*.

Kommer du fra Stavanger?	*Do you come from Stavanger?*
Ja, jeg kommer fra Stavanger.	*Yes, I come from Stavanger.*
Kommer du ikke fra Stavanger?	*Don't you come from Stavanger?*
Jo, jeg kommer fra Stavanger.	*Yes, I come from Stavanger.*
Liker du norsk mat?	*Do you like Norwegian food?*
Jo, jeg liker norsk mat.	*Well – yes, I like Norwegian food.*

2 Verbs – talking about events in the past

The tense of the verb relates to when the action takes place, in the past, present or future. When you want to talk about something which happened in the past, the verb will have to be in the past tense.

Jeg var i London i går.	*I was in London yesterday.*

The present tense of the verb *to be* is *am/are/is*, and in the past tense: *was/were* in English. In Norwegian, the present tense of **å være** is **er**, and the past tense is **var**.

Jeg er i England.	*I am in England.*
Jeg var i Oslo i går.	*I was in Oslo yesterday.*

It makes sense to list verbs in the following order:

Infinitive		*Present tense*		*Past tense*	
å være	(*to be*)	**er**	(*am/are/is*)	**var**	(*was*)
å reise	(*to travel*)	**reiser**	(*travel/travels*)	**reiste**	(*travelled*)
å kjøre	(*to drive*)	**kjører**	(*drive/drives*)	**kjørte**	(*drove*)
å spise	(*to eat*)	**spiser**	(*eat/eats*)	**spiste**	(*ate*)

The last three verbs in this list follow the normal rules and are described as regular. There are four groups of regular verbs, which you will meet in the following units. But there are also many irregular verbs, which don't follow the normal patterns. Here are some useful ones:

å gå	**går**	**gikk**	(*to go*)
å ha	**har**	**hadde**	(*to have*)
å drikke	**drikker**	**drakk**	(*to drink*)

3 Adverbs

Do you remember *here* and *there*? These are examples of adverbs. Adverbs are words which give extra information, such as how, when or where the verb takes place.

There are two words for *here* and two words for *there*, one to use when there is movement, and one for stationary situations.

Kom hit!	*Come here!*
Gå dit!	*Go there!*
Jeg er her.	*I am here.*
Du er der.	*You are there.*

There are some more adverbs like this.

With movement:		**Stationary:**	
bort	(*away/off*)	**borte**	
han kjører bort	(*he drives off*)	**de er borte**	(*they are away*)
opp	(*up*)	**oppe**	(*up/upstairs*)
ned	(*down*)	**nede**	(*down/downstairs*)
ut	(*out*)	**ute**	(*out/outside*)
inn	(*in*)	**inne**	(*in/inside*)
hjem	(*home*)	**hjemme**	(*at home*)

4 Doing arithmetic

+	og/pluss	3 + 5 = 8	tre og fem er åtte
–	minus	6 – 2 = 4	seks minus to er fire
×	ganger	7 × 3 = 21	sju ganger tre er tjueen
÷	dividert med/ delt på	24 : 8 = 3	tjuefire dividert med åtte er tre

QV

å dividere/å dele *to divide*
å gange/å multiplisere *to multiply*
å legge sammen *to add*
å trekke fra *to take away*

Exercises

1 These statements are in the present tense. Change them into the past tense:

CD1, TR 36

a John reiser til Bergen.
b Han spiser reker og majones.
c Bente drikker en kopp kaffe.
d Hun har en liten rød bil.
e De går til Turistinformasjonen.

2 Insert the correct adverb (see the English in brackets), remembering that some are used for movement and some not:
a Tante Maiken er ___ (*at home*)
b Bente sitter ___ (*there*)
c Kom ___! (*Come in!*)
d Det regner ___ (*outside*)
e Bente vil reise ___ (*home*)

3 Make these statements into questions:
a John liker øl.
b Han kommer fra York.
c Bente vil reise til Bergen.
d Bentes bror heter Tom.

4 Answer these questions starting with **ja** or **jo**:
a Liker du ikke kaffe?
b Vil du komme med meg til Bodø?
c Vil han ikke ringe til Bente?
d Heter han ikke Per?

5 Fill the gaps using the correct forms of the adjectives:

a	en blå bil	den ___ bilen	___ biler	de ___ bilene
b	et stort hus	det ___ huset	___ hus	de ___ husene
c	en lang gat	den ___ gaten	___ gater	de ___ gatene
d	en fin dag	den ___ dagen	___ dager	de ___ dagene

6 Which numbers are these? Write them in figures!

- **a** seksten
- **b** tjuefem
- **c** femtini
- **d** syttifire
- **e** tohundreogto

7 Write out the following numbers in Norwegian:

a 7 **b** 17 **c** 18 **d** 80 **e** 632

8 Can you write out these sums in words, or say them out loud? And then give the answer in Norwegian, too. (Remember to use **er** for =!)

CD1, TR 37

a 4 + 5 =
b 15 − 7 =
c 3 × 6 =
d 28 ÷ 7 =
e 12 + 2 =

Telephoning in Norway

All telephone numbers are eight digits, and you use all eight, whether you dial a local number or long distance. The two first digits specify the town or area, Oslo numbers start with 22, Bergen with 55 and so on.

To phone Norway from abroad you dial 00 + 47 followed by the eight digits.

Telephone numbers are normally said in twos:

22 45 96 37: **tjueto førtifem nittiseks trettisju.**

Cheaper rate starts at 5 p.m.

The majority of mobile numbers start with 9. All mobile numbers have eight digits.

Text messaging (SMS) is widespread, and people will often use shortened words. Much used words are:

180	**trenger mer informasjon** (need more info)		
7k	**syk** (ill)	oxo	**også** (also, as well)
å	**og** (and)	pm	**privat melding** (private message)
d	**det** (it)	prt	**party**
dg	**deg** (you)	qlt	**kult** (cool)
g9	**geni** (genius)	r	**er** (am/are/is)
gid	**glad i deg** (love you)	sik	**skal i kveld** (shall/will tonight)
jg	**jeg** (I)	td	**til deg** (for/to you)
ik	**ikke** (not)	thx	**takk** (thanks)
mld	**melding** (message)	z	**sett** (seen)

Have a go!

Bergensbanen

The Oslo–Bergen railway is a major tourist attraction. The train takes you from Oslo through the farming valleys and beautiful forests and lakes. The train climbs steadily to the bare mountain plateau at more than 1,000 m, where the views over glaciers and mountain peaks are breathtaking. The train descends to the fjord country of Western Norway. The railway is kept open right through the winter, and the trip takes about six hours.

The popular 'Norway in a nutshell' tour can be booked. In one day you travel from either Bergen or Oslo, get off at Myrdal high in the mountains, and take the steepest railway in the world, Flåmsbana, via hairpin bends down to the tiny port of Flåm. Board a fjordboat for a memorable trip on the water through narrow fjords, then onto a coach for more breathtaking scenery to Voss. Take the train back to the starting point.

Do you understand?

You are in Oslo and you urgently need to see a dentist. You look in the telephone directory, and pick one: you dial the number.

Damen	Tannlege Per Hansen, vær så god?
Du	(Translate!) *My name is ___. I would like to book an appointment.*
Damen	Er du pasient hos oss?
Du	*No. I come from England. I am on holiday here.*
Damen	Et øyeblikk, så skal jeg se … Jo, du kan få time på torsdag klokken ti over tolv. Det er torsdag niende juli.
Du	*Can I come a little later? I come back from Hamar that day.*
Damen	Et øyeblikk. Jeg har en time klokken fem på fredag tiende juli.
Du	*That is fine. You are in Storgaten. How do I get (use come) there from Oslo S?*
Damen	Det beste er å gå opp Karl Johans gate. Gå til høyre når du ser Domkirken. Gå forbi Domkirken. Da ser du Storgaten. Vi er i nummer sekstini. Det er kanskje femten minutter fra Oslo S.
Du	*Thank you. I shall be there on Friday.*
Damen	Adjø.
Du	*Goodbye.*

QV

Domkirken *the Cathedral Church*
opp *up*
oss *us*
pasient (en) *patient*

***

You are now well into the course. How are you getting on? It would be a good idea now to look back through the **Language patterns** sections to check that you have understood everything. You could even re-do some of the exercises you found difficult and re-read some of the dialogues. You'll be surprised to see how much you have learnt. Good luck with the rest of the course!

Test yourself

You have three choices, but only one is correct.

1 Hva heter Arnes lillebror?
  a Odd. **b** Knut. **c** Tom.
2 Hvem vil Arne snakke med?
  a mor. **b** far. **c** Odd.
3 Vil Arne reise med fly til Bergen?
  a Ja, med fly. **b** Nei, med motorsykkel. **c** Nei, med tog.
4 Når går toget til Bergen?
  a Klokken 15.05. **b** Klokken 14.55. **c** Klokken 14.45.
5 Arne ringer til tante Maiken: tjueto tjuesju nittifem førtifire
  a 22 25 95 44. **b** 22 27 95 44. **c** 22 27 95 45.
6 Vil Sue reise til Bergen med Arne?
  a Ja, hun vil reise med Arne.
  b Nei, hun vil kjøre motorsykkel.
  c Nei, hun vil reise til London.
7 Tante Maiken sier at Arne er en hyggelig gutt.
  a Ja, Arne er en hyggelig gutt.
  b Nei, Arne er en kjedelig gutt.
  c Nei, Arne er en sint gutt.
8 Hvem er tante Maiken?
  a Sues tante. **b** Arnes tante. **c** Norsklæreren.
9 Hvor kommer Arne fra?
  a Han kommer fra York. **b** Han kommer fra Oslo.
  c Han kommer fra Bergen.
10 Hva gjør Arne?
  a Han er frisør. **b** Han er tannlege. **c** Han er student.

7

Familie

Family

In this unit you will learn

- ***About family relationships***
- ***How to talk to children***
- ***How to express irritation***
- ***How to set up a family tree***

Insight

There are many words for family members in this unit. It may be an idea to look up some of them before starting. Look at the section on Norwegian families which follows the Exercises.

Text 1

CD2, TR 1

Arne is now back in Bergen with his family.

Arnes foreldre har et stort, gammelt, gult hus i en stor hage. Foreldrene bor der med Arnes lillebror, Tom, som er atten år og går på skole. Farmor bor der også. Farfar ble drept av en lastebil for fem år siden.

Arne har fire søsken, tre søstre og den ene broren, Tom. Den eldste søsteren heter Liv og er gift med Geir. De bodde i Bergen, men nå bor de i Trondheim. De kom til Trondheim for sju år siden. Arne liker svogeren sin. De har mye til felles.

Søsteren Bente har en hyggelig leilighet i byen. Hun har ikke giftet seg. Hun er mor til Per på fire år og Pål som er femten måneder. Arne og Bente er gode venner, og Arne hjelper Bente med barna hennes når han er i Bergen.

Den yngste av søstrene heter Elisabeth. Hun arbeider i Kristiansand. Da kan hun treffe mormor og morfar ofte. Hun er glad i besteforeldrene, og de liker at hun forteller om jobben sin.

Arnes far arbeider i en stor bank. Moren hadde jobb på et legekontor, men da farmor kom til dem og Bente ble alene-mor, var de glade for at mor var hjemme.

Liv og Geir har to barn. Gutten er tretten år og heter Trond og piken er ti år og heter Anne. Arne har en niese og tre nevøer.

Familiens etternavn er Vik. Liv har Geirs etternavn, Berg, og mormor og morfar heter Hansen.

Insight

'Søsken', meaning *sibling/siblings*, is a word used much more in Norwegian than in English, where it sounds a bit technical.

The use of **'farfar'** and **'farmor'** for father's parents and **'morfar'** and **'mormor'** for mother's parents is a good way of distinguishing between grandparents, and is very common in Norway.

QUICK VOCAB

av *by*
barna (et barn) *the children*
besteforeldre *grandparents*
ble (å bli) *became/was*
bodde (å bo) *lived/used to live*

bror (en) *brother*
da *when*
drept (å drepe) *killed*
eldste *eldest*
etternavn (et) *surname*
farfar (en) *grandfather, paternal*
farmor (en) *grandmother, paternal*
for ... siden *ago*
foreldre *parents*
forteller (å fortelle) *tell/tells*
gift med *married to*
giftet seg (å gifte seg) *got married*
glad i *fond of/love*
glade (glad) *glad/happy* (plural)
hadde (å ha) *had*
hage (en) *garden*
jobb (en) *job*
legekontor (et) *doctor's surgery*
leilighet (en) *flat*
morfar (en) *grandfather, maternal*
mormor (en) *grandmother, maternal*
måneder (en måned) *months*
nevøer (en nevø) *nephews*
niese (en) *niece*
ofte *often*
om *about*
svogeren (en) *the brother-in-law*
søsken *siblings*
søstre (en søster) *sisters*
til felles *in common*
yngste *youngest*
år (et) *year*

True or false? 1

a Arne har tre eldre brødre.
b Arnes svoger heter Tom.
c Elisabeth har to barn.
d Tom er eldre enn Arne.

Dialogue 2

Arne can't find his jacket.

Arne skal ta en tur til byen for å treffe noen venner. Han finner ikke jakken sin.

CD2, TR 2

Arne	Mor, hvor er jakken min?
Mor	Hvilken jakke?
Arne	Den nye, blå jakken som jeg kjøpte i London!
Mor	Tom hadde den da han gikk ut. Jeg trodde han hadde spurt deg om å få låne den.
Arne	Han skal få juling når jeg får tak i ham! Har han ikke en jakke selv? I går tok han sykkelen min. Nå er den ikke i orden. Den … den drittungen!
Mor	Ikke vær sint, Arne. Jeg skal si et alvorsord til ham når han kommer tilbake.
Arne	Kan jeg ta bilen din, mor? Jeg er sen, og jeg når ikke bussen. Hvor er bilnøklene?
Mor	Bilen? Nei … nei, Tom har lånt bilen. Han kommer ikke hjem før klokken åtte.
Arne	Han er mors lille engel! Når kommer far hjem?
Mor	Far skulle besøke Bente og barna før han kommer hjem i dag.
Arne	Jeg tror jeg reiser tilbake til tante Maiken!!

Insight

Here is rather an offensive way to address someone: **'drittunge'** consists of two words, **'dritt'** meaning *manure/ muck/dirt* and **'unge'** meaning *animal offspring*, but can also mean *kid*. **'Drittunge'** is not the very worst insult you can use, but it is not very nice. Much worse would be **'Drittsekk'**, meaning: *dirt/manure bag*, but we don't use such words in our nice book!

If you want to insult somebody you would usually say **'din drittunge'**, meaning *you …!*

QUICK VOCAB

alvorsord (et) *serious word*
besøke *visit*
bilnøkkelen (en) *the car key*
drittungen (en drittunge) *the 'dirty kid'* (see This is how we say it, in this unit)
engel (en) *angel*
får (å få) tak i *get/gets hold of*
gikk (å ga) *went*
ham *him*
hvilken *which*
i dag *today*
i går *yesterday*
i orden *in order*
jakken (en jakke) *the jacket/coat*
juling (en) *hiding/beating*
låne (å låne) *borrow*
nye (ny) *new*
når (å nå) *reach/reaches*
selv *himself/herself*
skulle *should*
spurt (å spørre) *asked*
trodde (å tro) *thought/believed*
tur (en) *trip*

True or false? 2

a Arne tar bussen til byen.
b Mor kjører Tom til byen.
c Arne er i dårlig humør.
d Tom har Arnes nye jakke.

Dialogue 3

CD2, TR 3

It is raining. Arne visits Bente.

Livs barn, Trond og Anne, er på besøk hos besteforeldrene. De skal være der i en uke. I dag tar Arne dem med til Bente. Det regner og Bente og barna er inne. Pål skriker.

Bente	Trond, vil du holde Pål.
Trond	Han er våt!
Bente	Han skal snart få en tørr bleie.
Per	Jeg er sulten! Jeg vil ha mat!
Bente	Det heter ikke 'jeg vil', Per. Du må spørre pent. Du må si: 'Kan jeg få litt mat'.
Per	Jeg vil! Jeg vil!

Bente	Da får du ikke mat. Du får ikke mat før du er snill!
Per	Jeg vil ikke være snill!!

Nå skriker både Per og Pål. Begge guttene skriker.

Bente	Jeg vil gjerne skrike også!!
Arne	Jeg skal hjelpe deg. Jeg skal ta meg av Per* mens du skifter på Pål.

Bente vasker Pål og skifter på ham. Snart sover Pål. Bente må skifte skjørtet sitt også.

Trond	Per, jeg var alltid snill da jeg var liten! Anne og jeg var alltid snille da vi var små!

Per ser på Trond og Anne. Så ser han på Arne.

Per	Kan jeg få litt mat, Arne?
Arne	Det kan du, Per. Vil du ha en bolle med geitost og et glass saft?
Per	Ja takk!
Arne	Det var bedre, Per! Hva med dere to? Vil dere ha boller og saft?
Trond	Ja takk! Mange boller! Anne og jeg vil gjerne ha saft også.
Bente	Og is? Vil dere ha is?
Barna	Ja!!!
Bente	Takk, Arne! Du er en god bror.

Bente gir Arne en klem. Arne lager mat og de spiser. Etterpå vasker Bente opp og rydder. Trond hjelper henne, mens Anne og Per leker med Lego. Alle er i godt humør. Snart skinner solen og de kan ta en tur ut.

Bente	Trond, jeg passet deg da du var liten. Du var ikke bedre enn Per!

*Arne actually said '... ta av meg Per'. This is colloquial.

Insight

Dear oh dear, – Bente isn't having an easy time with her two small children, is she! Trying to instill good manners isn't easy. The polite phrase: **'kan jeg få ...'** equals the English *may I have ...* Of course you remember: **'jeg vil gjerne ha ...'** meaning *I would like to have ...*

QUICK VOCAB

besøk (et) *visit*
bleie (en) *nappy*
bolle (en) *bun*
enn *than*
gir (å gi) *give/gives*
i en uke *for a week*
inne *inside*
is (en) *ice-cream*
klem (en) *hug*
lager (å lage) *make/makes*
leker (å leke) *play/plays*
mens *while*
passet (å passe) *looked after/minded*
pent *nicely*
rydder (å rydde) *tidy/tidies*
saft (en) *juice/squash*
sitt *his/her own*
skifter (å skifte) *change/changes*
skjørtet (et) *the skirt*
skriker (å skrike) *scream/screams*
snill *good/kind*
sover (å sove) *sleep/sleeps*
spørre *ask*
ta meg av *take care of*
tørr *dry*
vasker (å vaske) *wash/washes*
vasker opp *wash/washes up*
våt *wet*

True or false? 3

a Arne besøker Bente.
b Bente har to små piker.
c Bentes bror heter Trond.
d Bente vasker opp.

This is how we say it

▸ Looking at a baby:

Så søt hun er!	*How sweet she looks!*
Hun likner tante Kari!	*She looks like Aunt Kari!*
Hun skriker ofte!	*She cries often!*
Jeg liker ikke små barn!	*I don't like small children!*
Hun er våt!	*She is wet!*
Hun likner en liten engel når hun sover!	*She looks like a little angel when she's asleep!*

▸ Exasperated parent to small child:

Hvis du er snill, skal du få en stor is!	*If you are good, you will get a big ice-cream!*
Du får ikke is hvis du ikke gjør som jeg sier!	*You will not get an ice-cream if you don't do what I tell you!*
Det heter ikke: 'jeg vil ha', – det heter: 'kan jeg få'.	*It isn't: 'I want', – it is 'may I have'.*
Du likner faren din!	*You are like your father!*

▸ One child hurling abuse at another:

Din drittunge!	*You dirty kid!* (**dritt** = *dirt/muck,* **unge** = *kid/baby animal)*
Din tufs!	*You feeble thing!*
Din gris!	*You pig!*

▸ Instructions:

Vask hendene!	*Wash your hands!*
Sitt pent!	*Sit nicely!*

Ikke snakk med mat i munnen!	*Don't talk with food in your mouth!*
Ti stille!	*Keep quiet!*

▶ And some kind words:

Du er verdens beste gutt.	*You are the best boy in the world.*
Du er en snill, liten gutt.	*You are a good little boy.*
Skal jeg lese for deg?	*Shall I read to you?*
Skal vi spille Ludo?	*Shall we play Ludo?*
Skal vi leke med Lego?	*Shall we play with Lego?*
God natt, og sov godt.	*Good night, and sleep well.*

Insight

In Norway children learn from an early age to say **'Takk for maten'** meaning *Thank you for the food* after every meal. You must remember to say **'takk for maten'** to your hostess. Only badly brought up people don't!

Language patterns

1 Personal pronouns

The personal pronouns are as follows:

1st person singular	**jeg**	*I*
2nd person singular	**du**	*you*
3rd person singular	**han**	*he*
	hun	*she*
	den/det	*it*
1st person plural	**vi**	*we*
2nd person plural	**dere**	*you* (more than one)
3rd person plural	**de**	*they*

The personal pronouns have three forms. The list shows the subject forms. The subject tells you who or what is doing something.

Anne skriker.	*Anne cries.*
Hun skriker.	*She cries.*
Tom og Trond leker med Lego.	*Tom and Trond play with Lego.*
De leker med Lego.	*They play with Lego.*

Insight

Are you quite sure of the first-, second- and third-person forms (*I/we, you, he/she/it/they*) when it comes to pronouns? Just check – they are important for the next section, the possessives.

2 Possessives

The possessives give information about ownership:

Er det din far?	*Is that your father?*
Nei, det er min mann.	*No, it is my husband.*

min/mitt/mine		*my, mine*
din/ditt/dine		*your, yours*
hans	sin/sitt/sine	*his*
hennes		*her, hers*
dens		*its*
dets		*its*
vår/vårt/våre		*our, ours*
deres		*your, yours* (pl.)
deres	sin/sitt/sine	*their, theirs*

There are two important points to remember about possessives:

- If you put the possessive before the noun, the noun is in the indefinite; whereas if you put the possessive after the noun, the noun is in the definite.

Min tante er tykk.	*My aunt is fat.*
Tanten min er tykk.	*My aunt is fat.*
Hennes bror er i fengsel.	*Her brother is in prison.*
Broren hennes er i fengsel.	*Her brother is in prison.*

▶ When the possessive pronoun refers back to the subject, but is not itself the subject, you use the reflexive **sin** in the third person, singular and plural.

This point needs a little explaining. Look at the examples below:

1 Tanten min er tykk.	*My aunt is fat.*
2 Tanten din er tykk.	*Your aunt is fat.*
3 Tanten hans er tykk.	*His aunt is fat.*
4 Jeg liker tanten min.	*I like my aunt.*
5 Jeg liker tanten din.	*I like your aunt.*
6 Jeg liker tanten hans.	*I like his aunt.*
7 Han liker tanten sin.	*He likes his (own) aunt.*
8 Han liker tanten hans.	*He likes his (some other chap's) aunt.*

In Examples 1–3 the possessive is part of the subject. In the rest of the examples, the possessive is part of the object. In Examples 4 and 7 the ownership refers back to the subject. Both Examples 7 and 8 have the subject and the possessive in the 3rd person, but only in Example 7 does the ownership refer back to the subject. This is when one uses the reflexive **sin**, **sitt** and **sine** in the 3rd person singular and plural. It defines ownership better.

A good way of remembering this is if you think of the consequences:

Han er i sin seng.	*He is in his own bed.*
Han er i hans seng.	*He is in some other chap's bed.*
Han er i hennes seng.	*He is in her bed.*

The reflexive is never the subject of a sentence, but refers back to the subject.

This may seem a little complicated at first, but you will soon get to grips with it.

Insight

You may find this a little hard to start with. Just remember that the reflexive pronoun in the third person singular and plural identifies ownership. Also remember that the reflexive points back to the subject, but is never used with the subject.

3 Irregular nouns

Here is a reminder of the four forms of the regular nouns:

en gutt (*a boy*)	**gutten** (*the boy*)	**gutter** (*boys*)	**guttene** (*the boys*)
et hus (*a house*)	**huset** (*the house*)	**hus** (*houses*)	**husene** (*the houses*)

In Unit 5 you found some irregular nouns, nouns which don't follow the normal rules. Here are some more:

en far	**faren**	**fedre**	**fedrene**	(*father*)
en mor	**moren**	**mødre**	**mødrene**	(*mother*)
en bror	**broren**	**brødre**	**brødrene**	(*brother*)
en søster	**søsteren**	**søstre**	**søstrene**	(*sister*)

All **en** and **et** words have **ene** or just **ne** in the definite plural except for these two:

et barn	**barnet**	**barn**	**barna**	(*child*)
et ben	**benet**	**ben**	**bena**	(*bone/leg*)

They follow the normal pattern for short (one syllable) **et** words with no ending in indefinite plural, but get an **a** in the definite plural. This has nothing whatsoever to do with feminine endings.

Liv har to barn.	*Liv has two children.*
Barna heter Trond og Anne.	*The children are called Trond and Anne.*
Arne har lange ben.	*Arne has long legs.*
Hunden spiser bena.	*The dog eats the bones.*

4 Verbs

The really irregular verbs are called 'strong' verbs in Norwegian. The other verbs are 'weak' verbs. Weak verbs fall into four groups, and follow a definite pattern.

	infinitive	present	past	
Group 1:	å vente	venter	ventet	(*to wait*)
	å rydde	rydder	ryddet	(*to tidy*)
	å arbeide	arbeider	arbeidet	(*to work*)
Group 2:	å spise	spiser	spiste	(*to eat*)
	å drepe	dreper	drepte	(*to kill*)
	å reise	reiser	reiste	(*to travel*)

There is more on the two other groups in Unit 8.

Some more strong verbs:

å hete	**heter**	**het**	(*to be called*)
å komme	**kommer**	**kom**	(*to come*)
å ta	**tar**	**tok**	(*to take*)

5 *Leke/spille* to play

Å leke (*to play*) is used for playing with toys, whereas **å spille** (*to play*) is used for any other kind of playing, such as sport, games, gambling, musical instruments, theatre and so on.

å leke	**leker**	**lekte**
å spille	**spiller**	**spilte**

Both verbs are weak verbs, belonging to Group 2.

Notice the spelling of the past tense of **spille:** one **l** is left out.

Exercises

1 Fill in the missing forms of the nouns:

a	en søster	___	___	___
b	___	faren	___	___
c	___	___	___	barna
d	___	___	menn	___
e	en lærer	___	___	___

2 Adjectives and nouns:

a	en god venn	den___	___	___
b	et stort hus	det___	___	___
c	et lite barn	det___	___	___
d	en kjedelig film	den___	___	___

3 Use the possessive pronouns prompted in brackets:

a ___ mor er norsk. (*my*)
b Søsteren ___ er snill. (*her*)
c Dette er ___ familie. (*my*)
d Han spiser maten ___. (*his own*)
e Han tar sykkelen ___. (*her*)

4 Fill in the gaps in these phrases about family relationships:

CD2, TR 5

a Min farmor er gift med min ___.
b Jeg er tante til to piker. De er mine ___.
c Min søster er gift med Ole. Han er min ___.
d Mor og far er mine ___.
e Den gutten der er ___ min. (*Use 'son' or 'brother'*).

5 Set out your own family tree, using Norwegian words. Follow the example overleaf.

6 List all the members of your family by name: Min (aunt, uncle, grandmother (maternal), brother, etc.) heter ___, (using Norwegian names).

Norwegian families

Arnes familietre *(Arne's family tree)*

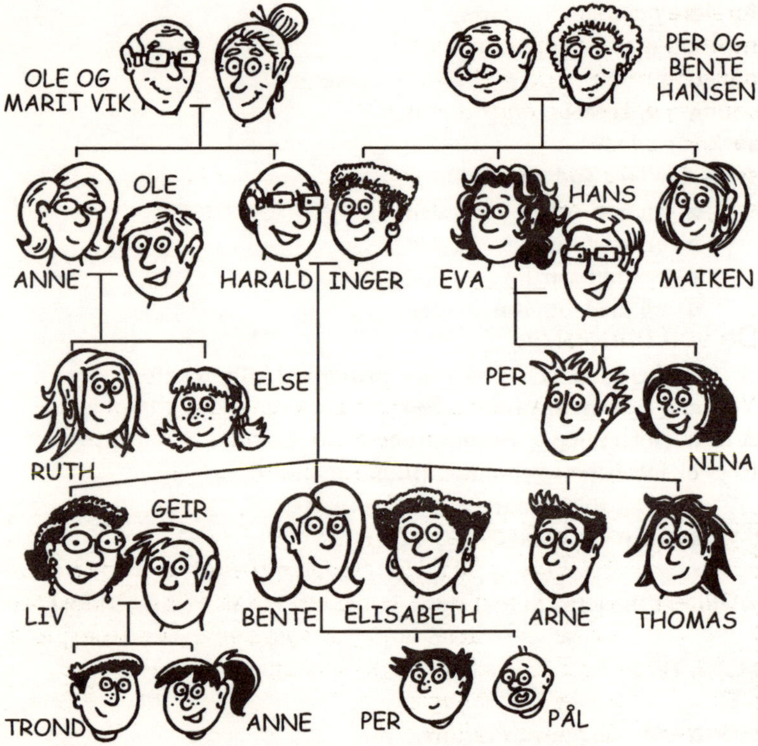

g. (gift med) *married to*
oldeforeldre *great-grandparents*
oldefar og oldemor *great-grandfather and great-grandmother*
bestefar og bestemor *grandfather and grandmother*

In Norway it is most usual to distinguish between father's parents and mother's parents by calling them: **farfar og farmor, morfar og mormor.**

barn *child*
barnebarn *grandchild*
bror og søster *brother and sister*
far og mor *father and mother*
fetter og kusine *male cousin and female cousin*
foreldre *parents*
nevø og niese *nephew and niece*
onkel og tante *uncle and aunt*
sønn og datter *son and daughter*
søsken *sibling*
svigerfar og svigermor *father-in-law and mother-in-law*
svoger og svigerinne *brother-in-law and sister-in-law*

QUICK VOCAB

Do you understand?

You are sitting on a seat in Frogner Park, enjoying the sunshine. A family is having a picnic on the grass. A small boy comes over to you, eating an ice-cream. He starts talking to you:

CD2, TR 5

Gutten	Hei, er du alene?
Du	*Yes, I like to be alone. (You hope he will go away.)*
Gutten	Familien min er der borte. Det er mamma og tante Kari, og det er søsteren min, hun som skriker. Den store piken er tante Karis barn. Jeg liker henne ikke.
Du	*What is your name?*
Gutten	Jeg heter Andrew.
Du	*Andrew is not a Norwegian name.*
Andrew	Min far er amerikansk. Mamma er fransk. Jeg heter Pierre også. Vennene mine kaller meg Anders. Det er et norsk navn.
Du	*And your sister, has she got an American and a French name as well?*
Andrew	Nei, hun heter Olga, fordi mormor er russisk.
Du	*Isn't your father here?*
Andrew	Jo, men han går en tur i parken fordi mamma snakker og snakker og Olga skriker.

(Contd)

Du	*Why are you not with him?*
Andrew	Fordi han liker å være alene også!

QUICK VOCAB

fransk *French*
heller *either*
hvit *white*
kaller (å kalle) *call/calls*
russisk *Russian*

Test Yourself

You have three choices, and only one is correct.

1 Hvem ble drept av en lastebil?
a Bente. **b** Farmor. **c** Farfar.
2 Hva heter den yngste søsteren?
a Elisabeth. **b** Liv. **c** Tom.
3 Hva heter Arnes svoger?
a Odd. **b** Geir. **c** Randi.
4 Hvor arbeider Arnes far?
a På en ferge. **b** På et hotell. **c** I en bank.
5 Hva er Geirs etternavn?
a Vik. **b** Berg. **c** Hansen.
6 Hvor bor morfar og mormor?
a Bergen. **b** Kristiansand. **c** Trondheim.
7 Hvem leker med Lego?
a Anne og Per. **b** Mor og far. **c** Arne og Bente.

From *Do you understand.*

8 Gutten heter Andrew. Hva kaller vennene ham?
a Andy. **b** Android. **c** Anders.
9 Er Andrews far norsk?
a Nei, han er fransk. **b** Nei, han er amerikansk.
c Ja, han er norsk.
10 Hva heter Andrews tante?
a Kari. **b** Bente. **c** Elisabeth.

8

Sue er på sykehus

Sue is in hospital

In this unit you will learn

- ***How to express pain and discomfort***
- ***Parts of the body***
- ***How to deal with being in hospital***
- ***How to describe symptoms of illness or pain***

Insight

Sue has now left poor old Arne and is travelling with Jan. All goes well to begin with. Notice in the first paragraph: **'det var sol'**, meaning: it was sunny. **'Sol'** really means *sun*, but may be used to mean both *sun* and *sunshine*. However, there is also a word for *sunshine*, namely **'solskinn'**.

Dialogue 1

Fredag trettende august (*Friday 13 August*) Disaster!

Sue og Jan hadde en fin reise sørover til Stavern på Sues motorsykkel. Stavern er en hyggelig liten by som ligger ved havet. Sue og Jan fant en campingplass. De satte opp teltet og så badet de i sjøen. Det var sol og fint vær, men sjøen var kald, syntes Sue.

CD2, TR 6

Jan	Vannet er ikke kaldt! Det er sikkert nitten grader! Det er varmt!
Sue	Det er for kaldt! Det er ikke varmt nok for meg. Jeg vil ikke bade mer!

De tok en tur til Stavern. Alle de små husene var hvite eller gule med vakre, små hager. Det var flere hyggelige ute-restauranter hvor folk hygget seg sammen.

Sue	Jeg liker Stavern. Her skulle jeg gjerne bo.
Jan	Stavern smiler til oss! Vil du ha en is?
Sue	Gjerne! Isen er god her i Norge!

Så kjørte de til fjellet. De stoppet der veien var over tusen meter over havet. De gikk til toppen av et høyt fjell. Utsikten var fantastisk.

De kjørte videre mot Kristiansand. Sue så på den vakre naturen og tenkte på hvor fint det var å være her. Hun så ikke den store lastebilen som kom mot dem før det var for sent. Sue hørte at hun skrek. Hun så et stort, rødt lys. Så ble alt mørkt.

Ambulansemannen	Kan du høre meg?
Sue	Hvor er jeg? Å, jeg har så vondt i hodet! Jeg har vondt alle steder.
Ambulansemannen	Ligg stille! Du er i en ambulanse på vei til Kristiansand.
Sue	Hvor er Jan?
Ambulansemannen	Jan? Han er også her. Dere har hatt en ulykke.
Jan	Å! Hodet mitt!

Insight

'Jeg har vondt i ...' meaning: *I have pain in/it hurts* is a bit hard to get to grips with. **'Vondt'** is an adverb, and not a noun, as is pain. This phrase crops up a lot in this unit, and there is an extensive list of uses in 'This is how we say it' after Dialogue 3.

alle steder *everywhere*
ambulanse (en) *ambulance*
badet (å bade) *swam/bathed*
campingplass (en) *campsite*
fant (å finne) *found*
fantastisk *fantastic*
fjellet (et) *the mountain*
flere *several*
folk *people*
for *too*
grader (en grad) *degrees*
har hatt (å ha) *have/has had*
havet (et) *the ocean*
hodet (et hode) *the head*
hvor *how*
hygget seg (å hygge seg) *had a good time*
høyt (høy) *tall/high*
kald *cold*
mot *towards*
mørkt (mørk) *dark*
naturen (en) *the landscape/scenery/nature*
rødt (rød) *red*
satte opp (å sette opp) *set up*
skrek (å skrike) *screamed*
sted (et) *place*
stille *quietly*
stoppet (å stoppe) *stopped*
sørover *southwards*
syntes (å synes) *thought/was of the opinion that*
så (å se) *saw/looked*
tenkte (å tenke) *thought*
toppen (en) *the top*
ulykke (en) *accident*
utsikten (en) *the view*
varmt (varm) *warm*
vondt *pain/hurt*

QUICK VOCAB

True or false? 1

a Sue kjører til Bergen.
b De reiser ikke til Stavern.
c Arne har en ulykke med motorsykkelen.
d De reiser med lastebil til Kristiansand.

Dialogue 2

Sue wakes up in hospital. She aches all over. Poor Sue!

Sue våkner i en sykeseng. Hun kan ikke røre seg. En sykepleier står ved sengen.

CD2, TR 7

Sykepleier	Hvordan har du det nå?
Sue	Dårlig! Hvor er jeg?
Sykepleier	Du er på sykehuset i Kristiansand. Husker du at dere ble påkjørt av en lastebil?
Sue	Nå husker jeg det! Hvordan går det med Jan?
Sykepleier	Ikke så verst. Han har brukket en arm. Du kan se ham senere. Men du må ligge så stille du kan til hodet ditt er bedre. Du har en kraftig hjernerystelse. Du får nok vondt i hodet i noen dager.
Sue	Jeg har vondt alle steder! Jeg har vondt i hele kroppen!
Sykepleier	Du har vært heldig. Du kunne ha blitt drept! Du har ikke brukket noe. Men du har mange sting. Ligg stille!
Sue	Jeg er veldig tørst. Kan jeg få litt vann?
Sykepleier	Ja, men bare litt. Jeg skal hjelpe deg.

Sue så ansiktet sitt i speilet da hun drakk.

Sue	Hjelp! Jeg er kvalm! Jeg må kaste opp!

Insight

Sue and Jan were struck by a lorry: **'påkjørt av en lastebil'**. Luckily they weren't killed by a lorry: **'drept av en lastebil'**, as Arne's granddad was! Do you remember this from the previous unit?

QUICK VOCAB

ansiktet (et) *the face*
arm (en) *arm*
blitt (å bli) *become/been*
brukket (å brekke) *broken*
drakk (å drikke) *drank*
hjernerystelse (en) *concussion*
kaste opp *be sick/throw up*
kraftig *strong/heavy*
kroppen (en) *the body*
kvalm *feeling sick/nauseous*
noe *something/anything*
nok here a 'tag' word, meaning *perhaps*
påkjørt av *hit by* (a car/bus etc.)
røre seg *move* (herself)
sengen (en) *the bed*
speilet (et speil) *the mirror*
sting (et) *stitch*
står (å stå) *stand/stands*
sykehuset (et) *the hospital*
sykepleier (en) *nurse*
sykeseng (en) *hospital bed*
våkner (å våkne) *wakes up*

True or false? 2

a Sue er på sykehuset.
b Hun har vondt alle steder.
c Hun er tørst og drikker vann.
d Hun blir kvalm når hun ser seg i speilet.

Dialogue 3

Sue is getting better. She talks to the nurse.

Sue er mye bedre. Hun snakker med sykepleieren.

CD2, TR 8

Sue	Jeg ser at du heter Elisabeth Vik. Jeg har en venn som heter Arne Vik. Han er student i London, og han kommer fra Bergen.
Elisabeth	Arne! Det er broren min. Han har snakket om en som heter Sue. Og du er Sue! Arne er en god bror. Vi kranglet mye da vi var barn, men nå er vi veldig gode venner.
Sue	Hils ham fra meg!
Elisabeth	Det skal jeg gjøre.

Sue vil se Jan. Han ligger på rom nummer sju i fjerde etasje. Sue går inn. Det er tre senger der. Men hvor er Jan?

I den første sengen ligger en gammel mann uten hår. I den andre sengen er en stor, tykk mann med langt, svart hår. Da må det være Jan i den tredje sengen. Men er det virkelig Jan?

Sue ser et rødt og blått ansikt med mange sår og mye plaster. Hun kan nesten ikke se øynene hans og nesen er som en potet. Munnen er helt skjev og håret er klippet bort. Stakkars Jan!

Jan Hei, Sue!

Han prøver å smile.

Sue Stakkars deg! Har du mye vondt?

Hun tar hånden hans.

Jan	Au!! Jeg har brukket en arm. Legen sier at jeg får noen arr på føttene. Jeg har mange sting. Hvordan har du det?
Sue	Ikke så verst. Jeg skal være her noen dager til.
Jan	Mor og far kommer på fredag. Jeg reiser hjem med dem. Vil du være med? De vil gjerne treffe deg. Vi kan være hjemme til vi begge er bedre.
Sue	Jeg vil gjerne treffe familien din. Og jeg må tenke på hva jeg skal gjøre. Jeg vil finne en jobb når jeg er helt frisk.

Insight

Here we have the first four of the ordinal numbers: **'første'**, **'andre'**, **'tredje'**, **'fjerde'**. The full list is in Unit 10.

QUICK VOCAB

andre *second*
arr (et) *scar*
au! *ouch!*
etasje (en) *floor*
fjerde *fourth*
frisk *healthy/well*
føttene (en fot) *the feet*
helt *quite/completely*
hånden (en) *the hand*
hår (et) *hair*
klippet (å klippe) *cut*
legen (en lege) *the doctor*
munnen (en) *the mouth*
nesen (en nese) *the nose*
plaster (et) *plaster*
potet (en) *potato*
prøver (å prøve) *try/tries*
rom (et) *room*
skjev *crooked*
som *as/like*
stakkars *poor*
svart *black*
sår (et) *sore/wound*
tredje *third*
treffe (å treffe) *to meet*
uten *without*
virkelig *really*
øynene (et øye) *the eyes*

True or false? 3

a Jan er Elisabeths bror.
b Jan ligger i den tredje sengen.
c Sue har brukket armen.
d Sue vil ikke treffe Jans familie.

This is how we say it

Expressions regarding how you feel:

▶ **Hva er i veien med deg?**	*What is the matter with you?*
▶ **Jeg har vondt i …**	*I have a pain in the …*
Jeg har vondt i hodet.	*I have a sore head.*
Jeg har vondt i en finger.	*I have a sore finger.*
Det gjør vondt …	*It hurts …*
Det gjør vondt i magen min.	*My stomach hurts.*
Det gjør vondt i hodet.	*My head hurts.*
Jeg har vondt alle steder!	*It hurts everywhere!*
Jeg har hodepine.	*I have a headache.*
▶ **Stakkars deg!**	*Poor you!*
▶ **Jeg er trett.**	*I am tired.*
Jeg er i dårlig humør.	*I am in a bad mood.*
Jeg føler meg dårlig.	*I feel bad/unwell.*
Jeg føler meg syk.	*I feel ill.*
Jeg har diaré.	*I have diarrhoea.*
Jeg er kvalm.	*I feel nauseous.*
Jeg føler meg kvalm.	*I feel nauseous.*
Jeg må kaste opp!	*I have to throw up/vomit!*
▶ **Jeg føler meg bedre i dag.**	*I feel better today.*
▶ **Jeg er frisk som en fisk!**	*I am healthy as a fish.*
▶ **God bedring!**	*Good/speedy recovery!*

Insight

Look carefully at these phrases. As you can see, you can either say **'jeg har vondt i ...'**, meaning: *I have pain in ...* or **'det gjør vondt i ...'** meaning: *it hurts in ...*

'Stakkars deg!' meaning: *poor you!* is used in every situation where you feel sorry for someone, whether they are ill, tired or just irritated for some reason.

'Jeg er frisk som en fisk', *I am as healthy/well as a fish* could only be a Norwegian expression!

Language patterns

1 Verbs

I have been, *He has gone*, *You have had*, all demonstrate the perfect tense of the verb. Past tense describes something which has already happened. Perfect tense is also about the past, but could still be going on:

Jeg har vondt i hodet.	*I have a headache.*	**Present**
Jeg hadde vondt i hodet i går.	*I had a headache yesterday.*	**Past**
Jeg har hatt vondt i hodet hele dagen.	*I have had a headache all day.*	**Perfect**

As in English, the perfect tense is formed with the verb **å ha** (*to have*) and the past participle of the verb. The past participle is sometimes the same as the past tense (as in Group 1 of the weak verbs listed below), but most often it is a different word.

2 Groups of weak verbs

	Infinitive	Present	Past	Perfect (*have* + past participle)	
Group 1:	å klippe	klipper	klippet	har klippet	(*to cut*)
	å kaste	kaster	kastet	har kastet	(*to throw*)
	å stoppe	stopper	stoppet	har stoppet	(*to stop*)

Group 2:	å smile	smiler	smilte	har smilt	(*to smile*)
	å røre	rører	rørte	har rørt	(*to move*)
	å tenke	tenker	tenkte	har tenkt	(*to think*)

Most weak verbs fall into these two groups. Less usual are these:

Group 3:	å leve	lever	levde	har levd	(*to live – be alive*)
	å prøve	prøver	prøvde	har prøvd	(*to try*)
Group 4:	å bo	bor	bodde	har bodd	(*to live – reside*)
	å nå	når	nådde	har nådd	(*to reach*)
	å tro	tror	trodde	har trodd	(*to believe*)

3 More strong verbs

å drikke	drikker	drakk	har drukket	(*to drink*)
å brekke	brekker	brakk	har brukket	(*to break*)
å hjelpe	hjelper	hjalp	har hjulpet	(*to help*)
å ligge	ligger	lå	har ligget	(*to lie*)
å se	ser	så	har sett	(*to see*)
å si	sier	sa	har sagt	(*to say*)

There is a complete list of strong and modal verbs in the **Grammar section** at the back of the book.

Insight

How can you find out if a verb is weak or strong? Look in the Norwegian–English vocabulary towards the end of the book. Look up a verb, say **'arbeide'**, meaning *to work*. After **'arbeide'** there is a 'v' indicating 'verb' followed by a bracket with a number, which here is (1). This means that the verb **'arbeide'** is a Group 1 weak verb. The list in this unit tells you how to conjugate the four groups of weak verbs, presented in the Vocabulary as (1), (2), (3), and (4). Similarly, a strong verb will be listed with (s). You can then look it up in Irregular verbs in the **Grammar section** towards the end of the book. All irregular, or strong, verbs used in this book will be listed.

4 Personal pronouns

In Unit 7 you came across the personal pronouns, and you looked at the possessives. Now look at the object form:

1st	jeg	*I*	meg	*me*	
2nd	du	*you*	deg	*you*	
3rd	han	*he*	ham	*him*	seg
	hun	*she*	henne	*her*	
	den	*it*	den	*it*	
	det	*it*	det	*it*	
1st	vi	*we*	oss	*us*	
2nd	dere	*you* pl.	dere	*you* pl.	
3rd	de	*they*	dem	*them*	seg

The pronouns are used in the same way as in English:

Bente liker John. Bente liker **ham.** Hun liker **ham.**
(John is the object)
Bente liker Kari og Per. Hun liker **dem.**
(Kari and Per are the objects)
Jeg skal ringe til **deg.** (you are the object)
Vil du skrive til **meg?** (I am the object)
Vi skal reise til **dem.**
De kommer til **oss.**

5 Reflexive pronouns

Just as the possessive pronoun has a **sin** used in the third person, when the ownership reflects back to the subject, but is not itself the subject, the same applies to the object form:

1st Jeg setter meg. *I sit (myself) down.*
2nd Du setter deg.

3rd	Han setter seg.
3rd	Hun setter seg.
1st	Vi setter oss.
2nd	Dere setter dere.
3rd	De setter seg.

If you say: Han setter **ham**, it would mean that he sits some other male down, a child perhaps.

6 Reflexive verbs

Many verbs are reflexive in Norwegian.

Jeg føler meg dårlig.	*I feel ill.*
Jeg skal gifte meg.	*I shall marry.*
Han skal gifte seg.	*He'll marry.*
Vi skal gifte oss.	*We'll marry.*
De skal gifte seg.	*They shall marry.*
Hun liker seg i Oslo.	*She likes to be in Oslo.*

7 Some more irregular nouns

et øye	**øyet**	**øyne**	**øynene**	*(an eye)*
en hånd	**hånden**	**hender**	**hendene**	*(a hand)*
en skulder	**skulderen**	**skuldre**	**skuldrene**	*(a shoulder)*
en finger	**fingeren**	**fingre**	**fingrene**	*(a finger)*
et kne	**kneet**	**knær**	**knærne**	*(a knee)*
en tå	**tåen**	**tær**	**tærne**	*(a toe)*
en fot	**foten**	**føtter**	**føttene**	*(a foot)*

8 *Au!, Æsj!* *Ouch!, Yuk!*

Exclamations and interjections express reactions or emotions:

Au!	an expression of pain *(ouch!)*
Æsj!	shows irritation or disgust *(yuk!)*
Isj!	more irritation and disgust!

Huff!	grumbling or being irritated
Fy!	showing strong disapproval, and mainly used when talking to children or dogs
Pytt!	*Never mind!*
Stakkars deg!	*Poor you!*
Åh!	expressing delight, amazement or horror, depending on the tone of voice

Exercises

1 Fill in the gaps with the past tense forms of the words in brackets:

CD2, TR 9

a (spise) Arne ______ reker med majones.
b (drikke) Han ______ et stort glass øl.
c (reise) De ______ på ferie til Amerika.
d (ta) Randi ______ trikken til Frognerparken.

2 Perfect tense this time:

CD2, TR 10

a (bo) De har ______ i Norge i fire måneder.
b (tro) Jeg har ______ på ham.
c (stoppe) Han har ______ for rødt lys.
d (brekke) Jan har ______ den høyre armen.

3 Translate the words in brackets into Norwegian, using the diagram overleaf for reference. Remember to use the correct forms of the nouns:

Jan har et (*head*) ______. Han har to (*eyes*) ______, to (*ears*) ______, en (*nose*) ______, og en (*mouth*) ______. Han har to (*arms*) ______ og to (*legs*) ______. Han har ti (*fingers*)

______ og ti (*toes*) ______. Han har vondt i (*the head*) ________ og i (*the stomach*) ________.

4 Insert the correct form of the adjective in brackets:
- **a** Sue har (**brun**) _______ øyne.
- **b** Arne har (**blå**) _______ øyne.
- **c** Jan har et (**stor**) ______ sår i hodet.
- **d** Mannen har (**rød**) ______ hår og en (**stor**) _____ nese.

5 Use the possessive pronouns to complete these phrases:
- **a** Sue har vondt i hodet ______.
- **b** Jan har mange sting på armene _______.
- **c** Nesen _______ er som en potet.
- **d** Den tredje sengen er _______.

6 Write the following passage in the present tense. (Use the **Vocabulary** at the back of the book. This will tell you which group the weak verbs belong to. There is a list of irregular verbs in the **Grammar** section at the back of the book.)

Jan våknet i en sykeseng. Han var på et stort sykehus. Han hadde vondt alle steder. Legen sa at han ville få noen arr på føttene. Han hadde mange sting i hodet og på armene og bena, men han var heldig som ikke var drept.

Sue var også på sykehuset. Hun så ansiktet sitt i speilet. Da måtte hun kaste opp. Sykepleieren sa at hun hadde en bror som het Arne.

7 Can you translate the passage in Exercise 6?

Looking after your health

Trygdekassen

This is the national health service in Norway. If you are British, you will get the same benefits as the Norwegians. It is advisable

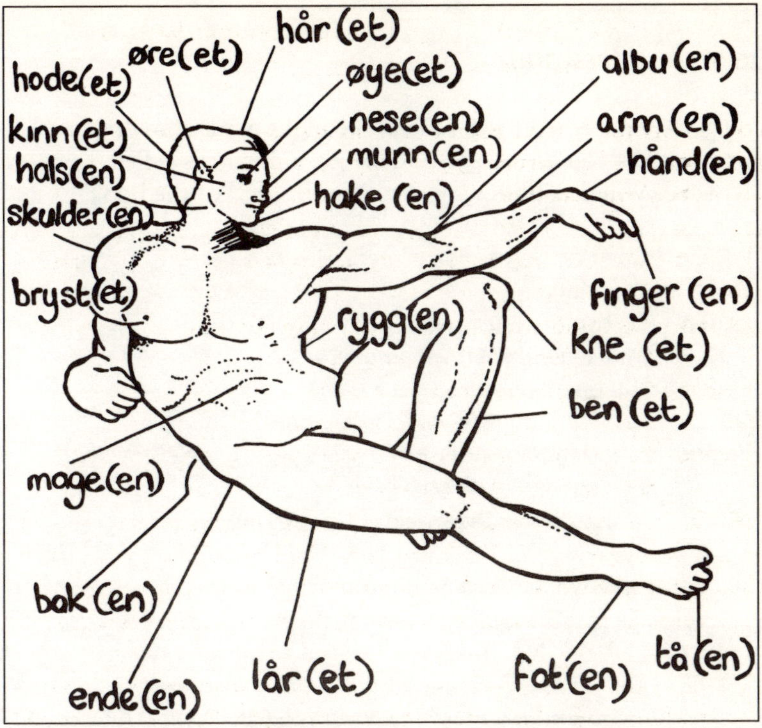

to find out about this, and take out travel insurance if necessary. British tourists should bring an EHIC-European Health Insurance Card.

In-patient treatment is free. At **legevakten** (*casualty*) there is a fixed, sum to pay, whatever the amount of treatment. If you go to a GP, you will pay part of his/her fee yourself, and the doctor will get the rest refunded from *Trygdekassen*. Dental treatment for adults is not covered, but certain treatments can be refunded.

Doctor in Norwegian is **lege**, but the title is **doktor**. You address the doctor as **doktor Berg, doktor Hansen**, and so on. When written, a capital D is used: Dr. Hansen.

Do you understand?

You get a terrible stomach-ache in the night, with vomiting and diarrhoea. As you are not getting better, a doctor is called. Look up any words you don't know in the list at the end of the book.

Legen	God dag. Jeg er doktor Berg. Hva heter du?
Du	*Your name.*
Legen	Og hva er i veien med deg?
Du	*I have a pain in my stomach.*
Legen	Har du diaré?
Du	*Yes, and I have vomited many times.*
Legen	Jeg vil gjerne undersøke deg. Er det i høyre eller venstre side av magen du har vondt?
Du	*I have pain in the whole stomach. Ow!*

The doctor gently examines your stomach.

Legen	Stakkars deg. Hva spiste du i går?
Du	*We went to a restaurant and had prawns and mayonnaise and white wine, then meatballs in gravy with potatoes and salad and red wine. Afterwards we had ice-cream. Then we walked in the streets and had two hot dogs with mustard and later we had some beers in a pub. We had one more hot dog and chips.*
Legen	Drikk mye vann og ring til meg hvis du ikke blir bedre. Men jeg tror du vil være frisk som en fisk i morgen.

Test Yourself

You know the procedure now:

1 Har Sue brukket noe?

a Sue har brukket et ben. **b** Sue har brukket en arm.
c Sue har ikke brukket noe.

2 Hvor er sykehuset?
  a I Stavern. **b** I Kristiansand. **c** I Bergen.

3 Hvilken seng ligger Jan i?
  a Den første sengen. **b** Den andre sengen.
  c Den tredje sengen.

4 Hva vil Sue gjøre når hun er helt frisk?
  a Finne en jobb. **b** Reise til England. **c** Ringe til Arne.

5 Sykepleieren heter Elisabeth Vik. Hva heter broren hennes?
  a Han heter Knut. **b** Han heter Jan. **c** Han heter Arne.

Now for some grammar. Here are some weak verbs:

6 What is the past tense of: å klippe – klipper – har klippet?
  a klippet. **b** klipt. **c** kluppet.

7 What is the past tense of: å bo – bor – har bodd?
  a bodd. **b** bode. **c** bodde.

8 What is the past tense of: å smile – smiler – har smilt?
  a smolte. **b** smilte. **c** smilt.

And some strong verbs:

9 What is the past tense of: å drikke – drikker – har drukket?
  a drikket. **b** drakket. **c** drakk.

10 What is the past tense of: å hjelpe – hjelper – har hjulpet?
  a hjalp. **b** hjulpet. **c** hjelpet.

9

Sue får jobb
Sue gets a job

In this unit you will learn

- ***How to buy clothes***
- ***How to describe clothes, colours and patterns***
- ***How to buy medicines***
- ***How to tell the time***

Dialogue 1

Now that Sue is better, she gets a job in a dress shop.

Nå er Sue helt frisk og hun har bare et lite arr på den høyre hånden. Hun bodde hos Jans familie i to uker. For noen uker siden fikk hun seg en jobb, og da fant hun seg en hyggelig liten leilighet.

Sue arbeider i en butikk som selger klær. Hun er interessert i klær og moter, og hun liker kontakten med kolleger og kunder. Når hun er på jobben bruker hun smarte klær og make-up.

Det er mandag morgen. En elegant dame kommer inn. Hun ser på kjolene.

CD2, TR 11

Sue	Kan jeg hjelpe Dem? Er det noe spesielt De ser etter?
Damen	Jeg skal i et stort selskap på lørdag. Jeg vil gjerne se på noen kjoler.
Sue	Disse kjolene er de siste vi har fått inn. Hvilken farge liker De best?
Damen	Jeg vil gjerne prøve den korallrøde kjolen der. Jeg liker stilen.
Sue	Hva med den turkise kjolen her? Den vil passe godt til håret Deres.
Damen	Jeg liker ikke turkis. Jeg blir blek i turkis. Turkis kler meg ikke.
Sue	Men denne mønstrete kjolen her? Det er smart med de korte ermene og det smale beltet.
Damen	Ja, den er pen. Men den korallrøde er penere. Jeg vil gjerne prøve disse to. Jeg liker begge.
Sue	Prøverommet er der borte.

QUICK VOCAB

belte (et) *belt*
blek *pale*
bruker (å bruke) *use/uses, wear/wears*
butikk (en) *shop*
Dem *you* (object form) (polite *you* = **De**)
Deres *yours* (polite *you*)
elegant *elegant*
ermer (et erme) *sleeves*
farge (en) *colour*
fikk (å få) *got* (past tense)
fått (å få) *got* (perfect tense)
interessert *interested*
kjolene (en kjole) *the dresses*
kler (å kle) *suit/suits*
klær *clothes*
kolleger (en kollega) *colleagues*
kontakten (en) *the contact*
korallrøde *coral red* (plural)
korte (kort) *short*
kunder (en kunde) *customers*
morgen (en) *morning*
moter (en mote) *fashions*

mønstrete (mønstret) *patterned*
passe til *go with*
penere (pen) *prettier*
prøve *try*
prøverommet (et prøverom) *the changing room*
selskap (et) *party*
siste (sist) *last*
skal i *shall attend*
smale (smal) *narrow*
smarte (smart) *smart*
spesielt (spesiell) *special*
stil (en) *style*
turkis *turquoise*

True or false? 1

a Sue bruker smarte klær på jobben.
b Damen vil kjøpe en turkis kjole.
c Sue skal i et stort selskap på lørdag.
d Sue liker ikke arbeidet sitt.

Dialogue 2

Bente wakes up feeling rotten. The children are not well either.

Bente følte seg ikke bra da hun våknet. Hun hadde vondt i hodet og halsen og hun hostet og nøs. Hun så seg i speilet:

CD2, TR 12

Bente	Huff! Jeg er stygg! Jeg er blek! Jeg har en rød nese! Jeg hoster og nyser! Jeg har vondt i halsen! Jeg skal ringe til mor. Hun må hjelpe meg med barna.

Bente ringte, men ingen svarte.

Bente	Mor, jeg savner deg! Hvor er du?

Ingen svarte telefonen.

Bente	Jeg må kle på meg og barna og gå til apoteket.

Hun kledde på seg og de to guttene, og så gikk de til apoteket.

Farmasøyten	God dag, kan jeg hjelpe deg?
Bente	Jeg føler meg dårlig. Jeg har vondt i hodet og halsen og jeg hoster og nyser. Den største gutten hoster også og den minste kastet opp.
Farmasøyten	Du er nok blitt forkjølet. Har du feber, tror du?
Bente	Nei, jeg har ikke feber.
Farmasøyten	Er du allergisk mot noe?
Bente	Nei, jeg har ikke noen allergier. Jeg tror ikke barna er allergiske heller.
Farmasøyten	Det er fint. Her har du en god hostesaft. Ta en skje tre ganger hver dag. Og disse pillene skulle hjelpe hodepinen din. Du må ikke ta flere enn det står skrevet på esken. Du må ikke drikke alkohol mens du tar denne medisinen.
Bente	Takk, og hva med barna?
Farmasøyten	Hvor gammel er gutten som hoster?
Bente	Han er fire år gammel.
Farmasøyten	Da passer denne hostesaften. Pass på at begge barna drikker mye vann. Hvis dere ikke er bedre om et par dager, må dere gå til legen.
Bente	Takk for hjelpen. Hvor mye koster medisinen?

Insight

In Unit 8 we touched on reflexive verbs. In this unit you will get some more practice.

'Bente føler seg ikke bra' in direct translation would be: *Bente feels herself not well*. What we really mean is: *Bente doesn't feel well.*

Jeg føler meg bra *I feel well.*
Hun føler seg bra *She feels well.*

QUICK VOCAB

allergier (en allergi) *allergies*
allergisk *allergic*
apotek (et) *chemist's*
esken (en eske) *the box*
farmasøyten (en) *the chemist/pharmacist*
feber (en) *fever/temperature*
flere *more*
forkjølet *suffering from a cold*
føler meg (å føle seg) *feel*
halsen (en hals) *the throat/neck*
hodepinen (en hodepin) *the headache*
hostesaft (en) *cough mixture*
hostet (å hoste) *coughed*
kle på *dress*
minste (liten) *smallest*
nese (en) *nose*
nyser (å nyse) *sneeze/sneezes*
nøs (å nyse) *sneezed*
pillene (en pille) *the pills*
savner (å savne) *miss/misses*
skje (en) *spoon*
skrevet (å skrive) *written*
stygg *ugly*
største (stor) *biggest*

True or false? 2

a Bente synes at hun er pen.
b Hun kaster opp.
c Den minste gutten hoster.
d Bente går til legen.

Dialogue 3

Elisabeth is shopping for clothes.

Fredag femtende oktober (*Friday 15 October*). Bentes søster, Elisabeth, er sykepleier på et stort sykehus i Kristiansand.

Nå skal hun ha ferie i en uke, og hun skal reise til Oslo og være hos tante Maiken. Broren, Arne, vil også ha noen dager i Oslo. Etter å ha studert engelsk et år i London, har han nå begynt på høstsemesteret på universitetet i Bergen. Han skal også bo hos tante Maiken. Elisabeth og Arne er gode venner og hun gleder seg til å se ham. Begge liker å bo hos den snille tanten.

Men først vil Elisabeth kjøpe noen nye klær. Hun går til en butikk:

Elisabeth	Hvor finner jeg noen smarte bukser? Jeg er lei av ola-bukser!
Piken	Vi har nettopp fått inn de buksene som henger der. Vi har alle størrelser i svart og mørkeblått og noen i grått.
Elisabeth	Jeg vil gjerne prøve de mørkeblå buksene der. Har dere en genser i samme farge?
Piken	Ja, kom med meg! Her er en genser i lammeull, og den der borte er i bomull.
Elisabeth	Genseren i lammeull er smartere enn den i bomull, synes jeg.
Piken	Vil du prøve den?
Elisabeth	Nei, jeg tror ikke den er stor nok. Jeg liker store gensere. Kan du finne en større genser i denne fargen?
Piken	Her har du en. Er det noe annet du ser etter?
Elisabeth	Ja, jeg vil gjerne se på noen skjorter. Jeg liker best rutete skjorter.
Piken	Liker du den mønstrete skjorten der?
Elisabeth	Nei, den er fæl! Den er virkelig stygg! Vil noen virkelig kjøpe den?
Piken	Ja, det er noen som synes at den er lekker. Heldigvis har ikke alle samme smak!
Elisabeth	Den grønne skjorten der er enda styggere. Men jeg liker den lyseblå skjorten der. Og den rødrutete der. Nå vil jeg gjerne prøve disse klærne.
Piken	Prøverommet er der borte.

QUICK VOCAB

begynte (å begynne) *began*
bomull *cotton*
bukser (en bukse) *trousers*
enda *even*
fæl *awful, gruesome*
gensere (en genser) *sweaters*
grått (grå) *grey*
heldigvis *fortunately*
henger (å henge) *hang/hangs*
høst (en) *autumn*
lammeull *lambswool*
lei av *tired of/fed up with*
lekker *super*
lyse- *light/pale*
mørke- *dark*
nettopp *just*
noe annet *something/anything else*
ola-bukser *jeans*
rutete (rutet) *checked*
rødrutete *red-checked*
samme *the same*
semesteret (et) *the term*
skjorter (en skjorte) *shirts*
smak (en) *taste*
smartere *smarter*
styggere *uglier*
større (stor) *bigger*
størrelser (en størrelse) *sizes*
ull *wool*
universitetet (et) *university*

True or false? 3

a Elisabeth vil gjerne kjøpe ola-bukser.
b Bente er lei av klærne sine.
c Elisabeth liker store gensere.
d Elisabeth synes at den rødrutete skjorten er fæl.

This is how we say it

Useful expressions for shopping:

▶ **Jeg vil gjerne se på ...**	*I would like to look at ...*
Jeg vil gjerne prøve ...	*I would like to try ...*
Jeg vil gjerne kjøpe ...	*I would like to buy ...*
▶ **Jeg liker denne kjolen.**	*I like this dress.*
Jeg liker ikke dette skjørtet.	*I don't like this skirt.*
▶ **Denne genseren er smart.**	*This sweater is smart.*
Denne jakken er lekker.	*This jacket is super.*
Denne skjorten er fæl!	*This shirt is awful!*
▶ **Jeg vil gjerne se på en rødstripet kjole.**	*... red striped dress*
Har dere en mørkeblå genser?	*... dark blue sweater*
Jeg vil heller prøve en mønstret jakke.	*... patterned jacket*
Jeg vil heller ha et lyseblått skjørt.	*... pale/light blue skirt*
▶ **Denne jakken er for liten.**	*This jacket is too small.*
Dette skjørtet er for stort.	*This skirt is too big.*
Har dere en større genser?	*Have you got a bigger sweater?*
Nei, vi har bare mindre størrelser.	*No, we only have smaller sizes.*
▶ **Denne jakken er stygg!**	*This jacket is ugly!*
Dette er en stygg genser!	*This is an ugly sweater!*
▶ **Den fargen kler deg.**	*That colour suits you.*
Jeg kler ikke gult.	*Yellow doesn't suit me/I don't suit yellow.*
Jeg blir blek i svart.	*I become pale in black.*

At the chemist's:

▶ **Jeg vil gjerne kjøpe hostesaft.**	*I would like to buy cough mixture.*
Jeg trenger hodepinetabletter.	*I need headache pills.*
▶ **Jeg hoster.**	*I cough.*
Jeg nyser.	*I sneeze.*
Jeg klør.	*I am itchy.*
Det klør alle steder!	*I itch all over!*
Jeg trenger noe beroligende!	*I need something to calm me down!*

Insight

After studying Dialogues 1 and 3 you should be able to go shopping. And if you are taken ill, the **apotek** is where to go, unless the situation is serious. In that case the hospitals have Accident and Emergency departments, called **Legevakt**.

Language patterns

1 Adjectives: colours/patterns

In Unit 4 there is a list of the adjectives used up to then. Here are some more adjectives as well as a repeat of relevant adjectives.

En	Et	*Definite Singular + Indefinite and Definite Plural*	
blå	**blått**	**blå**	*blue*
brun	**brunt**	**brune**	*brown*
grønn	**grønt**	**grønne**	*green*
grå	**grått**	**grå**	*grey*
gul	**gult**	**gule**	*yellow*
hvit	**hvitt**	**hvite**	*white*
oransje	**oransje**	**oransje**	*orange*

En	Et	*Definite Singular + Indefinite and Definite Plural*	
rød	**rødt**	**røde**	*red*
svart	**svart**	**svarte**	*black*
turkis	**turkis**	**turkise**	*turquoise*
lyseblå	**lyseblått**	**lyseblå**	*light blue*
mørkerød	**mørkerødt**	**mørkerøde**	*dark red*
fæl	**fælt**	**fæle**	*awful/gruesome*
fin	**fint**	**fine**	*fine*
pen	**pent**	**pene**	*pretty*
smart	**smart**	**smarte**	*smart*
stygg	**stygt**	**stygge**	*ugly*
blomstret	**blomstret**	**blomstrete**	*flower-patterned*
mønstret	**mønstret**	**mønstrete**	*patterned*
rutet	**rutet**	**rutete**	*checked*
stripet	**stripet**	**stripete**	*stripey*

A reminder of the adjective + noun combination:

en gul jakke	**den gule jakken**	**gule jakker**	**de gule jakkene** (*jacket*)
et gult skjørt	**det gule skjørtet**	**gule skjørt**	**de gule skjørtene** (*skirt*)
en rutet skjorte	**den rutete skjorten**	**rutete skjorter**	**de rutete skjortene** (*shirt*)

Insight

Did you put a marker at Adjectives in Unit 4, as I suggested? This is a good time to go back and revise the whole adjective and noun situation. At this point in Unit 9 you'll get a long list of adjectives and a reminder of how to use them.

2 Comparison of adjectives

In English you can compare adjectives like this:

big bigger biggest

Tom is big. Tim is bigger (than Tom). Titch is the biggest.

Norwegian is similar:

pen – penere – penest	*pretty – prettier – prettiest*
stygg – styggere – styggest	*ugly – uglier – ugliest*

As in English, some are irregular:

god – bedre – best	*good – better – best*
dårlig – verre – verst	*bad – worse – worst*

One can also compare by using **mer** (*more*) and **mest** (*most*):

Per er sulten.	*Per is hungry.*
Tor er sultnere enn Per.	*Tor is hungrier than Per.*
Tor er mer sulten enn Per.	*Tor is more hungry than Per.*
Kari er sultnest.	*Kari is the hungriest.*
Kari er mest sulten.	*Kari is the most hungry.*

3 The formal *De*

If you want to address somebody formally, you would use **De** instead of **du**. **De** has a capital **D**. In earlier times you would have always addressed adults as **De**, and used the surname with a title.

These days most Norwegians are informal, and it is natural to use **du** and first names immediately. If, however, you speak to an elderly person, to your solicitor, doctor, bank manager or child's headmaster, or meet a government minister, bishop or local dignitary, it would be appropriate to say **De** until you get to know each other better. Bente would say **De** to an elderly customer.

De (subject) (*you*) **Dem** (object) (*you*) **Deres** (possessive) (*yours*)

4 *Synes/tro* to think

These are two very useful verbs when you want to express your feelings:

å synes means *to think, be of the opinion* ... whereas **å tro** means *to think, believe.*

Synes du denne fargen kler meg?	*Do you think this colour suits me?*
Nei, jeg synes ikke det.	*No, I don't think so.*
Tror du det vil regne hele dagen?	*Do you think it will rain all day?*
Nei, jeg tror ikke det.	*No, I don't think so.*

5 Telling the time

How to tell the time will be covered fully with exercises in Unit 11. A little basic explanation at this point may be a good idea.

en klokke *a clock*
klokken er ... *the time is ... / it is ...*

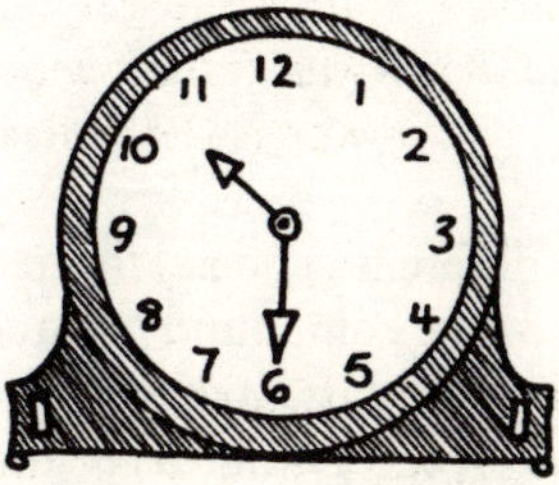

CD2, TR 13

Klokken er ti.	**10.00**
Klokken er fem over ti.	**10.05**
Klokken er ti over ti.	**10.10**
Klokken er kvart over ti.	**10.15**
Klokken er ti på halv elleve.	**10.20**
Klokken er fem på halv elleve.	**10.25**
Klokken er halv elleve.	**10.30**
Klokken er fem over halv elleve.	**10.35**
Klokken er ti over halv elleve.	**10.40**
Klokken er kvart på elleve.	**10.45**
Klokken er ti på elleve.	**10.50**
Klokken er fem på elleve.	**10.55**
Klokken er elleve.	**11.00**

Insight

Watch out for **'halv tre'**: it means 2.30 and not 3.30! In Norwegian we mean *'half before three'*, but we say *'half three'*, without the 'before'. Take care; you could easily get your important meeting wrong. And when we say **'fem på halv elleve'** we mean *10.25*. We're actually saying: *five to half before eleven!*

6 Compound nouns

Many nouns in Norwegian are long but you discover that they consist of two or three shorter words.

legekontor = lege (*doctor*) + **kontor** (*office*)	(*doctor's surgery*)
tannlege = tann (*tooth*) + **lege** (*doctor*)	(*dentist*)
hjernerystelse = hjerne (*brain*) + **rystelse** (*shaking*)	(*concussion*)

If the two words have different genders, the gender of the last word will decide the gender of the compound noun: **en lege, et kontor.** Here **kontor** is the last word. **Lege** just tells us what sort of office it is. The gender becomes **et: et legekontor, et tannlegekontor.**

You have had many compound nouns so far:

en bilnøkkel *a car key*
et sykehus *a hospital*
en sykeseng *a sickbed*
en sykepleier *a nurse*
en motorsykkel *a motorbike*
en turistinformasjon *a tourist information centre*

Insight

When you come across a frighteningly long word, it is a good idea to see if you can break it up into manageable pieces. Look at **'skinkesmørbrød'** meaning *open ham sandwich*. **'skinke'** is *ham*, **'smør'** is *butter* and **'brød'** is *bread*.

Exercises

1 Fill in the gaps with the correct forms of the adjectives (*a*) grønn, (*b*) blå, (*c*) stripet, (*d*) pen:

a	en **grønn** skjorte	den ___ skjorten	___ skjorter	de ___ skjortene
b	et ___ skjørt	det **blå** skjørtet	___ skjørt	de ___ skjørtene
c	en ___ sokk	den___ sokker	___ sokken	de **stripete** sokkene
d	en ___ bukse	den ___ buksen	**pene** bukser	de ___ buksene

2 These adjectives are all regular. Write out the comparative and superlative forms of each.

CD2, TR 14

Example: pen (*pretty*) – penere (*prettier*) – penest (*prettiest*)

a fæl (*awful*) –
b fin (*fine*) –
c smart (*smart*) –
d blek (*pale*) –

3 Here are some irregular adjectives:

stor	større	størst	(*big*)
liten	mindre	minst	(*small*)

Insert suitable forms of the adjectives:

a Bentes brødre heter Arne og Tom. Arne er ___ enn Tom.
b Tom er ___ enn Arne.
c Tom er ___.
d Arne er ___.

4 Do you remember these irregular nouns? Fill in the gaps:

a	en bror	broren	___	brødrene
b	___	faren	fedre	___
c	___	___	søstre	___
d	en mor	___	___	___
e	___	mannen	___	___

5 Insert the correct forms of the formal **De** in these sentences:

- **a** Kan jeg hjelpe ___?
- **b** Vil ___ ha en kopp kaffe?
- **c** Jeg synes at denne fargen kler ___.
- **d** Er denne jakken ___?

6 å synes synes syntes har syntes (*think, be of the opinion*)
å tro tror trodde har trodd (*think, believe*)

CD2, TR 15

Which verb would you use in the following?

- **a** Jeg ___ at den rutete jakken er stygg.
- **b** ___ du at det blir pent vær i morgen?
- **c** Jeg ___ ikke at han kommer i dag.
- **d** ___ du at han er hyggelig?

Norwegian *apotek* *chemist's*

These are completely different from British chemists' shops. They are not privately run, and sell only medicines and medical appliances. They are staffed by highly trained pharmacists, who are happy to give advice on everyday health problems.

There is not a standard prescription charge; you pay the full price of the medicine prescribed. Some medicines on prescription can therefore be very expensive. Patients with illnesses such as diabetes and various other chronic ailments are exempt from paying.

Many brands which are sold elsewhere in the world are available only on prescription in Norway.

Shampoos, soap, toothpaste and so on are sold at **parfymerier**, or in supermarkets.

hodepinetabletter *headache tablets/pills*
hostesaft (en) *cough mixture*
medisin mot diaré *medicine for diarrhoea*
medisin mot forstoppelse *medicine for constipation*
plaster (et) *plaster*
på apoteket *at the chemist's*
reisesykemiddel (et) *travel sickness remedy*
støttebandasje *elastic bandage*

Clothing

bh (en) *bra*
bluse (en) *blouse*
brystholder (en) *brassiere*
bukse (en) *trousers* (pair of)
bukser *trousers* (singular and plural)
dress (en) *suit* (don't be confused!)
frakk (en) *overcoat*
genser (en) *sweater*
hatt (en) *hat*
jakke (en) *jacket*
kjole (en) *dress*
klær *clothing*
kåpe (en) *overcoat* (female)
lue (en) *cap*
skjorte (en) *shirt*
skjørt (et) *skirt*
sko (en) *shoe*
sokk (en) *sock*
strømpe (en) *stocking*
strømpebukse (en) *tights*
støvel (en) *boot*
truse (en) *pants*
trøye (en) *vest*
underbukse (en) also *pants*

QUICK VOCAB

Note that all these articles of clothing take the **en** gender, **except** for **skjørt**!

Test Yourself

There is only one correct answer to these questions:

1 Hva selger Sue i butikken?
  a Fisk. **b** Kort og frimerker. **c** Klær.

2 Hva vil damen se på?
  a Kjoler. **b** Belter. **c** Biler.

3 Hvilken farge blir damen blek i?
  a Turkis. **b** Svart. **c** Korallrødt.

4 Hva er i veien med Bente?
  a Hun har brukket et ben. **b** Hun har hjernerystelse.
  c Hun hoster og nyser.

5 Er Bente allergisk ?
  a Ja. **b** Nei. **c** Hun eraller gisk mot barn.

6 Hvor skal Elisabeth være i Oslo?
  a Hos Bente. **b** Hos tante Maiken. **c** På hotell.

7 Hva vil Elisabeth kjøpe?
  a Olabukser. **b** En kjole. **c** Smarte bukser.

8 Hvilken skjorte liker Elisabeth?
  a Den grønne. **b** Den mønstrete. **c** Den lyseblå.

9 Hva gjør Elisabeth?
  a Hun er lærer. **b** Hun er sykepleier. **c** Hun er aupair.

10 Hvor arbeider Elisabeth?
  a I Kristiansand. **b** I Oslo. **c** I London.

10

Selskaper
Parties

In this unit you will learn

- ***About Norwegian party customs***
- ***What to say to your hosts during and after a party***
- ***How to say the months and dates***

Dialogue 1

Sue ringer til tante Maiken.

CD2, TR 16

Sue	Hallo, tante Maiken! Dette er Sue. Husker du meg?
Tante Maiken	Hallo Sue! Jeg husker deg godt! Hvordan har du det?
Sue	Bare bra. Det var veldig hyggelig å bo hos deg i sommer. Jeg vil gjerne hilse på deg igjen. Jeg vil gjerne besøke deg. Kan jeg ta med meg Jan, vennen min, og komme en liten tur?
Tante Maiken	Ja, det er bare hyggelig. Kan dere komme i kveld? Vi spiser aftens klokken åtte.
Sue	Tusen takk! På gjensyn!
Tante Maiken	På gjensyn i aften.

(Contd)

Sue ringer på dørklokken, og tante Maiken åpner døren:	
Tante Maiken	Kom inn! Velkommen til meg! Hyggelig å se deg, Sue! Jeg vil gjerne bli kjent med deg, Jan!

De går inn i den koselige leiligheten. Arne og Elisabeth er der.

Sue	Arne!! Er du her?
Arne	Hei Sue! Ja, jeg er på et kort besøk i Oslo.
Jan	Elisabeth!! Den søte sykepleieren min! Jeg er veldig glad for å se deg igjen!
Elisabeth	Hei, Jan! Jeg håper du er helt frisk igjen.
Jan	Ja, og det kan jeg takke deg for!!
Tante Maiken	Nå skal vi ha en drink. Vil dere ha vin eller eplesaft? Jeg skal ha et stort glass rødvin, men jeg vet at Arne heller vil ha eplesaft.

De har en drink og prater mens de beundrer den fine utsikten over Oslo og fjorden. Så setter de seg ved bordet på kjøkkenet, og tante Maiken har laget en deilig gryterett. Før de spiser løfter tante Maiken glasset sitt og sier:

Tante Maiken	Skål og velkommen hit!

Alle sier 'Skål', og smiler til hverandre.

Tante Maiken	Vær så god, forsyn dere!

Maten er god. Det er lys på bordet. De spiser og hygger seg. Til dessert er ost og frukt. Når de har spist, sier alle: 'Takk for maten' til tante Maiken, og Arne gir henne en god klem.

Elisabeth og Jan snakker sammen.

Elisabeth	Hva gjør du, Jan?
Jan	Jeg er ingeniør. Jeg arbeider i et stort firma.
Elisabeth	Er du og Sue samboere?

Jan	Nei, Sue har en liten leilighet i byen og jeg bor hjemme hos foreldrene mine. Og du? Har du en spesiell venn?
Elisabeth	Nei, men jeg har mange venner.

Insight

This was an informal supper. Even so, the hostess, tante Maiken, observes the little formality of saying 'Skål' to wish the guests welcome. The guests will answer 'Skål', and smile at each other before putting their glasses down. This little ritual is followed everywhere. Notice also that the guests say 'Takk for maten', meaning *Thank you for the food*, when they leave the table.

QUICK VOCAB

aftens (en) *supper*
beundrer (å beundre) *admire/admires*
bli kjent med *get to know*
deilig *delicious*
dessert (en) *dessert*
drink (en) *drink*
dørklokken (en dørklokke) *the doorbell*
eplesaft (en) *apple juice*
firma (et) *firm*
forsyn dere (å forsyne seg) *help yourselves*
frukt (en) *fruit*
gryterett (en) *casserole*
håper (å håpe) *hope/hopes*
ingeniør (en) *engineer*
kjøkkenet (et) *the kitchen*
koselige (koselig) *cosy/pleasant*
lys (et lys) *lights/candles*
løfter (å løfte) *lift/lifts*
ost (en) *cheese*
prater (å prate) *chat/chats*
setter seg (å sette seg) *sit down/sits down*
takke *thank*
velkommen *welcome*
åpner (å åpne) *open/opens*

True or false? 1

- **a** Tante Maiken husker ikke Sue.
- **b** Tante Maiken har laget en deilig gryterett.
- **c** Alle sier 'Takk for maten'.
- **d** Sue og Jan er samboere.

Dialogue 2

Sue holds a flat-warming party.

Sue liker å bo i den lille leiligheten sin. Hun bor i Oslo, og hun har kort vei til jobben. Om kvelden kan hun treffe vennene sine. Nå vil hun gjerne ha et lite selskap. Arne, Elisabeth og Jan skal komme, og hun har ringt til Randi og Odd.

Sue har bakt en stor bløtkake og hun har kjøpt mange pizzaer. Gjestene har med vin, øl og mineralvann. Pop-musikken fra stereo-anlegget er høy når gjestene kommer.

CD2, TR 17

Odd	Fint å se deg igjen, Arne! Hvordan liker du å studere i Bergen?
Arne	Bra. Men jeg savner London! Jeg likte veldig godt å bo der.
Jan	Når skal du reise tilbake til Kristiansand, Elisabeth?
Elisabeth	Jeg hører ikke hva du sier!!

Det ringer på døren. Sue åpner, og der står en nabo. Han er sint.

Mannen	Vil dere dempe musikken!! Jeg kan ikke høre TVen min!
Sue	Unnskyld! Musikken er visst litt for høy. Jeg skal dempe den med en gang.

Mannen går og Sue slår musikken ned. De spiser pizza og drikker øl og vin. De snakker om julen og hva de skal gjøre da. Sue vet ikke. Kanskje vil hun reise hjem til England. Men hun vil veldig gjerne ha en norsk jul.

Jan	Elisabeth, når skal du reise tilbake til Kristiansand?
Elisabeth	Jeg skal til Bergen først, for det er mors fødselsdag på lørdag. Jeg reiser til Kristiansand på søndag.
Jan	Jeg vil gjerne treffe deg før du reiser. Det er dumt at det er arbeidsdag for meg i morgen, men kanskje vi kan være sammen on kvelden?
Elisabeth	Fint. Jeg vil gjerne treffe deg.

De spiser kake og danser. Men siden det er arbeidsdag i morgen, går gjestene hjem tidlig. De sier 'god natt' og 'takk for i kveld'.

Arne	Dette var en kos kveld. Jeg ringer til deg, Sue.

Sue vasker opp og rydder. Hun tenker på Arne. Hun var glad for å se ham igjen og forbauset over at hun virkelig hadde savnet ham. Bare han ringer!

Insight

More pizza is eaten per person in Norway than anywhere else in the world. You could be forgiven for thinking that pizza is Norway's no.1 national dish.

'Bløtkake' actually translates as *softcake* and is a light sponge cake filled with fruit, chopped almonds etc. and smothered in whipped cream. It is traditional at birthdays and festivals.

QUICK VOCAB

anlegget (et) *the centre/installation*
arbeidsdag (en) *working day*
bakt (å bake) *baked*
bløtkake (en) *cream cake*
danser (å danse) *dance/dances*
dempe *dim/turn down*

dumt (dum) *silly/stupid/boring*
forbauset *surprised*
fødselsdag (en) *birthday*
gjestene (en) *the guests*
julen (en) *the Christmas*
kake (en) *cake*
kos *nice, lovely* (slang for **koselig**)
mineralvann (et) *mineral water*
musikken (en) *the music*
nabo (en) *neighbour*
siden *as*
slår ned (å slå ned) *turn/turns down*
tidlig *early*
TVen *the TV*
visst *certainly*

True or false? 2

a Sue skal ha et selskap.
b Elisabeth vasker opp og rydder.
c Gjestene går hjem tidlig.
d Sue vil gjerne være i Norge i julen.

Text 3

CD2, TR 18

Arne's mother is 50!

Lørdag tjuetredje oktober (*Saturday 23 October*). Det var mors fødselsdag. Hun var femti år, og hele familien var sammen. Mormor og morfar kom fra Kristiansand og Liv og hennes familie kom fra Trondheim. Elisabeth og Arne var kommet hjem fra Oslo.

Far hadde bestilt en stor middag på et hotell. Flere av mors venninner fra skoletiden var invitert, og mors og fars beste venner var der også.

Mor hadde en elegant, ny kjole, og alle barna syntes at hun var virkelig pen, med det lyse håret og de smilende blå øynene, selv om hun var veldig gammel.

Alle sa 'Gratulerer med dagen' til mor. Etter en drink satte gjestene seg ved det festlige bordet. Far sa 'Skål' og ønsket alle velkommen.

Maten var deilig. Til forrett var det røkelaks og eggerøre med gressløk. Så fulgte lammestek med poteter og grønnsaker. Til dessert var det karamellpudding.

Det var mange taler. Far holdt tale for sin kjære kone. Liv, som var den eldste av barna, holdt en vakker tale om det gode barndomshjemmet hun og søsknene husket så godt. Da ble mor rørt og måtte tørke bort en tåre. Noen av vennene talte også og det var mye skåling. Til slutt var det morfars tur. Han satt til venstre for mor, og da var det hans plikt å si 'takk for maten' på vegne av gjestene. Morfar var morsom og alle lo.

Etterpå var det kaffe og marsipankake i den store stuen.

'Jeg elsker å ha fødselsdag', sa mor med et stort smil da gjestene hadde gått.

Insight

'Big' birthdays are always celebrated with a more formal dinner. People just love giving speeches in Norway. At a wedding there could easily be 12 to 15 speeches, and often a song or two. The gentleman sitting to the left of the hostess will make a 'Takk for maten' speech on behalf of the guests. He will normally be notified in advance so that he can prepare his vote of thanks.

QUICK VOCAB

barndomshjemmet (et hjem) *the childhood home*
eggerøre (en) *scrambled eggs*
elsker (å elske) *love/loves*
festlig *great/festive*
forrett (en) *starter*
fulgte (å følge) *followed*
gratulerer (å gratulere) *congratulate/congratulates*
gressløk *chives*
grønnsaker (en grønnsak) *vegetables*
holde en tale *make a speech*
holdt (å holde) *held*
invitert (å invitere) *invited*
karamellpudding (en) *crème caramel*
kjære *dear*
kone (en) *wife*
lammestek (en) *roast lamb*
lo (å le) *laughed*
marsipankake (en) *marzipan cake*
morsom *amusing*
måtte (å måtte) *had to*
plikt (en) *duty*
på vegne av *on behalf of*
røkelaks (en) *smoked salmon*
rørt *moved/touched*
satt (å sitte) *sat*
skoletiden (en) *the schooldays*
skåling *drinking toasts*
smil (et) *smile*
smilende *smiling*
stuen (en stue) *the sitting-room*
taler (en tale) *speeches*
talte (å tale) *gave speeches, spoke*
til slutt *at the end*
tur (en) *turn*
tørke *wipe*
tåre (en) *tear*
venninner (en venninne) *friends* (female)
ønsket (å ønske) *wished*

True or false? 3

a Arne holdt en god tale for mor.
b Det var fars fødselsdag.
c Det var ingen taler.
d Alle sa 'Gratulerer med dagen' til Bente.

This is how we say it

- Congratulations:

Gratulerer med dagen!	*Happy birthday!*
Alt godt for dagen!	*All the best for 'the day'!*

- Greetings:

Velkommen!	*Welcome!*
Velkommen til oss!	*Welcome to us!*
Velkommen til bords!	*Welcome to the table!*
Skål og velkommen!	*Here's to the guests!*

- At dinner:

Vær så god.	*Please = come and eat.*
Vær så god forsyn deg.	*Please help yourself.*
Vil du ha litt mer?	*Would you like a little/some more?*
Vil du ha litt til?	*Would you like some more?*
Ja, takk!	*Yes, please!*
Nei takk.	*No, thank you.*
Nei takk, jeg er forsynt.	*No thank you, I am satisfied, I've had enough.*
Nei takk, nå har jeg spist nok.	*No thank you, I have eaten enough now.*
Det smaker godt/deilig.	*It tastes good/delicious.*

- The toast/after dinner:

Jeg vil gjerne holde en tale for ...	*I would like to make a speech/pay a tribute to ...*

Jeg vil gjerne si noen ord ...	*I would like to say a few words ...*
Skål for mormor!	*A toast for Granny!*
Skål for vertinnen!	*A toast for the hostess.*

▶ The 'thank-you's:

Takk for maten!	*Thank you for the food/meal.*
Velbekomme.	*'Don't mention it', 'You're welcome'.*
Takk for i dag!	*Thank you for today!*
Takk for i aften!	*Thank you for this evening!*
Takk for meg!	*Thank you for having me!*

▶ Phoning the host the next day:

Takk for i går!	*Thank you for last night/yesterday!*

▶ If some time has passed, or if you write a note:

Takk for sist!	*Thank you for last time!*
Det var en veldig hyggelig aften.	*It was a very pleasant evening.*

Insight

Look carefully at these phrases. You won't put a foot wrong if you are familiar with them!

Remember that there isn't such a word as 'please'. The hostess may say 'Vær så god' when the food is going to be served. 'Vær så god' is also used when you hand a plate or platter to someone, or when pouring wine.

Language patterns

1 Ordinal numbers

Perhaps you have noticed that at the beginning of some texts there is a date where an ordinal number is used. The ordinal numbers are as follows:

1st	første	11th	ellevte	21st	tjueførste
2nd	andre	12th	tolvte	22nd	tjueandre
3rd	tredje	13th	trettende	30th	trettiende
4th	fjerde	14th	fjortende	40th	førtiende
5th	femte	15th	femtende	50th	femtiende
6th	sjette	16th	sekstende	60th	sekstiende
7th	sjuende	17th	syttende	70th	syttiende
8th	åttende	18th	attende	80th	åttiende
9th	niende	19th	nittende	90th	nittiende
10th	tiende	20th	tjuende		

2 The months

januar	juli
februar	august
mars	september
april	oktober
mai	november
juni	desember

The months, like the days of the week, do not have capital letters, except at the start of a sentence.

3 Dates

This is how you write the date:

Fredag trettende august 2010. *Friday thirteenth August 2010*
or
13. august 2010
or
13.8.10.

4 Prepositions

Til (*to*), **fra** (*from*), **på** (*on*), **i** (*in*, *for*), **med** (*with*), **ved** (*by*), **etter** (*after*, *behind*), **om** (*about*, *in*), **over** (*over*), **under** (*under*), **av** (*of*), are called prepositions.

Kari sitter ved bordet.	*Kari sits/is sitting at the table.*
Kari sitter på bordet.	*Kari sits on the table.*
Kari sitter under bordet.	*Kari sits under the table.*

In Norwegian, as in many other languages, prepositions can have more than one meaning. This can be confusing. Some preposition phrases are worth remembering:

Min tykke tante skal være her om tre uker.	*My fat aunt will be here in three weeks.*
Min tykke tante skal være her i tre uker.	*My fat aunt will be here for three weeks.*

Insight

We have been using prepositions throughout the book. They can be a bit irritating. No sooner have you learnt one meaning of a preposition than you find that the preposition has a different meaning as well! In many situations it doesn't matter a great deal, but sometimes it does. Imagine if you invite your mother-in-law to come to stay **in** two months and she comes **for** two months!

* 'om' can mean *in*
* 'i' can mean *for*–but not always!

5 Time expressions

Prepositions are also used to express time.

i dag	*today*
i morgen	*tomorrow*
i går	*yesterday*
på torsdag	*on Thursday*
om morgenen	*in the morning/mornings*
om kvelden	*in the evening/evenings*
i morges	*this morning*

Insight

Take a good look at these time expressions using prepositions. They are really useful.

If you want to learn more about prepositions go to Unit 16, where all will be revealed!

6 Verbs: *legge/ligge* lay/lie, *sette/sitte* set/sit

å legge (*to lay/put*)	legger	la	har lagt
å ligge (*to lie*)	ligger	lå	har ligget

Jeg legger boken på bordet. *I lay/put the book on the table.*
Boken ligger på bordet. *The book lies on the table.*

å sette (*to set/place*)	setter	satte	har
å sitte (*to sit*)	sitter	satt	satt

Jeg setter glasset på bordet. *I place/set the glass on the table.*
John sitter ved bordet. *John sits by the table.*

If you put something flat or wide, like a book, on the table, you would use **legge**. If you place something which stands, like a vase or a glass, you would use **sette**.

In Unit 8 you looked at the reflexive verbs: **legge** and **sette** also have reflexive forms:

Jeg legger meg. *I lie down/go to bed.*
Hun legger seg. *She lies down/goes to bed.*
Vi setter oss. *We sit down.*
De setter seg. *They sit down.*

7 Past participles as adjectives

In Unit 8 you saw that the perfect tense consisted of **ha** *have* + the past participle of the verb:

å brekke (*to break*)
han brekker (*he breaks*)

han brakk (*he broke*)
han har brukket (*he has broken*)

Brukket is the past participle of the verb.

Some past participles, but not all, can be used as adjectives. **Brukket** is one of these:

et brukket ben	*a broken leg/bone*
en forbauset mann	*a surprised man*
dempet musikk	*soft, quiet music*
en invitert gjest	*an invited guest*

Exercises

1 Insert a suitable preposition to complete these sentences. The first two are suggested for you:

- **a** Kari vil gjerne reise (*to*) ___ Amerika.
- **b** Flasken er (*on*) ___ bordet.
- **c** John kjørte ___ byen.
- **d** Han har et kart ___ Oslo.
- **e** De sitter ___ bilen.

2 Time expressions:

- **a** Jeg kommer ___. (*today*)
- **b** Tom var her ___. (*yesterday*)
- **c** ___ spiste jeg frokost. (*this morning*)
- **d** Jeg spiser frokost___. (*in the morning*)
- **e** Han skal komme hit ___ onsdag. (*on*)

3 Insert ordinal numbers following the guide in brackets:

- **a** Jeg skal reise til New York (*4th*) ___ august.
- **b** Min fødselsdag er (*16th*) ___ september.
- **c** John kom til Bergen (*26th*) ___ juni.

d Det var (*1st*) ___ gangen han var i Norge.
e I dag er det torsdag (*9th*) ___ mars.

4 Do you remember the cardinal numbers? Write these out in words in Norwegian:

a 5
b 12
c 14
d 47
e 69

5 What would you say in these situations?

CD2, TR 19

a Wish someone a 'Happy birthday'.
b Welcome someone to your house.
c Ask your guest if s/he would like some more to eat.
d Say that you have had enough.
e Thank someone for a meal.

6 What are the definite singular forms of these adjectives and nouns?

a en sint nabo den ...
b et spesielt selskap
c en koselig kveld
d en deilig bløtkake
e et stort smil

7 What are the indefinite singular forms of these adjectives and nouns?

a gode venner en ...
b kjedelige gjester
c store kaker
d snille søstre
e dårlige brødre

8 Insert the verbs **ligge/legge, sitte/sette** as required by the English prompts in brackets:

a John (*puts/places*) ___ glasset på bordet.
b Bente (*sat*) ___ ved bordet.
c Gutten (*lies*) ___ i sengen.
d Bøkene (*lay*) ___ der.
e De (*sit*) ___ i bilen.

9 Insert the missing verbs (look at Unit 8 if you are not sure):

	Infinitive	Present	Past	Perfect
	å være	**er**	**var**	**har vært**
a	å smile	___	smilte	___
b	å tenke	___	___	har tenkt
c	___	kaster	___	har kastet
d	å drikke	___	___	___
e	å se	___	så	___

Special occasions

Significant birthdays are celebrated in Norway – usually the 18th, 21st, 50th, 60th, 65th, 70th and 80th. These birthdays are often marked with a big dinner party, either at home or in a private room in a restaurant.

Other occasions are christenings, confirmation parties, weddings and funerals. They tend to follow a certain pattern and can be rather formal.

In Unit 3 you read about how to say **Skål**. This is done frequently at dinners. The host will usually wish everyone welcome and say **skål** before the food is served. Then the guests will pick out whoever they want to drink with throughout the meal. Saying **skål** can be friendly or flirtatious – that is up to you!

Norwegians love making speeches, and there are often many of them – perhaps too many. The speeches also follow a special order, and it is common that one person is asked to be 'toastmaster' in order to keep the proceedings under control.

At the end of the meal, the gentleman sitting in the place of honour to the left of the hostess will make a speech to thank the hostess for the meal on behalf of the other guests. Sometimes the guest will be told in advance and can prepare a speech.

When leaving the table, everyone will shake hands with, or kiss, the host and the hostess, saying **takk for maten**.

Do you understand?

You are in Oslo and you have met up with Martin, the lorry driver from Unit 5. He invites you to go with him to see some friends of his.

Du	*I hope you can find where your friends live! You didn't know Oslo very well in July!*
Martin	Jo, jeg vet hvor pikene bor. De er søstre og heter Else, Mai og Liv. De har en stor, gammel leilighet ved Frognerparken.

You take the tram to Frognerparken, and Martin finds the girls' flat. He rings the doorbell and the door is opened.

Martin	Hei, Mai! Dette er min engelske venn, ___. Vi håper å få en kopp kaffe.
Mai	Så hyggelig å se dere. Kom inn! Else er ikke hjemme, men Liv og jeg er her.
Du	*Martin asked me to come. I hope it is all right (in order).*
Mai	Velkommen til oss! Kanskje vi kan snakke engelsk senere. Her er Liv.
Liv	Fint at dere kom! Nå skal jeg lage vafler og kaffe, og så kan du fortelle oss om London. Jeg skal reise dit snart.
Martin	Jeg er sulten, og jeg elsker vafler!

You have a pleasant evening eating waffles and drinking coffee. You remember to say: **takk for maten.** As you leave, you say:

Du	*Thank you for having me.*
Liv og Mai	På gjensyn!

QV

kjente (å kjenne) *knew, was/were familiar with*
spurte (å spørre) *asked*
vafler (en vaffel) *waffles*

Test yourself

As always you will find three answers to the questions, but only one is correct.

1 Når skal tante Maiken spise aftens?
a Klokken sju. **b** Klokken åtte. **c** Klokken ni.
2 Hva skal de spise?
a Fisk og poteter. **b** Reker og majones.
c En deilig gryterett.
3 Hva skal de ha til dessert?
a Ost og frukt. **b** Is. **c** Bløtkake.
4 Hva gjør Jan?
a Han er lærer. **b** Han er tannlege. **c** Han er ingeniør.
5 Hva heter Arnes venner?
a Randi og Odd. **b** Randi og Knut. **c** Odd og Knut.
6 Mor er 50 år! Et av barna holder tale. Hvem er det?
a Liv. **b** Elisabeth. **c** Tom.
7 Hvem sa 'Takk for maten' på vegne av gjestene?
a Far. **b** Arne. **c** Morfar.
8 Hvilken dato er fjortende april totusen og ni?
a 15. 4. 2009. **b** 14. 4. 2009. **c** 14. 4. 2008.
9 Hvilken dato er tjuetredje februar to tusen og elleve?
a 23. 2. 2011. **b** 25. 2. 2011. **c** 3. 7. 2011.

10 I *Do you understand?* møter vi Martin fra Unit 5 igjen. Hva gjør han?

a Han kjører buss. **b** Han kjører lastebil. **c** Han kjører sykebil.

Slottet, Oslo

11

God Jul! Godt Nyttår!

Happy Christmas! Happy New Year!

In this unit you will learn
- ***What to write on Christmas cards***
- ***How to enjoy a Norwegian Christmas***
- ***More about telling the time***

Dialogue 1

Torsdag tjuende desember (*Thursday 20 December*). Sue and Arne have been spending a lot of time together, and Sue was delighted when Arne's family invited her to spend Christmas with them.

Sue og Arne sitter på kjøkkenet og skriver julekort. Far ser på Dagsnytt, mens mor leser avisen.

CD2, TR 20

Arne	Hvis vi poster disse kortene i kveld, kommer de kanskje frem til julaften. Vi skulle ha skrevet dem før!
Sue	Jeg er alltid sen med julekortene mine. Hvorfor sier du ikke God Jul og God Nyttår?
Arne	Så dum du er! Du vet da at det er 'en' jul og 'et' nyttår! Et år!
Sue	Ja, selvfølgelig. Men jeg kan ikke huske alt!

Arne	Du er veldig flink til å snakke norsk, Sue. Du kan skrive: 'God Jul og Godt Nyttår' eller 'Alle gode ønsker for Julen og det Nye Året'. Vil du skrive navnet ditt på disse kortene som jeg har skrevet?
Sue	Ja, og så må du skrive en hilsen på dette kortet til bestemor i Australia. Jeg tror ikke hun får det til jul! Men hun blir sikkert glad for bildet av snø og fjell.
Arne	Odd og Randi skal få kortet med den tykke julegrisen.

Tom kommer inn.

Tom	Skal vi lage marsipan nå?
Sue	Marsipan?
Tom	Ja, vi lager alltid marsipan til jul. Vi farger den gul, grønn og lyserød og former den til små frukter. Det er en hyggelig juleskikk og den smaker veldig godt!

Mor kommer inn.

Mor	Nå skal jeg lage kaffe til oss og så skal vi smake på julekakene. Fint at dere vil lage marsipan.
Sue	Når pynter dere juletreet?
Mor	Vi pynter aldri juletreet før den tjuetredje desember. Lysene blir tent på selve julaften.
Sue	Jeg gleder meg til å feire en norsk jul. Det skal bli både festlig og interessant. Tusen takk for at jeg fikk komme hit.

Mor smiler. Arne gir Sue et kyss.

Arne	Jeg er glad du er her.

Insight

You may find a fat pig on a Christmas card a bit surprising, but it is as common on Norwegian Christmas cards as the robin is on English cards. Christmas is a time for good and plentiful food, and roast pork or a side of ribs of pork is traditional food in the south-east of Norway.

(Contd)

An old tradition is to serve a dish of rice porridge with one blanched almond hidden in it on Christmas Eve. The person who gets the almond will receive a marzipan pig.

QUICK VOCAB

aldri *never*
avisen (en) *the newspaper*
bildet (et bilde) *the picture*
Dagsnytt *the main news on TV*
farger (å farge) *colour/colours*
feire *celebrate*
flink *clever*
former (å forme) *shape/shapes*
hilsen (en) *greeting*
interessant *interesting*
julaften (en) *Christmas Eve*
julegrisen (en gris) *the Christmas pig**
julekakene (en kake) *the Christmas cookies*
juleskikk (en) *Christmas tradition*
juletreet (et) *the Christmas tree*
kommer frem (å komme frem) *get/gets there*
kyss (et) *kiss*
leser (å lese) *read/reads*
marsipan (en) *marzipan*
nyttår (et) *New Year*
poster (å poste) *post/posts*
pynter (å pynte) *decorate/decorates*
selve *itself*
selvfølgelig *of course*
smake *taste/tastes*
snø (en) *snow*
tenner (å tenne) *lit*
tre (et) *tree*
ønsker (et ønske) *wishes*

(*Pigs are associated with Christmas as pork is probably eaten by most Norwegians on Christmas Eve)

True or false? 1

- **a** Far lager marsipan, som han former til frukter.
- **b** Arne skriver julekort til Odd og Randi.
- **c** Sue er alltid tidlig med julekortene sine.
- **d** Mor vil gjerne ha en kopp te.

Dialogue 2

Julaften, mandag tjuefjerde desember (*Christmas Eve, Monday 24 December*). Klokken er halv elleve. Sue står ved vinduet og ser på alle lysene i byen. Det har vært en fin dag, og Sue er glad for at hun har fått oppleve en norsk julaften.

Klokken fire gikk hele familien i kirken til den tradisjonelle barnegudstjenesten. Kirken var full og Sue kjente mange av julesangene. Da de kom ut, ringte alle kirkeklokkene i byen.

CD2, TR 21

Tom	Nå ringer alle kirkeklokkene i hele Norge. Nå er det jul. God jul, alle sammen!

Da de kom hjem, ble juletreet tent. De hadde pyntet det i går kveld. Nå sto det der og lyste med glitter og små, norske flagg, og med pynt som barna hadde laget da de var små. Under treet lå det mange presanger.

Bente og barna var der, og Elisabeth hadde nettopp kommet hjem. Liv og hennes familie skulle feire jul i Trondheim med Geirs familie.

Klokken sju spiste de julemiddag. Det var tradisjon å ha 'pinnekjøtt' med øl og dram. Til dessert var det multer og krem. Sue syntes det var et deilig og spesielt måltid.

Nå var Per utålmodig. Men han måtte vente til alt var ryddet og kaffe og julekaker var på bordet. Da gikk far bort til juletreet.

Far	Er det noen snille barn her, da?
Alle	Ja! Ja! Ja!!

Presangene ble delt ut i tur og orden. Alle gledet seg over hva de andre fikk og over sine egne presanger. Sue fikk en fin, norsk genser, fire høye glass og flere bøker.

Mor	Da barna var små, gikk vi alltid rundt juletreet og sang julesanger. Men nå gjør vi ikke det lenger.
Per	Jeg skal synge: 'Jeg er så glad hver julekveld'.

Per sang, og lille Pål sov.

QUICK VOCAB

barnegudstjenesten (en) *the children's service*
bøker (en bok) *books*
delt ut (å dele ut) *handed out*
(å dele *to share***)**
dram (en) *tot of aquavit*
egne (egen) *own*
flagg (et flagg) *flags*
glitter *tinsel*
halv elleve *half past ten*
i tur og orden *one by one*
julekveld (en) *Christmas Eve*
julesangene (en julesang) *the Christmas carols*
kirken (en kirke) *the church*
kirkeklokkene (en kirke klokke) *the church bells*
krem (en) *whipped cream*
lengen *any longer*
lyste (å lyse) *glowed*
multer (en multe) *cloudberries*
måltid (et) *meal*
oppleve *experience*
pinnekjøtt *steamed lamb* (see 'Preparations for Christmas' section)
presanger (en presang) *presents*
pynt (en pynt) *ornaments*
sang (en) *song*
sang (å synge) *sang*

sov (å sove) *slept*
sto (å stå) *stood*
synge (å synge) *sing*
tradisjon (en) *tradition*
tradisjonelle (tradisjonell) *traditional*
under *under*
utålmodig *impatient*
vinduet (et) *the window*

True or false? 2

a Familien spiste middag før de gikk til barnegudstjenesten.
b Alle presangene lå under juletreet.
c Barna hadde laget pynt til juletreet da de var små.
d Arne fikk en fin genser.

Dialogue 3

Nyttårsaften, mandag trettiførste desember (*New Year's Eve, Monday 31 December*).

Etter jul reiste Sue og Arne til Oslo. Sue har begynt å jobbe igjen, men Arne har ferie fra universitetet noen dager til. De bor i Sues lille leilighet.

I dag er nyttårsaften, og de skal feire den sammen med Odd og Randi. Arne er flink til å lage mat, og han har laget en deilig middag. Det er så vidt plass til fire rundt bordet i det koselige, lille kjøkkenet. Ute er det kaldt, og det har snødd hele dagen.

Nå er klokken ti på tolv. Arne åpner en flaske musserende vin. Sue finner de høye glassene som hun fikk til jul og setter dem på bordet. Hun åpner døren til balkongen. Plutselig begynner et fantastisk fyrverkeri. Himmelen lyser i alle farger, og det smeller og bråker.

CD2, TR 22

Arne	Klokken er tolv. Godt nyttår, alle sammen! Godt nyttår, Sue!
Sue	Godt nyttår, Arne!

Arne kysser Sue.

Sue	Godt nyttår, Odd! Og Randi!

De klemmer hverandre. Nå ringer kirkeklokkene mens rakettene farer mot den mørke himmelen. Klokken er kvart over tolv. Det blir kaldt å stå i den åpne døren. Sue lukker den. De drikker vinen og skåler med hverandre.

Arne har armene rundt Sue.

Arne	Godt nyttår, søte, lille Sue, og takk for det gamle!
Sue	Takk i like måte. Jeg er glad jeg har truffet deg.
Arne	Tror du vi skal være sammen neste nyttårsaften?
Sue	Det håper jeg. Skål for oss, Arne!

Klokken er ett og selskapet er over. Randi og Odd går hjem med armene rundt hverandre. Arne og Sue står ved vinduet og ser dem ute i snøen. Snøfnuggene danser i luften.

Insight

Beware of 'false friends'! Sometimes you come across Norwegian words that are similar to English ones. Often they have the same meaning, but not always. Look at the description of the fireworks: 'Himmelen lyser i alle farger, og det smeller og bråker', meaning *The sky is lit up in all colours, and it bangs and make noises.* No *smell* at all! The noun 'et smell' means *a bang*.

QUICK VOCAB

balkongen (en) *the balcony*
bråker (å bråke) *make/makes a noise*
farer (å fare) *travel/travels*
fyrverkeri (et) *fireworks*
himmelen (en) *the sky/heaven*

klemmer (å klemme) *hug/hugs*
kvart over *a quarter past*
kysser (å kysse) *kiss/kisses*
luften (en) *the air*
lukker (å lukke) *shut/shuts*
musserende *sparkling*
nyttårsaften *New Year's Eve*
rakettene (en rakett) *the rockets*
setter (å sette) *put/puts*
smeller (å smelle) *bang/bangs*
snødd (å snø) *snowed*
så vidt *just about*
takk i like mate *thank you, the same to you*
ti på *ten to*
truffet (å treffe) *met*

True or false? 3

a Sue feirer nyttårsaften i Bergen.
b De hører ikke kirkeklokkene fordi døren til balkongen er lukket.
c Det er et fantastisk fyrverkeri fordi det er nyttår.
d Randi og Odd går klokken to.

This is how we say it

▶ Wishing people a Merry Christmas and a Happy New Year:

God jul!	*Happy Christmas!*
Godt nyttår!	*Happy New Year!*
Alle gode ønsker for julen og det nye året!	*All good wishes for Christmas and the New Year!*
Godt nyttår og takk for det gamle!	*Happy New Year and thank you for the old one!*

Takk det samme!	*Thank you, the same to you!*
Takk i like måte!	*Thank you, the same to you!*
Jeg håper du får et godt nytt år!	*I hope you will have a good New Year!*

Insight

After Christmas and New Year greetings we get back to telling the time. You may remember we started looking at this in Unit 9. In this unit we explain it all once more.

- Expressions concerning the time:

Hva er klokken?	*What is the time?*
Hvor mange er klokken?	*What is the time? How many is the time?*
Klokken er kvart på seks.	*It is a quarter to six.*
Den er kvart på seks.	*It is a quarter to six.*
Den er halv ni.	*It is* (half to nine) *half past eight.*
Er den halv ni alt?	*Is it half past eight already?*
Det er sent!	*It is late!*
Jeg skal reise tidlig i morgen.	*I shall travel early tomorrow.*
Jeg skal reise klokken halv sju.	*I shall travel at half past six.*
Når skal du legge deg?	*When will you go to bed?*
Jeg skal legge meg klokken tolv.	*I shall go to bed at twelve.*
Han legger seg kvart på ti.	*He goes to bed at a quarter to ten.*
Når står du opp?	*When do you get up?*
Jeg står opp ti på åtte.	*I get up at ten to eight.*
Jeg vil helst sove hele dagen!	*I would rather sleep the whole day!*

Language patterns

1 *Å få, får, fikk, har fått* *to get/receive*

This verb can have several different meanings:

a Asking or giving permission:

Får jeg komme inn?	*May I come in?*
Kan jeg få snakke med Kari?	*May I speak to Kari?*
Du kan få lov til å spise hele kaken.	*You have permission to eat the whole cake.*

b To manage, be able to or to get a chance to:

Han får ikke sove når det er lyst.	*He can't sleep when it is light.*
Jeg fikk høre at hun var syk.	*I heard/learnt that she was ill.*
Han fikk henne til å smile.	*He managed to make her smile.*

c A softly expressed order:

Du får gjøre som jeg sier.	*You will do what I say.*

d Future:

Vi får se.	*We shall see.*

2 Verbs: *å legge seg* *to go to bed,* ***å sette seg*** *to sit down*

In Unit 10 you looked at these reflexive verbs å **legge seg** (*to go to bed*), and å sette seg (*to sit down*). Here are more examples:

Jeg legger meg klokken ti.	*I go to bed at ten o'clock.*
Hun legger seg sent.	*She goes to bed late.*
John la seg klokken ti på elleve.	*John went to bed at ten to eleven.*
Bente setter seg ved bordet.	*Bente sits down by the table.*

Vil du sette deg her?	*Will you sit down here?*
De satte seg ved vinduet.	*They sat down by the window.*

Remember that you use the reflexive **seg** in the 3rd person (he, she, it and they) only, and only when it reflects back to the subject.

3 Verbs: the '-ing' ending

In English the *-ing* ending for verbs is called the present participle. In Norwegian it is formed by adding **-ende** to the stem of the verb.

å smile stem = **smil** present participle = **smilende** (*smiling*)

The present participle is not used so much in Norwegian. Look at the examples below:

Bente sitter.	*Bente sits/Bente is sitting.*
John ligger.	*John lies/John is lying.*

The present participle is used only after verbs which express movement, like **å komme** and **å gå.**

Han kom syklende til byen.	*He came cycling to the town.*
Hun gikk smilende mot ham.	*She went smiling towards him.*

4 '-ing' as an adjective

The present participle is used more as an adjective in Norwegian:

en glitrende stjerne	*a twinkling star*
et skrikende barn	*a screaming child*
en smilende dame	*a smiling lady*

These adjectives do not take endings in comparison. When comparing, you must use **mer** or **mest.**

en lovende student	*a promising student*
den mest lovende studenten	*the most promising student*

5 Nouns

Here are some more irregular nouns:

et tre	treet	trær	trærne	(*a tree*)
en bok	boken	bøker	bøkene	(*a book*)

Nouns ending in **er** usually follow this pattern for plurals:

(You looked at some in Unit 8.)

en lærer	læreren	lærere	lærerne	(*a teacher*)
en skulder	skulderen	skuldre	skuldrene	(*a shoulder*)
en finger	fingeren	fingre	fingrene	(*a finger*)
en vinter	vinteren	vintre	vintrene	(*a winter*)
en genser	genseren	gensere	genserne	(*a sweater*)

6 *Ikke* *not*: position

You have seen that **ikke** usually comes immediately after the verb:

John liker ikke Bente. *John doesn't like Bente.*

If the verb consists of two words, **ikke** comes after the first:

Bente vil ikke reise til Bergen. *Bente will not travel to Bergen.*

There are some situations where **ikke** moves around:

- In a subordinate (or 'dependent') clause, **ikke** comes in front of the verb:

  Fordi han ikke var syk, gikk han på kino. *Because he wasn't ill, he went to the cinema.*
  Da John ikke kom, spiste Bente all maten. *As John didn't come, Bente ate all the food.*

- If the object of the sentence is a pronoun, **ikke** moves to the end.

Bente så ikke John.	*Bente didn't see John.*
Bente så ham ikke.	*Bente didn't see him.*
Jeg leste ikke boken.	*I didn't read the book.*
Jeg leste den ikke.	*I didn't read it.*

▸ **Ikke** can come first if you want to stress something:

Ikke spiser han og ikke drikker han.	*He doesn't eat or drink.*
Ikke fikk hun lest brevet.	*She didn't get to read the letter.*

▸ **Ikke** comes first when giving an order (imperative):

Ikke sitt der!	*Don't sit there!*
Ikke drikk mer!	*Don't drink any more!*

Exercises

1 What is the time?

- **a** Ti over seks.
- **b** Kvart over ti.
- **c** Fem på elleve.
- **d** Halv åtte.
- **e** Ti over halv to.

2 Study 'Telling the time' at the end of this unit, then write out, or say, in Norwegian the times shown on these clocks:

CD2, TR 23

a

b

c

d

e

3 Which dates are these?

- **a** Tjuetredje i fjerde.
- **b** Sjuende i første.
- **c** Tiende i tiende.
- **d** Ellevte i femte.
- **e** Attende i åttende.

4 Write out these dates in Norwegian using ordinal numbers, and the names of the months:

- **a** 5 February
- **b** 12 March
- **c** 14 June
- **d** 16 July
- **e** 26 September

5 Give the appropriate greeting/expression of gratitude:

- **a** Wish someone a happy birthday.
- **b** Say Happy Christmas, Grandmother (paternal).
- **c** Wish someone a Happy New Year.
- **d** Thank your host/hostess for a meal.
- **e** Say: Thank you, the same (to you).

6 Use **sette/sitte, legge/ligge, sette seg/legge seg** in the present tense:

a Kari ___ boken på bordet.
b Erik ___ ved bordet.
c John ___ klokken tolv.
d Han ___ ved vinduet.
e Jeg ___ klokken ti på elleve.

7 These sentences are in the present tense. Change the verbs to past tense:

a Jeg sitter ved bordet.	Jeg ___ ved bordet.
b John legger seg klokken kvart på tolv.	John ______.
c Vi setter oss ved vinduet.	Vi ______.
d Du legger boken på bordet.	Du ______.
e Bøkene ligger på bordet.	Bøkene ______.

Preparations for Christmas

In Norway these get under way in early December. Homes are cleaned from cellar to loft, and the traditional seven kinds of cookies are baked. It is a time for the family to enjoy evenings together, writing Christmas cards and making sweets and Christmas decorations.

The Christmas tree is decorated the evening before Christmas – and Christmas is celebrated on Christmas Eve, the 24th. The tree is never lit before the evening of the 24th.

An old tradition is to have rice porridge for lunch. A blanched almond is hidden in the porridge, and the lucky finder receives a marzipan pig.

Vast numbers of people attend the children's service in the churches. The church bells ring at the same time all over the country to signal the beginning of Christmas.

Christmas Eve is a family time. Food traditions vary from place to place, with roast rib of pork in the south-east and lamb or cod, even **lutefisk** (described below) in the west, and grouse in the far north.

The custom of forming a circle round the Christmas tree and singing carols is slowly dying out as families become smaller. At larger family gatherings and other Christmas parties, however, this tradition is still very much alive. Traditional carols are sung, ending with action/dance songs similar to 'Here we go round the mulberry bush'.

The presents are arranged under the tree, and are distributed one at a time so that everybody can enjoy and admire them and share in the pleasure of the recipient.

There are usually many parties and family reunions between Christmas and the New Year. New Year is celebrated with parties and fireworks. Church bells also chime for the New Year.

Pinnekjøtt
Twigs of birch are placed in a large pan; the lamb, cut into pieces, is placed on the twigs; a little water is added; the meat is steamed through the twigs until tender. Season with salt and pepper and serve with plenty of chopped parsley and boiled new potatoes.

Lutefisk
Fillets of dried cod are soaked for some time in a potash lye. They are then soaked, boiled and served with crisply fried diced bacon, and the bacon fat is liberally poured over. A gourmet dish!

Telling the time

Hvor mange er klokken?	*What is the time?*
Hva er klokken?	*What is the time?*
Klokken er åtte.	*It is eight o'clock.*
Klokken er fem.	*It is five o'clock.*

Klokken er fem over fem.	*It is five past five.* (The time is five past five.)
Klokken er ti på fem.	*It is ten to five.* (The time is ten to five.)
Klokken er kvart på sju.	*It is a quarter to seven.*
Klokken er kvart over sju.	*It is a quarter past seven.*
på	*to*
over	*past*

So far it is easy to tell the time.

Klokken er halv ti.	*It is half past nine.* (Half *to* ten.)
Klokken er halv tre.	*It is half past two.*
Klokken er ti på halv tre.	*It is twenty past two.* (Ten to half to three.)
Klokken er fem over halv tre.	*It is twenty-five to three.* (Five past half to three.)

TV programmes, train and bus timetables and so on use the 24-hour clock, but, as in English, you don't normally say: **Jeg skal legge meg klokken tjuetretretti** (23.30), rather **Jeg skal legge meg klokken halv tolv** (*I shall go to bed at half past eleven*).

When written, **klokken** is shortened to **kl.**

Do you understand?

It is January the first. You are talking to your friend's grandmother. She has never been outside Norway, and she is a difficult old woman.

Bestemor	Savner du ikke familien din i julen?
Du	*Yes, a little. But I like to be here in Norway at Christmas.*
Bestemor	Feirer dere julen?

Du	*Yes, but not Christmas Eve. Christmas Day, 25 December, is our Christmas.*
Bestemor	Ikke julaften! Det er dumt, synes jeg. Det er ikke jul uten julaften!
Du	(thinking to yourself: better not upset the old lady!) *I like celebrating Christmas Eve. I like the Norwegian food and traditions.*
Bestemor	Jeg håper du har spist lutefisk!
Du	*No, and I will not eat it! I don't think that I will like it.*
Bestemor	Du er dum hvis du ikke vil smake lutefisk. Det ser ikke godt ut, men det smaker deilig. Du må ha et glass akevitt sammen med lutefisken.
Du	*I would like to have a dram, but not lutefisk!*
Bestemor	Jeg håper ikke du drikker for meget! Jeg tror julen er bedre i Norge enn andre steder.
Du	(beginning to get impatient) *Christmas is fine everywhere, if you are together with those you like. It was nice to talk with you, but now I must go.*
Bestemor	Du må snakke høyere! Jeg hører ikke hva du sier. Det er sikkert fordi du ikke snakker godt norsk.
Du	*Goodbye!*

Insight

The grumpy grandmother asks: **'Savner du ikke familien din i julen?'** meaning *Don't you miss your family at Christmas?* She asks if he is missing his family, but the question is in a negative form. The positive (*yes*) answer to a negative question is: 'jo' rather than 'ja'.

'Jo' can also mean *actually*. 'Han har jo vært her før', meaning *He has actually been here before*.

You can also use 'jo' as a reluctant *yes*. 'Vil du spise lutefisk?' You could answer: 'Jo, men jeg vil heller ha pinnekjøtt'.

QV

akevitt (en) *aquavit*
juledag *Christmas Day*
ser godt ut *look/looks good*

Test yourself

10 questions, three answers for each, but two are wrong!

1 Hvor skal Sue være i julen?
a Hos Arnes familie. **b** Hos tante Maiken.
c Hos Odd og Randi.
2 Hvem skal få kortet med julegrisen?
a Bestemor i Australia. **b** Odd og Randi.
c Tante Maiken.
3 Når pynter familien juletreet?
a Tjuetredje desember. **b** Tjuefjerde desember.
c Tjuefemte desember.
4 Når spiser familien julemiddag?
a Julaften. **b** Tjuefemte desember. **c** Nyttårsaften.
5 Hvor feirer Sue og Arne nyttårsaften?
a I Bergen. **b** I Oslo. **c** I Kristiansand.
6 Hvem er de sammen med?
a Tante Maiken. **b** Bente og barna. **c** Odd og Randi.
7 Hva drikker de klokken tolv?
a Kaffe. **b** Eplesaft. **c** Musserende vin.
8 Når går Odd og Randi?
a Klokken tolv. **b** Klokken ett. **c** Klokken halv to.

Two different types of questions:

9 What is the definite plural of *teacher*?
a Lærer. **b** Læreren. **c** Lærerne.
10 What is the indefinite singular of *Christmas*?
a Jul. **b** Julen. **c** Juler.

12

Brev
Letters

In this unit you will learn
- ***How to write formal and informal letters***
- ***How to use titles***
- ***How to describe the weather***
- ***How to describe the seasons***

In this unit you will find five short letters. Look in the **This is how we say it** and **Writing letters** sections, where you will find letter-writing in Norwegian explained.

Text 1

Personalsjefen
Johns Hotell
Storgaten 599
Bodø

Leilighet 16
Lillegaten 7
0123 Oslo

10. februar 2010

Jeg så Deres annonse i Aftenposten fredag sjette februar. Jeg er interessert i opplysninger om den ledige stillingen i resepsjonen.

Jeg er engelsk, tjuetre år, og for tiden arbeider jeg i en forretning i Oslo. Her selger jeg klær. Jeg snakker og skriver norsk ganske bra.

I London arbeidet jeg for økonomisjefen på et kontor. Jeg hadde jobb to kvelder i uken i en pub mens jeg var student. Jeg har også hatt jobb som kjøkkenhjelp på et sykehus.

Hvis denne stillingen allerede er besatt, vil jeg gjerne vite om det er andre muligheter for en jobb i dette hotellet. Jeg kan komme til samtale når som helst.

Attester vedlegges.

Ærbødigst

Sue Smith

Insight

This is a very formal letter. Notice the formal 'De' meaning *you*. This formal pronoun isn't used all that much any more, but in a letter of this kind it would certainly be correct. Look up the formal *you* in Unit 9.

Notice that the letter has no heading, like *Dear Sir or Madam*. You use 'Kjære', meaning *Dear*, only in private letters.

'Ærbødigst' meaning *Yours faithfully/yours truly* is the most formal way to end a letter.

QUICK VOCAB

Aftenposten *The Evening Post*, Norwegian newspaper
allerede *already*
annonse (en) *advert*
attester (en attest) *references/recommendations*
besatt *taken*
for tiden *at the moment*
forretning (en) *store/shop*
ganske *quite*
i uken *per week*
interessert *interested*
kjøkkenhjelp (en) *kitchen hand*
kontor (et) *office*
muligheter (en mulighet) *possibilities*

når som helst *at any time*
om *if/whether*
opplysninger *information*
personalsjefen (en) *the personnel manager*
resepsjonen (en) *the reception*
samtale (en) *interview, conversation*
sjef (en) *boss/director/manager*
stillingen (en) *the position*
vedlegges *is/are enclosed*
ærbødigst *yours respectfully*
økonomi *economics*
økonomisjefen (en) *the accountant*

True or false? 1

a Sue vil gjerne arbeide på et hotell.
b Hun arbeidet på et kontor i London før hun reiste til Norge.
c Hotellet er i Stavern.
d Det er en ledig stilling i resepsjonen.

Text 2

Johns Hotell
Storgaten 599
Bodø

Sue Smith
Leilighet 16
Lillegaten 7
0123 OSLO

15. februar 2010

Ref JKH / 15.02.10 / bn

Jeg må dessverre meddele deg om at stillingen i resepsjonen er besatt. Vi fikk mange kvalifiserte søkere med mange års erfaring innen hotellbransjen.

Vi vil gjerne treffe deg likevel, hvis du er interessert i å arbeide på kontoret. Vi skal også snart åpne et nytt hotell, så det er muligheter innen vår stadig voksende organisasjon.

Jeg foreslår at du kommer til en samtale 26. februar klokken 11. Jeg ser frem til å møte deg da.

Med hilsen

J. K. Hearst

Direktør

Insight

Again, no heading as this is a business letter. Notice also that there is no formal 'De' here. Sue is only 23 years old and the manager would naturally say 'du' to her.

'Med hilsen' meaning *With greetings* is impersonal, and suitable for business letters.

QUICK VOCAB

bransje (en) *line of business*
dessverre *unfortunately/sadly*
erfaring (en) *experience*
foreslår (å foreslå) *suggest/suggests*
hotellbransjen *the hotel business*
innen *within*
kvalifiserte (kvalifisert) *qualified*
likevel *all the same*
meddele *inform*
organisasjon (en) *organization*
ser frem til (å se frem til) *look/looks forward to*
stadig *ever/all the time*
søkere (en søker) *applicants*
voksende (å vokse) *growing*

True or false? 2

- **a** Stillingen i resepsjonen er allerede besatt.
- **b** Sue kan få jobb på kontoret.
- **c** Hotellet er i Bodø.
- **d** Sue har fått stilling som personalsjef.

Text 3

CD2, TR 24

Sue sender e-post til Randi:

Hei R!

Takk for sist! Skulle ha takket før. Er litt tankeløs. Veldig hyggelig kveld med deg og Odd.

Vil du høre hva som har hendt? Noe veldig spennende!!

Har nettopp vært i Bodø og skal jobbe på Johns hotell! Flytter dit om 4 uker. Er lei av å bo i Oslo og lei av jobben min her. Treffer bare gamle damer! På tide å flytte.

Mannen som eier Johns hotell, heter John og er engelsk. Kom til Norge for 10 år siden. Han er kjempekjekk! Kanskje 'Mannen med stor M'! Tror han liker meg.

Kan få et bittelite rom på hotellet, men vil leie en leilighet snart. Liker å stå på egne ben.

John er veldig sportsinteressert og er på ski hele tiden. Jeg vet heldigvis litt om engelsk fotball.

Nå må jeg skrive et brev til Arne. Han vet ikke noe.

Klem S x

Insight

E-mails to friends are very informal. 'Hei!' is a much-used was to start both e-mails and letters. Very often sentences are without a subject, but generally not as compressed as text messages.

'Klem' or 'klem fra' meaning *hug/hug from* is equivalent to *love/love from.*

QUICK VOCAB

ben (et) *leg*
bittelite (bitteliten) *very small/teeny weeny*
brev (et) *letter*
e-post *e-mail*
er på ski *skis*
flytter (å flytte) *move/moves*
fotball (en) *football*
hendt (å hende) *happened*
jobbe (å jobbe) *work*
kjempekjekk *very handsome*
leie *rent*
Mannen med stor M *the Man with a capital M*
på tide *time to*
spennende *exciting*
sportsinteressert *interested in sport*
stå på egne ben *stand on one's own feet*
tankeløs *thoughtless*

True or false? 3

a Sue sender en e-post til Randi.
b Arne vet at Sue skal flytte til Bodø.
c Sue liker jobben sin.

Text 4

CD2, TR 25

Sue skriver til Arne:

Kjære Arne *5 mars 10*

Det er lenge siden jeg skrev til deg. Jeg har hatt et veldig travelt liv og jeg har ikke hatt tid til å ringe heller.

I februar svarte jeg på en annonse i Aftenposten om jobb på et hotell i Bodø. Jeg har fått jobb der, og jeg reiser om to uker. Jeg skal arbeide på kontoret og jeg har fått et lite rom på hotellet. Snart skal jeg leie en leilighet, og da håper jeg at du kommer og besøker meg.

Jeg er lei av jobben min i Oslo, og jeg vil gjerne se mer av Norge. Jeg er interessert i turisme og jeg vil gjerne treffe flere nordmenn. Oslo er ikke en hyggelig by, synes jeg. Jeg gleder meg til å bo i en liten by.

Håper det går fint med studiet ditt. Du er sikkert glad for at det går mot slutten og at du snart er ferdig. Vil du ha jobb som lærer? Det sa du i fjor.

Du kan tro at det er kaldt her for tiden. Jeg liker ikke vinteren. Er det blitt vår i Bergen? Jeg er sikker på at det regner der.

Hils foreldrene dine og Tom.

Ha det godt, Arne!
Kjærlig hilsen fra Sue

Insight

Sue must now tell Arne about what she is up to. She starts her letter in the traditional way, using 'kjære' meaning *dear*, and ends it with 'kjærlig hilsen fra Sue' meaning: *loving greetings from Sue*. She is a bit worried about Arne's reaction, and he is not pleased, as you will discover when you read on.

QUICK VOCAB

du kan tro at ... *you can't believe how/what ...*
ferdig *finished*
i fjor *last year*
kjærlig hilsen *loving greetings*
liv (et) *life*
nordmenn (en nordmann) *Norwegians*
sikker på *sure*
slutten (en slutt) *the end*
studiet (et studium) *the study/course*
travelt (travel) *busy*
turisme (en) *tourism*
vinter (en) *winter*
vår (en) *spring*

True or false? 4

a Sue har fått jobb som personalsjef.
b Sue tror at det regner i Bergen.
c Sue liker å bo i Oslo.

Text 5

CD2, TR 26

Kjære Sue   Bergen, 10. mars 10

Jeg var ikke glad da jeg leste brevet ditt. Hvorfor har du ikke snakket med meg om dette? Jeg visste ikke noe før jeg fikk brevet ditt.

Jeg har ringt til deg mange ganger, men du tar aldri telefonen. Jeg har sendt SMS til deg hver dag, men jeg får ikke svar. Hva er i veien med deg?

Hva med påsken? Vi skulle reise på fjellet og gå på ski. Men du reiser til Bodø like før påske.

Jeg vet ikke hva jeg skal tro. Jeg var veldig sint på deg i sommer og nå er jeg sint igjen!

Arne

Insight

Arne starts his letter with 'kjære Sue', but he ends with just his name. No hugs or kisses here! And Sue has ruined his Easter holiday. Perhaps he should look for somebody else.

gå på *ski* **ski like før** *just before* **påske (en)** *Easter*

QV

This is how we say it

- Here are some useful phrases when writing letters:

Takk for sist!	*Thank you for last time.*
Jeg skal hilse fra mor.	*Mother sends her greetings.*
Jeg skal hilse fra John.	*John sends his greetings.*
Hils onkel Hans fra meg.	*Give my greetings/love to Uncle Hans.*
Du må hilse din tante.	*Give my greetings/love to your aunt.*
Hilsen ...	*Greetings ...*
Hilsen fra ...	*Greetings from ...*
Mange hilsener fra ...	*Many greetings from ...*
Tusen hilsener fra ...	*A thousand greetings from ...*
Kjærlig hilsen fra ...	*Loving greetings/love from ...*
Klem fra ...	*Hugs from ...*
Mange klemmer fra ...	*Many hugs from ...*
Kyss fra ...	*Kiss/kisses from ...*

- Business letters:

Takk for Deres brev.	*Thank you for your letter.*
Takk for brev av 15. november.	*Thank you for (your) letter of 15th November.*
Vi har dessverre ikke noen stilling ledig.	*Unfortunately we have no vacant position.*

Vi ser frem til å møte Dem fredag 3. januar.	*We look forward to meeting you on Friday 3rd January.*
Banksjefen vil gjerne treffe Dem neste torsdag.	*The bank manager would like to meet you next Thursday.*
Ærbødigst ...	*Yours faithfully/respectfully ...*
Med hilsen.	*With greetings.*

Insight

Look at these phrases. Writing letters should be no problem. Remember the polite phrase 'takk for sist', meaning *thank you for last time*, whenever that was. If you know some family member or close friend it is very nice to write 'hils Kari fra meg' meaning *greetings to Kari (from me)*, or 'hils din mor', meaning: *greetings to/remember me to your mother.*

Start friendly letters with 'kjære' or 'hei' and end with 'hilsen fra/klem fra' and a few XXX if appropriate!

Language patterns

1 *På* *on*

The preposition **på** normally means *on*.

Boken ligger på bordet.	*The book lies on the table.*
De er på vei til Nord-Norge.	*They are on their way to north Norway.*

In Norwegian you can often express where you are, using **på**. This may sound a bit strange:

Vi spiser frokost på kjøkkenet.	*We eat breakfast in the kitchen.*
John er på universitetet.	*John is at the university.*
Mor arbeider på et legekontor.	*Mother works at a doctor's surgery.*
Barna er på skolen.	*The children are at school.*
Vi er på fjellet i påsken.	*We are in the mountains at Easter.*

Note these too:

Vi er på landet (*in the countryside*)
Vi er i byen (*in town*)

There are more expressions with **på**:

Jeg er sikker på at ...	*I am sure/certain that ...*
Du må ta på deg en genser.	*You must put on a sweater.*
Klokken er kvart på tre.	*The time is a quarter to three.*
Det er på tide at jeg ...	*It is time that I ...*
På søndag skal vi gå på ski.	*On Sunday we shall go skiing.*
Han søker på en stilling.	*He is applying for a position.*

2 *Å gå* *to go/walk/travel*

Det er bare fem minutter å gå til stasjonen.	*It takes only five minutes to walk to the station.*
Toget går klokken fem på fire.	*The train leaves at five to four.*
Fergen går til Harwich.	*The ferry goes to Harwich.*
Jeg må gå nå.	*I have to leave now.*
Skal vi gå på kino?	*Shall we go to the cinema?*

You use **gå** for ferries, trains and so on, but for people only when you are actually walking.

Vi skal reise til Norge i sommer.	*We shall go/travel to Norway this summer.*

3 Words ending in *-m*

Words must not end with a double **m** in Norwegian, even if there should be a double consonant for the pronunciation. This means that you have to add the **m** if there is an ending to follow:

Nouns				
et rom	rommet	mange rom	rommene	(*a room*)
et hjem	hjemmet	mange hjem	hjemmene	(*a home*)
en klem	klemmen	mange klemmer	klemmene	(*a hug*)

Verb				
å komme	kommer	kom	har kommet	(*to come*)

Adjective				
en dum gutt	den dumme gutter	mange dumme gutten	de dumme guttene	(*a stupid boy*)

Adverb	
hjem	(*home*)
hjemme	(*at home*)

4 *Annen/annet/andre* *second/(an)other*

Andre is the second ordinal number. It also means *other*.

en annen dag	den andre dagen	andre dager	de andre dagene
et annet hus	det andre huset	andre hus	de andre husene

Notice the difference:

Jeg vil gjerne ha en annen kopp.	*I would like another/different cup.*
Jeg vil gjerne ha en kopp til.	*I would like another/one more cup*
Jeg vil gjerne ha den andre koppen.	*I would like the other cup.*

5 Nouns of foreign origin

Nouns ending in **-um** are declined this way:

et museum	museet	museer	museene	*(museum)*
et studium	studiet	studier	studiene	*(academic course)*
et laboratorium	laboratoriet	laboratorier	laboratoriene	*(laboratory)*
et sentrum	sentret	sentrer	sentrene	*(centre)*

Notice that they are all **et** words.

Exercises

1 Can you find a contrasting word – meaning the opposite? Look at the words below:

a nei
b nesten
c interessant
d stor
e stygg
f mørk
g sol

2 Do you remember the adverbs which have one form for movement and one for non-movement? If you are not sure, look back to Unit 6.

a John reiser ___ (*home*).
b Bente er ___ (*inside*).
c Han kjører ___ (*away*).
d Hun sender brevet ___ (*there*).
e De kommer ___ (*here*).

3 Insert a suitable pronoun:

a Jeg legger ___ i sengen.
b De setter ___ ved bordet.
c De gifter ___ på lørdag.
d Han følte ___ dårlig.

4 How would you end a letter to these people?

a Your aunt.
b A good friend.
c Your bank manager.
d Your boyfriend/girlfriend.

5 Write out, or say, these sentences in the present tense:

CD2, TR 27

a John drakk en kopp kaffe.
b Bilen stoppet plutselig.
c Vi bodde i Oslo i tre år.

d Brevet lå på bordet.
e Hun smilte til den lille gutten.

6 Insert in the gaps the correct forms of the adjectives in brackets:

a	(god)	en ___ dag
b	(rød)	et ___ hus
c	(liten)	den ___ bilen
d	(stygg)	de ___ klærne
e	(blå)	mange ___ skjorter
f	(vond)	det ___ kneet

7 Write a letter to a friend, thanking him/her for a Christmas present.

Writing letters

Starting a letter

Informal letters to friends and relatives start with **Kjære …** (*Dear …*); very informal letters start with **Hei …**

In a business letter it is not common to write *Dear Sir* or anything at all; you just write the name of the organization, with perhaps the title of the person you want to contact:

Personalsjefen (*the personnel director/manager*)
Bankdirektøren (*the director/manager of the bank*)

These are then followed by the address.

If you have met the person you are writing to, you could start with:

Hr. Ole Larsen (hr. = herr *Mr*)
Fru Kari Berg (fru = *Mrs*)
Frk. Liv Grorud (frk. = frøken *Miss*)

Ending a letter

The common greetings are:

Hilsen ... (*greeting ...*)
Hilsen fra ... (*greetings from ...*)
Mange hilsener fra ... (*many greetings from ...*)
Kjærlig hilsen ... (*loving greeting ...*)
Klem fra ... (*hugs from ...*)

Formal endings are:

Med hilsen ... (*greetings ...*) formal
Ærbødigst ... (*yours respectfully ...*) very formal

In a business letter one should use the formal **De**. It looks more professional.

Job titles

These are used much more in Norway than in England, both on letters and when one makes formal introductions.

Dette er tannlege Knut Berg. (*dentist*)
Dette er min kollega, veterinær Solveig Dale. (*veterinary surgeon*)
Har du truffet urmaker Ole Vik? (*watchmaker*)

Addresses on letters and envelopes:

Snekker Peter Linderud (*carpenter*)
Doktor / (Dr.) Elisabeth Nilsen (*Dr.*)
Kunstmaler Håkon Nordnes (*artist/painter*)
Operasanger Agnes Rud (*opera singer*)
Vaktmester Harald Olsen (*caretaker*) – just to mention a few!

In the telephone directory people are listed with their job/profession.

Royal titles

There is no aristocracy in Norway, so there are no titles apart from those used by the royals:

Hans Majestet Kong Harald *His Majesty King Harald*
Hennes Majestet Dronning Sonja *Her Majesty Queen Sonja*

If you meet them, you should address them as:

Deres Majestet *Your Majesty*

The King's two children and two sisters are addressed as:

Deres Kongelige Høyhet *Your Royal Highness*

Norwegians can be knighted for services to the nation. In this event, they receive the insignia from the King, but there is no title or letters after the name.

Årstidene *The seasons*

vinter	*winter*
vår	*spring*
sommer	*summer*
høst	*autumn*

Norway is a very elongated country with extreme temperatures and climate, and the seasons are very different. Winter is cold and dark, but the snow gives a lot of pleasure, as both old and young enjoy skiing and other winter activities.

Spring is usually dramatic. In a very short time the snow melts, the ground thaws out and the countryside becomes lush and green. The days grow noticeably longer.

Summer can be as hot and sunny as in southern Europe. But in a bad year it can be like a 'green winter'. Most of the time it is a mixture, and most years there will be several weeks of hot, sunny weather. The coast is ideal for water sports, and the temperature in the fjords and lakes can be surprisingly pleasant for swimming.

Norwegians love the outdoor life and hiking in the mountains and through the forests.

Autumn again is short and dramatic, with beautiful autumn colours and special golden light, soon to be replaced by storms and high seas round the jagged coastline. November often seems to be the darkest month, before the snow again covers the countryside, usually in December.

A great part of Norway lies north of the Arctic Circle (**Polarsirkelen**). Here part of the winter is without daylight, and in the summer the Midnight Sun (**Midnattssolen**) keeps everyone awake.

Do you understand?

You are one of Bente's old friends. You arrive in Oslo and you phone her old number.

CD2, TR 28

Girl	22 64 35 98 (say it in Norwegian!)
Du	*May I speak to Bente?*
Girl	Bente bor ikke her. Hun bor i Bergen. Hvem er du? Heter du John?
Du	*No, I am not John. I am (your name). I am one of Bente's friends from America.*
Girl	Du er flink til å snakke norsk. Bente bodde her før, men hun har flyttet til Bergen. Jeg heter Nina. Jeg er Bentes kusine.
Du	*Hi, Nina! Bente said that I could stay for a week or two. Is that in order?*
Nina	Ja, det er fint. Det er god plass her. Jeg deler leiligheten med broren min, og vi krangler hele tiden.
Du	*Why is that?*
Nina	Han er bare interessert i fotball. Og han sier at jeg bare er til bry fordi jeg ikke liker å rydde eller vaske opp. Bare kom, så skal jeg lage noen vafler.
Du	*Who is John?*

(Contd)

Nina	Bente hadde en engelsk venn som het John. Det var før hun møtte Knut. Alle likte John. Knut var dum og kjedelig, men Bente syntes at han var deilig. Huff!
Du	*I am looking forward to meeting you, Nina. Bye bye!*
Nina	Hei hei.

til bry *a nuisance*

Test Yourself

Try these questions. Only one of the three answers given is correct.

1 You are writing to your bank manager. How would you end the letter?
a Kyss fra ... **b** Klem fra ... **c** Ærbødigst ...

2 You are writing to your lover. How would you finish?
a Ærbødigst. **b** Med hilsen. **c** Klem og kyss fra ...

3 Sue vil gjerne ha jobb på Johns Hotell. Hvor er Johns Hotell?
a I Bergen. **b** I Bodø. **c** I Oslo.

4 Kan Sue få jobb på Johns Hotell?
a Nei. **b** Ja, i resepsjonen.
c Ikke i resepsjonen, men kanskje en annen jobb.

5 Når skal Sue komme til samtale på hotellet?
a Tjuesjette februar. **b** Sjette februar.
c Tjuesjuende februar.

6 Hvorfor vil Sue reise til Bodø?
a Hun er lei av klærne sine. **b** Hun er lei av jobben sin.
c Hun er lei av Arne.

7 Er Arne sint på Sue?
a Ja. **b** Nei. **c** Nei, han er sint på Tom.

8 Hvor skulle Sue og Arne reise i påsken?
a Til London. **b** På fjellet. **c** På campingtur.

9 Hvor kommer John fra?

a Fra Wales. **b** Fra Skotland. **c** Fra England.

10 Hva skriver Sue om John til Randi?

a Han er kjempekjekk. **b** Han er kjempedum.

c Han er kjempestor.

Sinnataggen, Vigeland Sculpture Park, Oslo

13

Påske
Easter

In this unit you will learn

- ***How to ask for advice on skiing***
- ***How to express delight***
- ***How to express fear***
- ***How to describe winter scenery***

Insight

Even though all Norwegians ski from a very early age, surprisingly there isn't a verb *to ski* in the Norwegian language. You have to say 'jeg liker å gå på ski' or 'vi skal gå på ski i påsken'.

Cross-country skiing is 'langrenn' when you take part in a race. As a sport just for pleasure one usually says 'skitur' meaning: *skiing trip*.

'Slalom' is a well-known term. The word for *downhill* is 'utfor'.

Dialogue 1

Sue enjoys her job in Bodø.

Sue tok imot tilbudet om en stilling på Johns Hotell og nå har hun flyttet til Bodø. Hun har ikke snakket med Arne, og hun vet at det er galt av henne.

Sue liker arbeidet på hotellet. Det har vært en veldig travel tid. Nå er det påske, og i dag har John invitert henne til en dag på fjellet. De skal på ski på høyfjellet.

Det har snødd mye de siste dagene, og det er høye brøytekanter langs veiene. Sue liker å sitte ved siden av John i den store bilen hans.

CD2, TR 29

Sue Synes du det er vanskelig å kjøre når det er så mye snø?
John Nei, jeg er vant til det nå, vet du. Jeg har gode piggdekk, og dette er en god, tung bil. Men jeg har vært i noen farlige situasjoner her i Norge. Mange bilister er idioter. De tenker ikke på at en må være veldig forsiktig når det er glatt.
Sue Bruker du piggdekk hele året?
John Nei, etter en bestemt dato er det forbudt å bruke vinterdekk. De ødelegger veiene, vet du. Jeg skifter til sommerdekk like etter påske. Men det er mye snø i år.
Sue Det er vakkert med den hvite snøen. Se, der kommer solen frem også! Jeg håper vi får fint vær i dag. Jeg gleder meg til å prøve skiene! Det skal bli gøy!
John Det er fint å gå på ski. Jeg har brukt skiene mye siden jeg kom til Norge. Jeg liker slalom best, men jeg liker også å gå lange skiturer.
Sue Jeg gikk på ski-kurs i Oslo, men jeg er ikke flink.
John Det blir du sikkert. Du skal sikkert fly fort. Du er en livlig jente!

Insight

Did you notice 'De skal på ski ...' in the first paragraph? Remember that the modal verbs are verbs in their own right. You don't have to have another verb, as you do in English. In Norwegian the modal verbs are conjugated in the same way as other verbs. Have a look in the **Grammar** section towards the end of the book. The section on *Modal verbs* follows that on *Irregular verbs*.

QUICK VOCAB

bestemt *set/decided*
bilister (en bilist) *drivers*
brøytekanter (en brøytekant) *banks of snow*
dato (en) *date*
dekk (et) *tyre*
farlige (farlig) *dangerous*
fly *fly, rush*
forsiktig *careful*
fort *fast*
galt *wrong*
glatt *slippery*
gøy *fun* (slang)
høyfjellet (et) *the high mountain* (usually above the tree limit)
idioter (en idiot) *idiots*
jente (en, ei) *girl*
langs *along*
livlig *lively*
piggdekk (et piggdekk) *studded tyres*
situasjoner (en situasjon) *situations*
skiene (en ski) *the skis*
skiturer (en skitur) *skiing trips*
tilbudet (et) *the offer*
tok imot (å ta imot) *accepted*
tung *heavy*
vant til *used to*
ved siden av *next to*
ødelegger (å ødelegge) *damage/damages, ruin/ruins*

True or false? 1

- **a** Sue sitter bak John i bilen.
- **b** Det er forbudt å bruke piggdekk om sommeren.
- **c** John liker ikke slalom.
- **d** De kjører til høyfjellet.

Dialogue 2

Our friends spend Easter in a mountain cabin.

Arnes familie har en hytte på fjellet. Det er påske, og Arne reiser dit med Bente, søsteren sin. Mor og far skal passe Per og Pål slik at Bente kan ha litt ferie. Elisabeth har en ferieuke, så hun og Jan er der også.

Det er en koselig tømmerhytte. I gangen er det plass til støvlene og anorakkene. Stuen er stor med peis og gode stoler. Det er trepanel på veggene og rødrutete gardiner ved vinduene. Det er flere bokhyller med mange bøker. Kjøkkenet er stort, men de tre soverommene med køyer er små.

Det har vært en fin dag. Solen skinte fra en blå himmel da de var på ski. Nå er det kveld. De er trette etter dagens skitur, og koser seg foran peisen.

CD2, TR 30

Jan	Dette er en kjempekos hytte. Hvor lenge har dere hatt den?
Bente	Mor og far kjøpte den for seks år siden.
Arne	Husker dere hytten vi var på i påskeferiene da vi var barn?
Elisabeth	Den var veldig primitiv.
Bente	Jeg husker hvor langt det var å gå på ski gjennom den dype snøen fra parkeringsplassen til hytten. Vi hadde ryggsekker med alt vi skulle bruke hele uken.

(Contd)

Elisabeth Og så kaldt det var da vi kom frem! Det første far gjorde var å tenne på peisen og i ovnen. Og mor tente lys og parafinlamper. Ikke elektrisitet.

Arne Og jeg måtte spa ren snø i flere store bøtter og fat, som vi hadde i stuen. Vi smeltet snø hele tiden. Tom og jeg vasket oss ikke!

Jan Ikke hele påsken?

Arne Nei! Det var et vaskerom, men det var ikke vann der. Ute var det en brønn, men den var frosset om vinteren.

Bente En gang var det så mye snø at vi ikke kunne åpne døren. Far spadde og spadde vekk snø mens vi frøs.

Elisabeth Det verste var utedoen. Det var en biologisk do, og vi måtte gå ut.

Jan Jeg liker de gamle hyttene. Mange hytter har verken vann eller elektrisitet, men folk koser seg likevel. Dette er en kjempefin hytte. Dere er heldige! Jeg er glad vi har en hel uke her!

Elisabeth Vi kan gå ned til hotellet en kveld. Der er det badstue og svømmehall. Vi kan ta en pizza og et glass øl.

Insight

Easter in Norway is a very important holiday. Read more about it towards the end of this unit. The sun is high in the sky, the days are getting longer and skiing is at its best. There is a special term for the suntan you get at this time of year: 'påskebrun', meaning *Easter brown.*

QUICK VOCAB

anorakkene (en anorakk) *the anoraks*
badstue (en) *sauna*
biologisk *biological*
bokhyller (en bokhylle) *book-cases*
brønn (en) *well*
bøtter (en bøtte) *buckets*
dype (dyp) *deep*
elektrisitet (en) *electricity*
fat (et fat) *basins*

foran *in front of*
frosset *frozen*
frøs (å fryse) *froze*
gang (en) *passage/entrance*
gardiner (en gardin) *curtains*
gjennom *through*
hytte (en) *cottage, cabin*
koser seg (å kose seg) *enjoy themselves*
lampe (en) *lamp*
ovnen (en) *the stove*
parafinlamper (en) *paraffin lamps*
parkeringsplassen (en) *the parking place*
peis (en) *fireplace*
primitiv *primitive*
ren *clean*
ryggsekker (en ryggsekk) *rucksacks*
slik at *so that*
smeltet (å smelte) *melted*
soverommene (et soverom) *the bedrooms*
spadde (å spa) *dug/shovelled*
stoler (en stol) *chairs*
svømmehall (en) *swimming pool*
trepanel (et) *wood panelling*
trette (trett) *tired*
tømmerhytte (en) *log cabin*
utedo (en do) *outside loo*
vaskerom (et) *washroom*
veggene (en vegg) *the walls*
vekk *away/off*
verken ... eller *neither ... nor*

True or false? 2

a Bente og barna er på fjellet.
b Det er dårlig vær.
c Hytten har tre små soverom.
d Jan er sammen med Elisabeth og to av hennes søsken.

Dialogue 3

Sue and John go skiing.

Da Sue bodde i Oslo deltok hun i et skikurs for begynnere. Først holdt hun seg til de minste bakkene. Men hun var ivrig etter å lære, og hun ble flinkere til å gå på ski for hver gang.

Nå er hun på ski med John. Solen er sterk, og hun er glad hun har smarte solbriller og en lekker, ny, rød anorakk. De er på toppen av en stor bakke.

CD2, TR 31

Sue	John, jeg tør ikke! Denne bakken er altfor bratt! Jeg er livredd!!
John	Ikke vær dum, Sue! Du kan ta det langsomt. Kjør på skrå og plog når du vil svinge. Du kan kjøre så langsomt du vil! Jeg visste ikke at du var en sånn reddhare!
Sue	Så ekkel du er! Jeg skulle ikke ha kommet!
John	Men du er her, og ned må du! Det er bare å sette i gang!
Sue	Bare ikke noen kjører på meg!
John	Jeg skal kjøre med deg. Bøy knærne dine godt, og husk å bøye deg forover. Det er mye snø, så det gjør ikke vondt om du faller.
Sue	Så dum jeg var som kom med deg! Men nå kjører jeg!
John	Du skal få en kopp sjokolade på veien tilbake. Kjør på, din tulling!

QUICK VOCAB

bakkene (en bakke) *the slopes*
begynnere (en begynner) *beginners*
bratt *steep*
bøy (å bøye) *bend*
deltok (å delta) *took part*
ekkel *awful*
faller (å falle) *fall/falls*
forover *forward*
holdt seg til *kept to*

ivrig *eager*
langsomt *slowly*
livredd *scared stiff/frightened for your life*
plog (å ploge) *plough*
på skrå *across*
redd *frightened/afraid*
reddhare (en) *coward, 'frightened rabbit'*
sette i gang *get started*
sjokolade (en) *chocolate*
solbriller *sunglasses*
sterk *strong*
svinge *turn*
sånn *such*
tulling (en) *idiot*
tør (å tore) *dare/dares*
visste (å vite) *knew*

True or false? 3

a Sue deltok i et skikurs for begynnere.
b Sue har ikke solbriller.
c Sue sier at John er en reddhare.
d John vil ha en kopp kaffe når de er på veien tilbake.

This is how we say it

- Expressions about skiing:

Skal vi gå på ski?	*Shall we go skiing?*
Vil du hjelpe meg med skiene mine?	*Will you help me with my skis?*
Passer støvlene til bindingene?	*Do the boots fit the bindings?*
Er disse stavene lange nok?	*Are these sticks long enough?*
Er det farlig?	*Is it dangerous?*
Jeg er redd!	*I am afraid!*
Jeg tør ikke!	*I dare not!*
Jeg faller!!	*I am falling!!*

Ikke vær redd!	*Don't be afraid!*
Det er ikke farlig!	*It is not dangerous!*
Bøy knærne!	*Bend your knees!*
Bøy deg forover!	*Bend (yourself) forward!*
Kjør ned!	*Ski down!*
Det gjør ikke vondt om du faller.	*It doesn't hurt if you fall.*
Du er en reddhare!	*You are a chicken!*
Jeg vil heller sitte i solen!	*I would rather sit in the sun!*

▶ Some slang expressions:

Dette er gøy!	*This is great!*
Det er kjempegøy!	*It is great fun!*
Det er en kjempekos hytte dere har.	*It is a super cottage you have.*
Vi hadde en kjempefin ferie!	*We had a super holiday!*
Kult!	*Cool!*

▶ Some useful expressions:

Gi deg!	*Give in!/Stop it!*
Din tulling!	*You idiot!* (affectionately)
Din tufs!	*You idiot!* (not affectionately)
Din idiot!	*You idiot!*

Insight

Do you recognize the imperative? When giving orders or instructions you use a short, snappy form of the verb. 'å kjøre', meaning *to drive*, has the imperative 'kjør!' If you want your dog to sit, the verb 'å sitte' becomes: 'sitt!' Some verbs cannot be made shorter, like 'å gå', so the imperative must be: 'gå!' Have a look back at Unit 5, where this is all explained.

Language patterns

1 Verbs

You may have noticed the use of **hadde** + a past participle: hadde invitert (*had invited*), hadde snødd (*had snowed*).

This tense is called the pluperfect, and is used in much the same way as in English.

Han hadde vært der før.	*He had been there before.*
De hadde hatt en fin ferie.	*They had had a fine holiday.*

2 Nouns

There are a few nouns where the feminine gender is commonly used, especially in the definite singular:

en/ei jente	*(a girl)*	**jenta**	*(the girl)*
en/ei hytte	*(a cabin)*	**hytta**	*(the cabin)*
en/ei geit	*(a goat)*	**geita**	*(the goat)*

The plurals follow the normal pattern for common gender nouns:

mange jenter	*(many girls)*	**jentene**	*(the girls)*
mange hytter	*(many cottages)*	**hyttene**	*(the cottages)*
mange geiter	*(many goats)*	**geitene**	*(the goats)*

Insight

As you know, we use neither *masculine* nor *feminine* gender in this book, but *common gender*, and *neuter*. This is the same as in the other two Scandinavian languages, Danish and Swedish. This two-gendered form of Norwegian is called **Bokmål**, which actually means *bookspeak*. Many dialects use three genders, and **Nynorsk**, *New Norwegian*, which is also an official language and is used by about 10–15% of Norwegians, is a three-gender language.

3 Adverbs

You have already seen adverbs which have one stationary and one movement form, such as **ut – ute, hit – her** and so on. (See Units 4 and 6.)

There are two main groups of adverbs:

a Adverbs formed from adjectives by adding a **t**:

Adjective		**Adverb**	
høy	(*high*, *loud*)	høyt	(*highly*, *loudly*)
fin	(*fine*)	fint	(*finely*)
pen	(*pretty*)	pent	(*prettily*)
gal	(*crazy*)	galt	(*crazily*)

In English the equivalent is making adverbs by adding *-ly* to adjectives.

b Independent adverbs. See below.

4 Independent adverbs

This is a big group of words. Somebody once said that all the words which can't be put into clear groups (adjectives, nouns, verbs, conjunctions, etc.) are adverbs, and that isn't far wrong!

You will find all the adverbs used in this book in the **Vocabulary** at the back of the book. Here are a few to start you off:

QUICK VOCAB

ikke *not*
alltid *always*
aldri *never*
for *too*
altfor *much too*
meget *very*
veldig *very*
etterpå *afterwards*
igjen *again*
kanskje *perhaps*

5 Word order

A sentence can have several clauses. A main clause can stand on its own as a sentence.

Hun satt ved bordet.	The normal word order in a Main Clause puts the subject before the verb.
Da han kom inn,	This is also a clause, but it cannot stand on its own as a sentence. It is called a Subordinate Clause.

You can join these two clauses to form a sentence:

Hun satt ved bordet da han kom inn.

You can also put the subordinate clause in front of the main clause with this result:

Da han kom inn, **satt hun** ved bordet.

The rules for inversion are:

The subject and verb in the main clause are inverted if:

- the subordinate clause comes before the main clause
- the main clause starts with an adverb
- the main clause starts with a preposition phrase

Take a look back at Unit 3 where you looked at word order in sentences.

6 Joining clauses into sentences

To link together sentences, clauses, phrases or words you use a group of words called conjunctions. You are familiar with many of them. Here are some:

og	(*and*)	men	(*but*)	så	(*so*)

There are two kinds of conjunctions:

a Coordinating conjunctions

- linking main clauses:

Kari spiser.	*Kari eats.*
Knut drikker.	*Knut drinks.*
Kari spiser og **Knut drikker.**	*Kari eats and Knut drinks.*
Kari spiser, men **Knut drikker.**	*Kari eats, but Knut drinks.*
Jeg har ingen penger så **jeg kan ikke reise.**	*I have no money so I can't travel.*

b Subordinating conjunctions

- joining a subordinate clause to a main clause:

Kari sto på hodet da **Knut kom inn.**	*Kari stood on her head when Knut came in.*
Hun spiste ikke fordi **hun kastet opp.**	*She didn't eat because she vomited.*

- starting a subordinate clause:

Da **Knut kom inn, sto Kari på hodet.**	*When Knut came in, Karistood on her head.*
Fordi **hun kastet opp, spiste hun ikke.**	*Because she vomited, she didn't eat.*

Notice inversion in the main (second) clause.

7 Punctuation

The rules for puncuation are not very different from English.

Full stop is used after a complete sentence, and after some abbreviations:

kl. = klokken, bl. a. = blant annet (among other things)

No full stop after measurements – km (kilometre), kg (kilogram or kilo)

Colon is used to introduce speech or information:

Han sa: så pen du er! *He said: how pretty you are!*

Exclamation mark is used when something is shouted or commanded or needs emphasizing:

Din idiot!	*You idiot!*
Ti stille!	*Keep quiet!*

Semicolon is somewhere between a comma and a full stop, but used only to link two main clauses.

Hyphen is used to divide words at the end of a line, and to clarify a point. Many first names are hyphenated, e.g **Anne-Lise, Per-Erik, Liv-Bente.**

Comma is used:

- to list items: **Hun kjøpte skjørt, jakke, genser og støvler.**
- between two clauses connected by a coordinating conjunction: **Han spiste først, og så sov han.**
- before the main clause if it is preceded by a subordinate clause: **Da de kom, ble mor glad.**

Exercises

1 Join these clauses with conjunctions to form single sentences:

a Det er sol. Det er kaldt.
b Den ene stolen er blå. Den andre stolen er rød.
c De ringte på døren. Han var ikke hjemme.

2 Start these sentences with the adverb, and adjust the word order:

CD2, TR 32

a	Kari er på ferie.	Nå ______
b	Vi kan gå på ski.	Her ______
c	Hilde og Erik kommer.	Der ______
d	Jeg vil gjerne ha en kopp kaffe.	Nå ______
e	Hun skal studere i London.	Snart ______

3 Change the verb in these sentences to the pluperfect:

a Erik og Hilde (**invitere**) ___ John og Bente til hytten i påsken.

b Det (**snø**) ___ mye i vinter.

c John (**være**) ___ i Trondheim.

d Bente (**ha**) ___ det travelt.

4 Answer the questions with a complete sentence:

a Bruker John piggdekk om sommeren?

b Var det elektrisitet på den gamle hytta?

c Hvordan fikk de vann om vinteren?

d Hvor er toalettet?

5 The verbs in the following sentences are in the past tense. Change the verbs into present tense:

a Hotellet hadde skikurs for begynnere.

b Hilde gikk lange skiturer.

c Erik kjørte på ski ned bakken.

d Bente stod på toppen av bakken.

6 Use the list of adverbs from the **Language patterns** and insert suitable ones below:

a Det er lite (*not much*) snø, så vi kan ___ gå på ski.

b Erik er ___ flink til å kjøre slalom.

c Først skal vi gå på ski, og ___ skal vi drikke sjokolade.

d Hilde går ___ lange skiturer.

7 Imperatives!

a (å **bøye**) ___ knærne!

b (å **kjøre**) ___ ned bakken!

c (å **sitte**) ___ stille!

d (å **være**) Ikke ___ dum!

Easter

Easter is the time when the Norwegians take to the mountains for the best skiing holiday of the year. The days are getting longer, and the sun is warm. There is usually plenty of snow on the higher ground. **Høyfjell** (*high mountain*) are areas above the tree line, usually about 700 metres or more above sea level.

All the hotels are fully booked, and all the holiday log cabins and cottages are occupied. The hotels have all modern conveniences, but the cabins can seem a bit primitive at first. In summer, people use water from wells, from sparkling clean mountain streams and lakes or from rainwater tubs, but in winter they have to melt snow for water. Some cottages in the big skiing resorts may be connected to the main water supply, but this is not the norm. Outside chemical or biological loos are the usual thing. The cottages are cosy and warm, and there is nothing more pleasant than relaxing with friends or family in front of a roaring log fire after a good day's skiing.

The big ski resorts have slalom slopes, ski lifts and after-ski activities. But the majority of Norwegians prefer to spread themselves over the huge snow plains, trekking for miles up slopes and coming down fast, with tireless children, babies on sledges and rucksacks with Thermos flasks and food.

People usually take a week to ten days' holiday at Easter. Maundy Thursday is a public holiday as well as Easter Monday. But don't go to Oslo at Easter. There is nobody around!

påske	*Easter*
palmesøndag	*Palm Sunday*
skjærtorsdag	*Maundy Thursday*
langfredag	*Good Friday*
påskedag	*Easter Day*

Friends and family will wish each other:

God påske!	*Happy Easter!*

Skiing

The verb *to ski* does not exist in Norwegian; use the following phrases:

å gå på ski	*to go skiing*
å kjøre ned bakken	*to ski down the slope*

Do you understand?

Whilst skiing in the Norwegian mountains, you meet a Norwegian couple, Hans-Jakob and Anne-Marie Lund.

Hans-Jakob	Hvordan liker du å være på fjellet?
Du	*I like it! I am with some friends in a cottage. It is a little primitive. The loo is outside, and there isn't a bathroom.*
Anne-Marie	Det er vanlig på hytter som ligger på fjellet. Hyttene ved sjøen er ikke så primitive.
Hans-Jakob	Jeg liker å være på hytte. Jeg liker å sitte foran peisen om kvelden og lese en god bok. Og så liker jeg å gå på ski.
Du	*I like skiing! I like slalom best. In the beginning I was afraid, but now I go fast down the slope. I don't fall often.*
Hans-Jakob	Jeg liker best å gå lange skiturer. Noen ganger går Anne-Marie sammen med meg og andre ganger kjører jeg slalom sammen med henne.
Du	*Would you like a cup of chocolate at the hotel when we get down? I would like to hear more about Norwegian cottages.*

Test Yourself

You know the drill! Only one of the answers is correct.

1 Hvor er familiens hytte?
 a Ved sjøen. **b** På fjellet. **c** I Danmark.

2 Hvor mange soverom er det?
 a To. **b** Tre. **c** Fire.

3 Hvor er Sue?
 a I Bodø. **b** I Oslo. **c** I London.

4 Når bruker John piggdekk?
 a Om vinteren. **b** Om sommeren. **c** I september.

5 Hvem er Sue på ski med?
 a Bente. **b** Odd og Randi. **c** John.

6 Sue har en ny anorakk. Hvilken farge?
 a Gul. **b** Rød. **c** Grønn.

7 Hva gjør mor og far i påsken?
 a De er i Italia. **b** De er i Tromsø. **c** De passer Bentes barn.

8 Which of these words is a noun?
 a Kjøre. **b** Sitte. **c** Bil.

9 Which of these words is an adjective?
 a Stor. **b** Tog. **c** I.

10 Which of these words is a verb?
 a Reise. **b** Ferie. **c** Gammel.

14

Syttende mai

Seventeenth of May

In this unit you will learn

- ***Why and how Norwegians celebrate their National Day***
- ***How to ask about the past***
- ***How to express interest in a subject***
- ***How to say 'Sorry'***

Insight

Now the flighty Sue is sorry! Will Arne give in? Do you think he should find another girlfriend? Sue is using as many ways of saying *sorry* as she possibly can!

This unit is also about Norway's National Day, which is celebrated by all Norwegians, at home or abroad.

Dialogue 1

17 May, morning. Sue rings Arne's mobile.

Syttende mai (17 *May*). Klokken er ti over åtte om morgenen. Sue ringer til Arnes mobiltelefon.

CD2, TR 33

Sue	Hei, Arne! Det er meg. Husker du meg?
Arne	Hei, Sue! Selvfølgelig husker jeg deg! Det er lenge siden vi snakket sammen.
Sue	Arne, jeg er så lei meg. Jeg savner deg fryktelig. Kan du tilgi meg?
Arne	Liker du ikke å være i Bodø?
Sue	Jo, jeg liker å bo her og jeg liker jobben min. Men det var galt av meg at jeg ikke snakket med deg før jeg tok denne jobben. Og jeg skulle ha ringt til deg før. Er du sint på meg?
Arne	Jeg var veldig sint på deg. Men jeg er ikke sint lenger. Du må gjøre hva du vil.
Sue	Om forlatelse, Arne. Det hele kom av at jeg var ensom i Oslo. Du er jo i Bergen. Jeg skulle ønske jeg var sammen med deg nå.
Arne	Jeg er i Oslo i et par dager. Nå skal jeg til byen og se på barnetoget med Odd og Randi. Og så skal vi ta en øl eller to.
Sue	Barnetoget?
Arne	Det er syttende mai. Alle skolebarna i Oslo og omegn går i en stor prosesjon opp hele Karl Johans gate og forbi Slottet. På Slottsbalkongen står Kongefamilien og vinker til barna. Hver skole har sitt musikk-korps som spiller marsjer og norske melodier. Hele Oslos befolkning er i byen. Det er blitt vår, og varmt nok til sommerklær. 17.mai er alltid en festlig dag.
Sue	Jeg tror det er et barnetog her også. Men jeg arbeider i dag.
Arne	Er du forelsket i sjefen din?
Sue	Nei. Han er veldig kjekk og hyggelig, men han er veldig gammel. Sikkert nesten 35 år.
Arne	Fint. Jeg var litt sjalu. Og såret.
Sue	Si at du tilgir meg!
Arne	Jeg gjør vel det, din tulling. Nå må jeg løpe. Ringer til deg i kveld. Ha det!

QUICK VOCAB

barnetoget (et) *the children's parade/procession*
befolkning (en) *population*
ensom *lonely*
forelsket *in love*
fryktelig *terribly*
Kongefamilien *the Royal Family*
lei meg *sorry*
løpe *run*
marsjer (en marsj) *marches*
melodier (en melodi) *tunes*
musikk-korps (et) *brass band*
om forlatelse *sorry/please forgive me*
omegn (en) *surrounding area*
prosesjon (en) *procession*
sjalu *jealous*
skolebarna (et skolebarn) *the school children/pupils*
skulle ønske *really wish*
sommerklær *summer clothes*
spiller (å spille) *play/plays*
såret (å såre) *hurt/wounded*
tilgi *forgive*
tog (et) *train/procession*
vinker (å vinke) *wave/waves*

True or false? 1

a Sue sier at hun er lei seg.
b Sue spør om Arne vil tilgi henne.
c Barnetoget går til Aker Brygge.
d Det er fint vær og alle bruker sommerklær.

Dialogue 2

17th May! Arne is in Oslo with his friends.

Arne er i Oslo med Odd og Randi. Det er fint vær. Solen skinner og alle er ute.

CD2, TR 34

Randi	Så gøy å være i Oslo på syttende mai! Kult at du kom hit, Arne!
Arne	Jeg skulle ha vært i Bergen slik at jeg kunne hjelpe Bente med barna. Huff! Barn er bare til bry!
Odd	Se, der nede i gaten kommer barnetoget! Her skal du se tusener av barn, Arne!
Arne	Ja, men det er ikke jeg som skal holde orden på dem! Stakkars lærerne. De har en travel dag.
Randi	Er ikke musikken fin! Jeg synes politimennene på de store hestene sine er kjempekjekke.
Odd	Jeg synes ungene er litt søte.

Så går barnetoget forbi dem, skole etter skole, med musikk-korps foran og tålmodige lærere som holder orden på barna. Alle har flagg i hendene. Det er tusener av mennesker i gatene, som roper 'Hurra!' Alle har flagg og alle har røde-hvite og blå bånd på brystet.

Randi	Det er synd vi ikke kan se Kongefamilien herfra. Kronprinsen er helt super. Skulle gjerne treffe ham!
Odd	Skal vi prøve å komme litt nærmere Slottet?
Arne	Nei, nå har jeg sett nok unger. Skal vi gå til Aker Brygge og få oss en øl?
Odd	God idé. Har du hørt noe fra Sue?
Arne	Ja, hun ringte til meg i morges. Hun er veldig lei seg.
Randi	Sue er OK. Jeg liker henne.
Arne	Jeg er tørst. Nå vil jeg gjerne ha en øl. Tante Maiken har invitert oss til middag senere i dag. Hun lager verdens beste bløtkake.

Insight

Randi says: 'Det er synd vi ikke kan se ...' meaning *It's a pity we can't see ...* 'Jeg synes synd på ...' means *I feel sorry for ...* 'Synd' has another meaning as well. It is the word for *sin*. 'En synd' means *a sin*.

QUICK VOCAB

brystet (et) *the chest/breast*
bånd (et bånd) *ribbons*
hendene (en hånd) *the hands*
herfra *from here*
hestene (en hest) *the horses*
holde orden på *keep in order*
i morges *this morning*
idé (en) *idea*
kronprinsen (en) *the crown prince*
kult *cool*
mennesker (et menneske) *people*
nærmere *nearer*
politimennene (en politimann) *the policemen*
roper (å rope) *shout/shouts*
super *super*
synd *a pity*
tusener (et tusen) *thousands*
tålmodige (tålmodig) *patient*
ungene (en unge) *the kids*
verdens (en verden) *the world's*

True or false? 2

a Barnetoget går forbi Slottet.
b Ingen av skolene har musikk-korps.
c Arne er tørst og vil gjerne ha en øl.
d Tante Maikens bløtkake er dårlig.

Dialogue 3

Arne explains the 17th May festival.

Det er sent på kvelden. Arne ringer til Sue.

CD2, TR 35

Arne	Har du hatt en god dag?
Sue	Jeg har arbeidet. Jeg er helt utkjørt! Jeg har arbeidet i resepsjonen. Og du?
Arne	Det har vært en fin dag. Jeg har vært sammen med Odd og Randi. Vi spiste middag hos tante Maiken. Jeg har spist altfor mye. Jeg skal aldri spise så mye bløtkake mer!
Sue	Og jeg er trett! Jeg sitter med bena mine på bordet og nå drikker jeg et stort glass kaldt vann. Arne, hvorfor feirer dere egentlig syttende mai?
Arne	Norge hadde vært en dansk provins i hele firehundredeog trettifire* år. I 1814 da Napoleonskrigen var over, måtte Danmark gi fra seg Norge til Sverige. Norge ville ikke bli en del av Sverige. Norge fikk sin egen grunnlov den syttende mai 1814, og gikk inn i en union med Sverige. Denne unionen varte til 1905. Da ble Norge et selvstendig land. Og syttende mai er vår nasjonaldag.
Sue	Men Kongefamilien, da. Hvor kom den fra?
Arne	Kongens bestefar het egentlig Carl og var en dansk prins. Han var gift med Maud, som var et av Dronning Victorias barnebarn. Carl ble spurt om han ville bli Norges konge, og det ville han. I 1905 kom han til Norge som Kong Haakon. Det er et godt, gammelt navn fra vikingtiden. Hans sønn, Alexander, fikk navnet Olav. Olav var Kong Haralds far. Og som du vet, er Harald kongen vår nå.
Sue	Hvorfor heter hovedgaten Karl Johans gate?
Arne	Karl Johan var den svenske kronprinsen i 1814. Han aksepterte at Norge var i en union med Sverige og ikke ble en svensk provins, og at Norge hadde sin egen grunnlov. Karl Johan hadde også en interessant historie. Jeg skal fortelle deg mer en annen gang.
Sue	Fortell mer nå! Særlig om vikingtiden!
Arne	Ikke mas! Bor du på hotellet?
Sue	Nei, jeg har en bitteliten leilighet nå, bare litt større enn en hybel.
Arne	Jeg er glad du ringte til meg i dag. Jeg tror jeg savner deg litt!

(Contd)

Sue	Jeg savner deg. Jeg har vært veldig dum, det ser jeg nå.
Arne	Godnatt, din lille idiot! Jeg reiser tilbake til Bergen i morgen og ringer til deg når jeg er hjemme.
Sue	Sov godt, Arne.

*This is the old-fashioned way of saying 'firehundreogtrettifire'.

Insight

The most interesting period in Norwegian history is from 1814 to 1905. During these years Norway went from being a Danish province through a union with Sweden to becoming an independent country.

The final Napoleonic war was a main factor in the events to follow. Read about it, and about **17 Mai**, in this unit.

QUICK VOCAB

aksepterte (å akseptere) *accepted*
Danmark *Denmark*
dansk *Danish*
del (en) *part*
egentlig *really*
en annen gang *another time*
grunnlov (en) *constitution*
het (å hete) *was called*
historie (en) *history*
hybel (en) *bedsit*
krig (en) *war*
land (et) *country*
mas (å mase) *nag*
Napoleonskrigen (en) *the Napoleonic war*
nasjonaldag (en) *National day*
prins (en) *prince*
provins (en) *province*
selvstendig *independent*
svensk *Swedish*
særlig *especially*
union (en) *union*

utkjørt *exhausted*
varte (å vare) *lasted*
vikingtiden (en) *the Viking age*

True or false? 3

a Norge fikk sin grunnlov syttende mai 1814.
b Karl Johan tok navnet Haakon da han ble konge.
c Maud ble dronning i 1915.
d Dronning Victoria var Mauds bestemor.

This is how we say it

- On 17th May people say to each other:

Gratulerer med dagen!	*Congratulations of the Day!*
Gratulerer med syttende mai!	*Happy 17th May!*
Hurra!	

- How to say 'Sorry'

Unnskyld.	*Excuse me.*
Jeg er lei meg.	*I am sorry.*
Jeg er lei for at …	*I am sorry that …*
Om forlatelse.	*Forgive me.*
Tilgi meg!	*Forgive me!*
Kan du tilgi meg?	*Will you forgive me?*
Er du sint på meg?	*Are you cross with me?*
Ikke vær sint på meg!	*Don't be cross with me!*
Ikke mas!	*Don't nag!*

- I wish that …

Jeg skulle ønske …	*I wish …*
Jeg skulle ønske du var her nå.	*I wish you were here now.*
Jeg skulle ønske at jeg var rik.	*I wish I were rich.*

Note the different tense in Norwegian.

- How to describe your boyfriend:

Han er kjempekjekk.	*He is handsome, wonderful, etc.*
Han er super!	*He is super!*
Han er ikke så verst.	*He is not too bad.*
Han er kjempedum!	*He is very stupid.*

Insight

I hope you won't have to use all these terms for saying *sorry*. However, you want to be able to understand when somebody says *sorry* to you!

Notice that when you say: 'jeg skulle ønske ...' you are really saying *I should wish ...* 'Skulle ønske du var her' means *Wish you were here* – a useful phrase for the postcards!

Language patterns

1 *Da, da, da/når* *then, as/since, when*

Da *then* (tag word, explained in Unit 15)

Da *then* (adverb)

Da gikk han.	*Then he went.*

Da *as/since* (conjunction)

Da hun ikke likte norsk mat, reiste hun hjem til Amerika.	*As she did not like Norwegian food, she travelled ...*

Da *when* (conjunction)

Da de kom hjem, spiste de.	*When they came ...*

Når *when* (conjunction)

Når de kommer hjem, skal de spise.	*When they come …*

Da and **når** both mean *when*. **Da** is used about the past and **når** is used about the present and future, and stating something that happens regularly (see the examples above). *When* as a question is always **når** (**når kom han?/når kommer han?**).

Norwegians remember this by the following:

Den gang da – hver gang når	*That time when – every time when.*

Try to remember it!

2 *Gå* *to go*

You looked at **gå** in Unit 12. Here are some more examples:

Jeg går på ski.	*I go skiing.*
Toget går klokken seks.	*The train goes/leaves at six o'clock.*
Flyet går til New York.	*The plane goes to New York.*
Det går/er en god film på Odeon.	*There is a good film on at the Odeon.*
Dette går ikke.	*This won't do.*
Jeg går til tannlegen.	*I go to the dentist.*

In all these examples you use **å gå**, but remember that if you are travelling somewhere, you never use **gå** unless you are actually walking:

Jeg reiser til Los Angeles i kveld.	*I go to Los Angeles this evening.*
Jeg kjører til Newcastle nå.	*I am going to Newcastle now.*
Jeg drar til London på mandag.	*I am going to London on Monday.*

3 Verbs – the infinitive

There is one way of constructing sentences in English which does not exist in Norwegian, so you'll need to re-phrase:

I want you to come.	**Jeg vil at du skal komme.**
John didn't know what to do.	**John visste ikke hva han skulle gjøre.**
Bente doesn't know when to stop.	**Bente vet ikke når hun skal stoppe.**

The short infinitive in English must have a modal, or helping, verb in Norwegian.

4 Forming the future: the modal verbs *skal* and *vil*

You have seen in Unit 2 how future tense is formed from a modal verb + infinitive:

Vi skal reise til Amerika.

John vil ha sommerjobb på et hotell.

There is a tendency to use **skal** in the first person and **vil** in the second and third, but there is no rigid rule. Notice these uses of **skal**:

Jeg skal reise på torsdag.	*I shall go/travel on Thursday.*
Jeg skal kjøpe en sykkel.	*I am going to buy a bike.*
Jeg skal være der klokken ti.	*I am supposed to be there at ten o'clock.*

Peculiar to the Scandinavian languages and German is that you can omit the main verb in certain situations.

Jeg vil hjem.	*I want to go home.*
Jeg skal til tannlegen.	*I shall go to the dentist.*
Hvor skal du?	*Where are you going?*
Jeg må til byen.	*I have to go to town.*

Insight

Do you remember the mention of the modal verbs in Unit 13? Here you can see more examples of omitting the main verb when you use a modal verb. But don't think you can leave out verbs all together! This omission is correct only in certain situations.

5 Comparison of adverbs

Adverbs which come from adjectives are compared in the same way as the corresponding adjectives:

adjective	pen (*pretty*)	penere	penest
adverb	pent (*prettily*)	penere	penest

In English you would normally use *more* and *most* when comparing adverbs, as you would with some adjectives.

More adverbs

sent	senere	senest	*slowly*
stygt	styggere	styggest	*uglily*
fryktelig	frykteligere	frykteligst	*terribly*
langt	lenger	lengst	*far*
godt	bedre	best	*well*
vondt	verre	verst	*painfully*
dårlig	verre	verst	*badly*
Fort	fortere	fortest	*quickly*

John føler seg dårlig, men Erik er verre.	*John feels ill, but Erik is worse.*
Min tykke tante kjører fortere enn meg.	*My fat aunt drives faster than me.*

Note that **fryktelig** and **fort** are also adjectives:

adjective	en fryktelig dag	*a terrible day*
adverb	han skrek fryktelig	*he screamed terribly*

adjective	en fort bil	*a fast car*
adverb	Bente kjørte fort	*Bente drove fast*

Some independent adverbs can also be compared:

ofte (*often*)	oftere (*more often*)	oftest (*most often*)
gjerne (*willingly*)	heller (*rather*)	helst (*preferably*)

Han går ofte på kino.	*He often goes to the cinema.*
Vi er oftere hjemme.	*We are more often at home.*
Som oftest spiser jeg for meget.	*Most often I eat too much.*
Jeg vil gjerne reise til Norge.	*I would like to travel to Norway.*
Min mann vil heller reise til Amerika.	*My husband would rather travel to America.*
Min nye venn vil helst reise til Italia.	*My new friend would like best to travel to Italy.*

Exercises

1 Insert **da** or **når** in the gaps to complete these sentences:

- **a** ___ John kom til Bergen, regnet det.
- **b** Det regner alltid ___ han er i Norge.
- **c** ___ kommer du?
- **d** ___ kom dere til Norge?
- **e** Det var mørkt ___ Bente kom hjem.

2 Where would you use **gå** and where would you use **reise** to complete these sentences?

- **a** John liker å ___ på ski.
- **b** Bente vil gjerne ___ til Amerika.
- **c** Fergen ___ til Gøteborg.
- **d** Skal vi ___ på kino i kveld?
- **e** De skal ikke ___ til Nord-Norge denne sommeren.

3 These sentences are in the past tense. Change them to the future using **skal** and **vil**:

CD2, TR 36

- **a** Vi kjøpte en rød bil. Vi ______
- **b** Jeg reiste til Stavanger. Jeg ______
- **c** John sendte et brev og kort til York. John ______
- **d** Trond spiste en stor is. Trond ______
- **e** John drakk et glass saft. John ______

4 Mental arithmetic! What are the answers (in Norwegian)?

- **a** Tretten og seks er ...
- **b** Seksten og fjorten er ...
- **c** Sju og åtte og elleve er ...
- **d** Tolv og atten er ...
- **e** Nitten og femten er ...

5 Don't forget adjectives and nouns! Here are some regular ones:

en hvit bil	den hvite bilen	mange hvite biler	de hvite bilene
et hvitt huss	det hvite huset	mange hvite hus	de hvite husene

a en stor gutt	______	______	______
b et gult bord	______	______	______
c et langt tog	______	______	______
d en god klem	______	______	______
e en sint dame	______	______	______

6 That was too easy! How about these:

a en dårlig far	______	______	______
b en liten søster	______	______	______

c en tykk mann ______ ______ ______
d et snilt barn ______ ______ ______

7 Saying sorry. What would you say in the following situations?
  a You have been really awful to someone.
  b You accidentally step on someone's foot.
  c You have made someone cross.
  d You have to interrupt a conversation.
  e You ask someone to forgive you.

8 Insert the correct form of the adverb:
  a John kom (*often*) ___ til Norge.
  b Bente kjørte (*faster*) ___ enn Erik.
  c Bente skriver (*more uglily*) ___ enn Hilde, men Kari skriver (*most uglily*) ___ .
  d Jeg vil (*rather*) ___ reise til Alaska.
  e Tom spiller fotball (*better*) ___ enn Arne.

Syttende mai *17th May*

Count Jean Bernadotte, one of Napoleon's marshals, had been adopted by the old, childless Swedish king some years before Napoleon's final war. The Count was now Crown Prince of Sweden and had taken the name Karl Johan. Napoleon had counted on the support of Sweden, and he was furious when he learnt that Sweden had joined the enemy.

When Napoleon lost his last big battle at the end of 1813, Denmark and Norway were on the losing side. Sweden had sided with the Allies, and after their victory, Sweden wanted Norway. Denmark had to hand over Norway to Sweden, as part of the peace agreement.

This was when the Norwegians revolted. With the help of the Danish prince, Christian Frederik, who was the Danish governor of Norway, Norwegian representatives formulated the new Norwegian Constitution. This was accepted on the 17th May,

1814, and since then **syttende mai** has been Norway's National Day. Norway entered into a union with Sweden, which ended in 1905, when Norway at last became fully independent.

Karl Johan became king of Sweden and Norway, and as far as Norway was concerned, he was a good and popular king.

Some useful expressions

Jeg er lei meg. *I am sorry.*
Don't get this mixed up with:
Jeg er lei av … *I am fed up with/tired of …*

Jada! *Yes I know!*
Så fint at … *How nice that …*
Så pen du er! *How pretty you are!*
Så hyggelig å se deg! *How lovely to see you!*

Tag word: *da*

Da means *then* but it is also a tag-word, i.e. it is not an absolutely necessary word, but adds a little flavour. There is more about 'tag' words in Unit 15.

Når kommer du? *When are you coming?*
Når kommer du, da? *When are you coming, then?*

The letter 'å'

Until 70 or so years ago, the letter 'å' was written 'aa'. It was the same in Denmark, where the change to 'å' happened much later. You will still come across the 'aa' in old family names.

King Harald's grandfather was **Haakon,** and the Crown Prince, named after his great-grandfather, is **Haakon Magnus.**

Do you understand?

CD2, TR 37

You are very tired after a busy 17th May in Oslo. Now you are having a cold beer with a Norwegian girl, an old friend of yours called Silje.

Silje	Så fint at vi kan sitte på en ute-restaurant. Det er plutselig blitt sommer. Det er ikke alltid så varmt i mai.
Du	*It has been a very good day. I am so tired! We must have walked many kilometres.*
Silje	Jeg tror at Kongen og hans familie må være trette også. De har stått på Slottsbalkongen i mange timer og vinket til barna.
Du	*Have you heard from Knut?*
Silje	Ja, han ringte til meg på torsdag. Han vil gjerne treffe meg igjen. Det er slutt med ham og Bente. De var sammen i flere år og har to små barn. Du vet jo at Knut og jeg var sammen før han og Bente fant hverandre. Nå vil han treffe meg igjen. Bente var veldig dum. Hun hadde den engelske vennen sin, John. Alle likte John.
Du	*Would you like to see Knut again?*
Silje	Nei! Jeg vil ikke se ham igjen. Først var jeg sjalu på Bente. Stakkars Bente! Det er sikkert ikke lett å være alene-mor. Knut tenker bare på jenter og fotball. Jeg liker ham ikke.
Du	*You will soon meet a pleasant young man. 'Skål' for you, Silje, and 'Skål' for Norway!*
Silje	'Skål' for syttende mai!

QV **kilometer (en)** *kilometre(s)*

Test Yourself

Questions and answers. Only one answer is correct.

1 Når er Norges nasjonaldag?
a Femtende mai. **b** Sekstende mai. **c** Syttende mai.

2 Hva heter Norges konge?
a Haakon. **b** Harald. **c** Charles.

3 Hva het kongens bestemor?
a Maud. **b** Sue. **c** Victoria.

4 Hva heter Oslos hovedgate?
a Storgaten. **b** Kongens gate. **c** Karl Johans gate.

5 Karl Johan var svensk konge. Hvor kom han fra?
a Frankrike. **b** Hong Kong. **c** Argentina.

6 Hvor er Sue 17 mai?
a I Bodø. **b** I Oslo. **c** I Bergen.

7 Vil Arne tilgi Sue?
a Ja. **b** Nei. **c** Kanskje.

8 Hvor skal Arne spise middag?
a På Slottet. **b** På Aker Brygge. **c** Hos tante Maiken.

9 Hvor bor Sue i Bodø?
a På Johns Hotell. **b** I en bitteliten leilighet.
c I et stort hus.

10 Hva er et 'barnetog'?
a En stor buss. **b** En prosesjon av barn.
c Toget som går fra Oslo til Bergen.

15

Sankt Hans

Eve of St John

In this unit you will learn

- ***How to book a room in a hotel***
- ***How to pay the bill***
- ***How to complain***
- ***How to cope with another special day in Norway***

Dialogue 1

Sue is working on Reception.

Tjuende juni (20 *June*). Sue arbeider i resepsjonen på Johns Hotell. Hun skal arbeide i dag og i morgen, og så har hun fri i en uke. Da skal hun reise til Bergen og feire Sankt Hans med Arne. Hun gleder seg, men først har hun to travle dager.

En familie kommer inn i resepsjonen.

CD2, TR 38

Sue	God dag. Kan jeg hjelpe dere?
Mannen	Hei. Har dere et rom ledig for en natt? Siden barna er små, vil vi helst ha ett rom for alle fire. Med bad, selvfølgelig.

Sue	Alle rommene har dusj og toalett. Nå skal jeg se. Ja, vi har et stort rom ledig. Det er i tredje etasje. Det er det siste rommet vi har ledig i dag. Dessverre er det ikke utsikt til sjøen.
Damen	Hvor mye koster det, da?
Sue	Det koster kr 800 for natten for to personer. Det koster ikke noe for barna hvis de er under tolv år og de bor i foreldrenes rom. Frokost er inkludert.
Damen	Det passer bra. Gutten er ni og piken er seks. Det er vel noe for barna å gjøre her på hotellet?
Sue	Det er et lekerom i andre etasje og svømmehall og badstue der borte ved siden av restauranten. Det er et trimrom der også. Men barn under tolv år må ikke bruke svømmehallen alene.
Damen	Når kan vi få frokost i morgen? Vi kan vel lage matpakke? Vi skal kjøre langt i morgen, og vi vil gjerne starte tidlig.
Sue	Frokost serveres fra klokken sju til halv ti. Si til servitøren at dere vil lage niste. Det koster litt ekstra. Han vil gi dere matpapir. Hvis dere har termos, kan dere få med dere kaffe eller te.
Mannen	Dette høres bra ut. Vi er sultne. Hvor kan vi spise?
Sue	Kafeteriaen der borte er åpen hele dagen. Restauranten er åpen for lunsj fra tolv til tre og for middag fra fem til elleve. Jeg skal fylle ut bestillingen, og så skal dere få nøkkelen til rommet. Det er rom nummer trehundreogfem. Hva er navnet?

Insight

At hotel breakfasts some people make sandwiches for lunch furtively, wrapping them in their napkins. This isn't really the done thing. You can always ask for some greaseproof paper, for which a charge will be made. You can then make your own gourmet lunch openly.

Read about Norwegian breakfasts later in this unit.

QUICK VOCAB

bad (et) *bath/bathroom*
bruke *use*
dusj (en) *shower*
ekstra *extra*
fylle ut *fill in*
har fri (å ha fri) *has/have time off*
høres bra ut *sounds good*
inkludert *included*
lekerom (et) *playroom*
lunsj (en) *lunch*
matpakke (en) *packed meal*
matpapir (et) *greaseproof paper*
natt (en) *night*
niste (en) *packed meal*
nøkkelen (en) *the key*
personer (en person) *persons*
serveres (å servere) *is served*
servitøren (en) *the waiter*
starte *start*
termos (en) *thermos flask*
toalett (et) *toilet*
trimrom (et) *gym*

True or false? 1

a Familien vil gjerne ha to rom for natten.
b Det koster ikke noe for barn under fem år.
c Det er ikke svømmehall der.
d Det koster kr 800 for natten uten frokost.

Dialogue 2

Sue has some unhappy guests to deal with!

Siste dag før ferien! Men ikke alle gjestene er fornøyde! En sint mann kommer i full fart til resepsjonen.

Mannen	Jeg vil snakke med direktøren! Jeg vil klage på dette dårlige hotellet!
Sue	Et øyeblikk, hr. Johansen. Jeg skal hente direktøren.

CD2, TR 39

Sue finner John. Han kommer til resepsjonen.

John	God dag, hr. Johansen. Kan jeg hjelpe Dem?
Mannen	Nå reiser vi, heldigvis. Jeg vil ikke betale regningen. Vi kommer ikke tilbake hit igjen!
John	Jeg vil gjerne vite hva det er De er så misfornøyd med. Våre andre gjester er meget fornøyde, både med maten og rommene.
Mannen	Rommet var for varmt. Jeg ville ikke åpne vinduet fordi det var trafikk på veien. Det var lyst hele natten.
John	Det er sommer i Nord-Norge. Da er det lyst om natten, hr. Johansen!
Mannen	Min kone likte ikke fargen på gardinene. De var for tynne også. Min kone syntes at badet var skittent og at sengen var for hard. I morges var frokosten dårlig også.
John	Hva var i veien med frokosten?
Mannen	Kaffen var for sterk og eggene var kokt for meget. Jeg likte ikke marmeladen, og jeg fikk en skitten kopp!
John	Jeg er lei for at dere har hatt en dårlig natt her. Var det noe mer?
Mannen	Ja! Det er for mange barn her. Barna skulle ikke ha lov til å bruke svømmehallen. Og heisen var ikke stor nok for min kone!
John	Jeg beklager. Men De må nok betale regningen. Jeg skal undersøke saken, og hvis De har rett i klagene, skal De få penger tilbake.
Mannen	Her er kredittkortet mitt. La meg få kvitteringen.

Insight

You know the preposition 'for', meaning: *for*. There is also the expression 'for ... siden', meaning: *ago*. Here two words in Norwegian become one in English. In this dialogue we have another use of 'for' meaning: *too*.

QUICK VOCAB

beklager (å beklage) *apologize/apologizes*
fornøyd *satisfied*
ha lov til *have permission to*
har rett (å ha rett) *to be right*
heisen (en) *the lift*
i full fart *at full speed*
klage *complain*
klagene (en klage) *the complaints*
kredittkortet (et) *the credit card*
la (å la) *let*
misfornøyd *dissatisfied*
regningen (en) *the bill*
saken (en) *matter, case*
skittent (skitten) *dirty*
trafikk (en) *the traffic*
tynne (tynn) *thin*
våre (vår) *our*

True or false? 2

a Den sinte mannen har en tynn kone.
b Mannen vil snakke med direktøren.
c Mannen er meget fornøyd med hotellet.
d Mannen sa at koppen var skitten og eggene var kokt for mye.

Dialogue 3

The longest day of the year! Sue is out with friends.

Tjuetredje juni (*23 June*). Sue har ferie, og hun er hos Arne i Bergen. De har savnet hverandre, og nå er de glade for at de kan ha en uke sammen.

Det er kveld. Sue og Arne drar ut på fjorden i en motorbåt sammen med noen av Arnes venner. De finner en liten holme hvor det ikke er noen andre. Her fortøyer de båten. Alle synes at det er for kaldt til å bade. De finner rekved og tenner et bål. Så griller de pølser på bålet. De spiser, prater og koser seg. En av guttene har en gitar med seg. Han spiller og de andre synger.

Sue ser ut over sjøen. Det er nesten midnatt, men det er ikke mørkt. Hun ser bålene som brenner på andre holmer. Hun hører latter og musikk over fjorden. For en fin kveld! Arne setter seg ved siden av henne.

CD2, TR 40

Sue	Arne, hvorfor feirer dere Sankt Hans?
Arne	Det er årets lengste dag. Vi gleder oss over at det er så lyst. Vinteren er lang og mørk i Norge, vet du. Vi drar alltid ut på sjøen og det er vanlig å brenne bål.
Sue	Det er så fint å sitte slik og se ut over fjorden. For en fin, stille kveld!
Arne	Og det er fint å være sammen med deg.
Sue	Du, jeg så at alle hadde redningsvester i båten. Har dere alltid det?
Arne	Nordmenn har respekt for sjøen. Det er forbudt å være i båt uten redningsvest. Som du ser, er det tusenvis av småbåter på fjorden, og mange barn er ute i båt alene. Og det er veldig bra. Nordmenn er født med ski på bena, heter det. De er født i båt også!

Sue tar hånden hans.

Sue	Skal vi gå tilbake til de andre? Jeg vil gjerne ha sjokoladekake.
Arne	Og kaffe. Og jeg trenger genseren min. Nå er det ikke varmt lenger!

QUICK VOCAB

brenner (å brenne) *burn*
bål (et) *bonfire*
båten (en) *boat*
drar (å dra) *go(es)/travel(s)*
fjorden (en) *the fjord*
fortøyer (å fortøye) *tie up/ties up*
født *born*

gitar (en) *guitar*
griller (å grille) *grill(s)/barbecue(s)*
heter det *the saying goes/it is said*
holme (en) *island/skerry*
latter (en) *laughter*
lengste (lang) *longest*
midnatt (en) *midnight*
motorbåt (en) *motor boat*
pølser (en pølse) *sausages*
redningsvest (en) *life jacket*
rekved (en) *driftwood*
respekt (en) *respect*
slik *like this*
småbåter (en) *small boats*
tusenvis *thousands*

True or false? 3

a De feirer Sankt Hans fordi det er årets lengste dag.
b Sue og Arne drar ut i motorbåt med noen venner.
c Alle bruker redningsvester i båten.
d Mange sier at nordmenn er født med ski på bena.

This is how we say it

▶ How to book a hotel room

Jeg vil gjerne bestille et rom.	*I would like to book a room.*
Jeg vil gjerne bestille et rom med bad.	*I would like to book a room with a bathroom.*
Har dere et rom ledig?	*Have you got a vacant room?*
Har dere et rom ledig for en natt?	*Have you got a room for one night?*
Hva koster det?	*What does it cost?*
Er frokost inkludert?	*Is breakfast included?*

Er det halv pris for barn?	*Is it half price for children?*
Vi vil gjerne ha et rom med utsikt.	*We would like a room with a view.*
Vi vil gjerne ha et rom med balkong.	*We would like a room with a balcony.*
Er det heis?	*Is there a lift?*
Er det svømmehall og trimrom?	*Is there a swimming-pool and gym?*
Jeg er sulten. Hvor kan jeg spise?	*I am hungry. Where can I eat?*
Kafeteriaen er åpen hele dagen.	*The cafeteria is open all day.*
Restauranten er åpen fra kl. 12 til kl. 11.	*The restaurant is open from 12 o'clock to 11 pm.*

▶ How to complain

Kan jeg få snakke med direktøren?	*May I speak to the manager?*
Jeg er ikke fornøyd!	*I am not satisfied!*
Jeg er misfornøyd med rommet!	*I am dissatisfied with the room!*
Det var for mye bråk i natt!	*There was too much noise last night!*
Maten var dårlig!	*The food was bad!*
Dette glasset er skittent!	*This glass is dirty!*

▶ How to pay

Kan jeg få regningen?	*May I have the bill?*
Jeg vil gjerne betale regningen.	*I would like to pay the bill.*
Kan jeg bruke kredittkort?	*May I use a credit card?*
Er service inkludert?	*Is service included?*
Jeg vil gjerne ha en kvittering.	*I would like a receipt.*

▶ **Velkommen tilbake!**	*Welcome back!*
Vi kommer ikke hit igjen!	*We are not coming here again!*

Language patterns

1 More about compound nouns

As you saw in Unit 9, many of the long words are actually two or more words joined together. There are many more of them in this unit. Here are some.

en sommerdag	*a summer's day*
en arbeidsdag	*a working day*
et lekerom	*a playroom*
et trimrom	*a gym*
en matpakke	*a packed meal*
et matpapir	*greaseproof paper*

The first part of the compound describes the word, but it is the last part which is the important one. The gender will be that of the last word.

et arbeid – en dag
en arbeidsdag
en mat – et papir
et matpapir

Some nouns can be either compounds or written with a preposition:

et trehus	*a wooden house*	et hus av tre	*a house of wood*
en ullgenser	*a woollen sweater*	en genser av ull	*a sweater of wool*
en gullring	*a gold ring*	en ring av gull	*a ring of gold*

2 Question words

Apart from **når** (*when*), all the question words start with **hv**.

hva	*what*	(pronoun)
hvem	*who*	(pronoun)
hvilken	*which*	
hvilket	*which*	(pronoun)
hvilke	*which*	
hvor	*where*	(adverb)
hvordan	*how*	(adverb)
hvorfor	*why*	(adverb)

Hvilken is used with common gender words:	**Hvilken dag er det idag?**
Hvilket is used with neuter words:	**Hvilket år er det?**
Hvilke is used for plural words:	**Hvilke bøker liker du?**

3 Tag words

vel *I suppose* (adverb)
nok *sure to*
da *then*
nok *enough* (adverb) is a different word
da *then/when* also has different uses

There is much use of the tag words in Norwegian. They are difficult to translate, but they do make a subtle difference to the meaning.

Vel indicates that there is a slight element of doubt:

Han kommer i dag.	*He comes/is coming today.*
Han kommer vel i dag.	*I suppose he comes/is coming today.*

Nok gives a feeling of confidence to this statement:

Han kommer nok idag.	*He is sure to come today.*

Da makes no difference at all to the meaning. It just gives a certain flow to the phrase:

Kommer han idag?	*Is he coming today?*
Kommer han idag, da?	*Is he coming today, then?*

4 The passive

The easiest way to see the difference between active and passive forms of the verbs is to compare these sentences.

Bente spiste kaken.	*Bente ate the cake.*	(active)
Kaken ble spist av Bente.	*The cake was eaten by Bente.*	(passive)
Kaken ble spist.	*The cake was eaten.*	(passive)

In the active form the subject carries out the action which the verb describes. In the passive form the 'object', i.e. the cake, becomes the subject. The active subject becomes the agent, or is perhaps left out.

The passive is expressed in two ways in Norwegian. The first is by using the verb **å bli – blir – ble – har blitt** (*to become/get*) and past participle, as above (**Kaken ble spist**).

5 The *s*-verb passive

Norwegian, like other Scandinavian languages, has passive forms with an s-ending:

Kaken spises av Bente.	*The cake is eaten by Bente.*
Bilen kjøres av John.	*The car is driven by John.*

Passive **s**-verbs have a rather limited use. They are mostly used in the present tense and with modal verbs:

Noe må gjøres.	*Something has to be done.*
Maten kan grilles ute.	*The food can be grilled outside.*

You can usually replace the passive **s**-verb with **bli** and the past participle.

Noe må bli gjort.
Maten kan bli grillet ute.

6 The non-passive *s*-verb

There are s-verbs in the active form as well:

Jeg synes at det er kaldt idag.	*I think that it is cold today.*
Det finnes ikke mat i huset.	*There is no food to be found in the house.*
Det føles rart å være i Norge.	*It feels strange to be in Norway.*
De skal skilles.	*They are getting divorced.*

A few s-verbs have reciprocal meaning (each other):

Vi sees på mandag.	*We will see each other on Monday.*
De møttes i London.	*They met each other in London.*

Exercises

1 Which gender are these compound nouns?

a kredittkort
b motorbåt
c lekerom
d bilnøkkel

2 Change these sentences from active to passive:

CD2, TR 41

Example: Bente spiser kaken. Kaken blir spist av Bente.

a John kjører bussen.
b Per liker Kari.
c Bente kjøper genseren.
d Mannen spiste frokost.
e Hilde leste brevet.

3 Change these sentences into the past tense. The verbs are all Group 1 verbs (å stoppe – stopper – stoppet – har stoppet).

a Bussen stopper ved hotellet.
b John arbeider i resepsjonen.
c Hilde venter på Erik.
d Mor rydder i stuen.
e Barna bråker på kjøkkenet.

4 These verbs are Group 2 verbs. Change these sentences into past tense. (å reise – reiser – reiste – har reist).

a Bente reiser til Amerika.
b John kjører ikke motorsykkel.
c De spiser deilige smørbrød.
d Han hører ikke hva jeg sier.
e Trond liker sjokoladekake.

5 Use the right form of *which* in each of these questions:

a ___ dag er det i dag?
b ___ glass vil du ha?
c ___ bøker liker du å lese?
d ___ ben har du brukket?
e ___ bil er din?

6 Make questions for these answers using *question words*:

a ______ ? Han heter Hans.
b ______ ? De kommer fra Alaska.
c ______ ? Hun har det bra.
d ______ ? Det er min tykke tante som sitter der.
e ______ ? Hun smiler fordi hun er glad.

7 What would you say in the following situations?

a You would like to book a room for two people.
b You want to know if breakfast is included.
c You want to know if there is a swimming-pool.
d You ask for the bill.
e You want to speak to the manager.

Sankt Hansaften *St John's Day*

St John's Day (Midsummer Day) is called St Hans in Norway. The eve of St Hans, 23rd June, is **Sankt Hans**, or **Sankt Hansaften**. This is the longest day, and it doesn't get properly dark at all, even in south Norway. In the north, of course, the midnight sun makes day and night the same.

The traditional way of celebrating **Sankt Hansaften** is for families and friends to go to the coast making bonfires and barbecues. There is music and singing well into the next day. Thousands of little boats chug along on the water, and people dance on the wooden jetties.

Norwegians are conscious of keeping their country litter-free, and the next day there is little evidence of the previous night's celebration.

Insight

This particular date is not celebrated in the English-speaking world. In the olden days, when people in Norway didn't know precisely which was the longest day, 23rd June seemed as good a date as any, and was celebrated as such. It's important to enjoy the light midsummer days as the long dark winter nights are not far off!

Breakfast

Breakfast in a hotel in Norway will consist of herring in various pickled varieties, sardines, cold meats, salami, liver pâté and cheese. You will also get cereal, jams, boiled eggs and different kinds of bread and crispbread. It is common to ask the waiter for greaseproof paper, and to make a packed lunch at the same time. And your Thermos can be filled with coffee too. (There is usually an additional charge for this.)

Skitt! *Dirt!*

Don't worry about saying 'skitt' (pronounced *shit*) or 'skitten'! These are perfectly good, useful Norwegian words:

skitt *dirt* (noun)

skitten *dirty* (adjective)

You can also say 'skitt!' as an expletive. It just means *dirt* and is no worse than saying *bother!* Your friend's grandmother won't even raise an eyebrow.

Do you understand?

You phone a hotel to make a booking:

Damen i resepsjonen	Nordlys Hotell. Vær så god?
Du	*I would like to book a room for tomorrow night, for one night.*
Damen	Nå skal vi se. Jo, vi har noen rom ledige. Er det for en eller flere personer?
Du	*I would like a double room with a bathroom.*
Damen	Vi har et rom i fjerde etasje med utsikt over sjøen. Rommet har bad og balkong. Dessverre er det ikke heis. Det andre rommet er i andre etasje. Parkeringsplassen er like utenfor. Det er fin utsikt til fjellene.
Du	*I will take the room with the sea view. May I bring my dog?*
Damen	Dessverre tar vi ikke hunder eller katter. Kommer dere med bil? Hunden må nok sove i bilen.
Du	*We will arrive at 9 o'clock, and we would like some dinner.*
Damen	Restauranten er åpen til klokken halv elleve. Kafeteriaen er åpen til midnatt.

Du	*Fine. We will come tomorrow.*
Damen	Velkommen til Nordlys i morgen.

QUICK VOCAB

ankomme *to arrive*
dobbel *double*
hunder (en hund) *dogs*
katter (en katt) *cats*
ta med *bring*

Test yourself

You know the drill!

1 Hvilken dato er St. Hans?
  a tjueførste juni. **b** tjueandre juni. **c** tjuetredje juni.
2 Sue har ferie. Hvor er hun?
  a I Oslo. **b** I Bergen. **c** I Bodø.
3 Hvem er Sue sammen med?
  a Jan. **b** Odd og Randi. **c** Arne.
4 De drar ut på fjorden i:
  a en motorbåt. **b** en ferge. **c** et vikingskip.
5 Hvorfor feirer de St. Hans?
  a Det er årets korteste dag. **b** Det er årets lengste dag.
  c Det er Arnes fødselsdag.
6 Hva har de med i båten?
  a Ski. **b** Sykler. **c** Redningsvester.
7 Er barn ute i båt alene i Norge?
  a Ja. **b** Nei. **c** De har med en hund.
8 Hva vil Sue gjerne ha?
  a Sjokoladekake. **b** Bløtkake. **c** Smørbrød.
9 Hva spiser nordmenn til frokost?
  a Brød. **b** Kaker. **c** Pizza.
10 Når er St. Hans?
  a Om vinteren. **b** Om sommeren. **c** Om våren.

16

Hva nå?

What now?

In this unit you will learn

- ***How to express thoughts***
- ***How to express feelings***
- ***How to be nostalgic***

Insight

We are back to John and Bente, who had a stormy relationship in the first two editions of this course. John is now a successful hotelier in Bodø. He is still single. But there is a new development. Read on!

Text 1

CD2, TR 42

Autumn in Bodø

Attende september (*18 September*). Det er blitt høst igjen. John trives i Bodø. Hotellet hans er godt, og han har tenkt å starte et nytt hotell lenger nord med det første. Sue er flink. Han er veldig fornøyd med henne.

Bodø er en hyggelig, liten by på kysten, nord for Polarsirkelen. Naturen er utrolig vakker, med høye, snødekte fjell mot sør og med fjorder og sjø. Verdens sterkeste tidevannstrøm, Saltstraumen, er ikke langt fra Bodø. Det er fint å fiske, og John har mye å tilby sine gjester.

John har blitt kjent med mange, og han har fått gode venner. Han har bodd i Norge i ti år, og føler seg helt norsk. Han kan ikke tenke seg å flytte tilbake til England nå. Heldigvis tar foreldrene hans ofte ferie i Bodø, og søsteren hans besøker ham hvert år med familien sin.

Livet er godt, men merkelig også, synes John. Han har aldri glemt Bente. Han og Bente var sammen i flere år.

Bente var student i Amerika. Hun studerte økonomi og moter. Men da hun kom tilbake, traff hun Knut igjen, som hun hadde vært forelsket i tidligere. De ble samboere, og fikk to barn. John har hørt at de er skilt og at Bente er alene med de to barna.

Sues spesielle venn er Bentes bror, Arne. Sue snakker ofte om Arne og om familien i Bergen. John trivdes sammen med Bentes familie, men han mistet kontakten med dem da det ble slutt med ham og Bente. Nå tenker han ofte på familien, og han savner Bente. Han fotograferte mye med det lille kameraet sitt det første året i Norge. Han finner frem det bildet som han liker best. Det viser Bente som smiler til ham. Det lyse håret hennes blåser rundt det solbrune ansiktet. De blå øynene er fulle av latter.

Skulle han ringe til henne?

Insight

Look at the final sentence in the third paragraph:

Søsteren hans besøker ham hvert år med familien sin.
His sister visits him every year with her family.

(Contd)

Do you remember how to use the reflexive pronoun? 'Søsteren hans', meaning *his sister*, is the subject of this phrase. The family belongs to her, so you have to use 'sin' to define ownership. Remember never to use 'sin' with the subject, but only when it refers back to the subject. If in doubt, have a look in Unit 7 **Language patterns.**

QUICK VOCAB

blåser (å blåse) *blow/blows*
fiske *fish*
finner frem (å finne frem) *get out/gets out*
fotograferte (å fotografere) *took photos*
kameraet (et) *the camera*
kysten (en) *the coast*
lenger *further*
med det første *soon/in the foreseeable future*
merkelig *strange*
mistet (å miste) *lost*
Polarsirkelen *the Arctic Circle*
sambœre (en samboer) *live-in partners*
skilt *separated*
snødekte (snødekt) *snow-covered* (plural)
solbrune (solbrun) *sun-tanned*
sør *south*
tenke seg *imagine*
tidevannsstrøm (en) *tidal current*
tilby *offer*
traff (å treffe) *met*
trives (å trives) *thrive(s)/like(s) to be*
utrolig *incredibly*
viser (å vise) *show/shows*

True or false? 1

a John trives i den lille byen nord for Polarsirkelen.
b Sue arbeider i Oslo.
c John kan ikke tenke seg å bo i Norge.
d John ser på bildet av en hest.

Dialogue 2

John is in his office when the phone rings.

John er på kontoret sitt. Han arbeider. Plutselig ringer telefonen.

CD2, TR 43

John	Johns Hotell, vær så god.
Bente	Hallo! Er det John? Husker du meg? Det er Bente.
John	Bente! Fint å høre stemmen din! Jeg har tenkt mye på deg. Hvordan har du det?
Bente	Jeg har det bra. Det er travelt med to barn, men familien min hjelper meg mye.
John	Hvor gamle er barna dine?
Bente	Per er fem og Pål er to. De likner på meg, sier alle. Begge har lyst hår og blåøyne.
John	Arbeider du?
Bente	Ja, jeg jobber halv dag på et kontor i byen. Men jeg vil gjerne ha tid med barna mens de er små. Men du, da? Er du gift?
John	Nei, jeg har det for travelt. Hotellet går fint, og nå skal jeg snart åpne et hotell til.
Bente	Det gikk som du ønsket. Du sa at du ville bli hotell-direktør!
John	Ikke alt har gått som jeg ønsket! Hva gjør lillebror Tom?
Bente	Han har begynt å studere i Australia og har det veldig bra. Han trives i utlandet, men han får nok et stort studielån. Mor savner ham, vet du.
John	Du kjenner jo Sue, som er Arnes venninne. Hun har jobb her. En livlig og flink jente.
Bente	Jeg liker henne. Og Elisabeth skal gifte seg med Jan til våren. Det er vi glade for.
John	Bente, kunne du tenke deg å besøke meg? Det er stille her nå. Ta med deg barna. Jeg vil veldig gjerne se deg.
Bente	Det er for sent å angre på at vi gled fra hverandre, John. Men jeg vil veldig gjerne besøke deg. Hvis du er sikker på at du virkelig vil treffe meg etter alt som har hendt.
John	Du kjenner da meg! Jeg sier det jeg mener! Når kommer du?

(Contd)

Bente	Jeg har en uke fri i oktober. Jeg ringer til deg i morgen. Ha det, John.
John	Ha det godt, Bente!

Insight

There are two words, 'både' and 'begge', both meaning: *both*. 'Både' is used when you mention two persons or items: 'både Per og Pål ligner på Bente', meaning *both Per and Pål look like Bente*. 'Begge' is used when you lump them together 'begge likner Bente', meaning *both look like Bente*.

QUICK VOCAB

angre (å angre) *regret*
fri *free*
gled fra hverandre (å gli) *drifted apart*
halv *half*
stemmen (en stemme) *the voice*
studielån (et) *study loan*
utlandet *abroad*

True or false? 2

a Bente er lei av barna sine.
b John vil at Bente skal besøke ham uten barna.
c Elisabeth skal reise til Australia.
d Bente jobber halv dag på et kontor.

Dialogue 3

CD2, TR 44

John and Bente are together again.

Sekstende oktober (*16 October*). Bente og barna reiste med fly til Bodø. John møtte dem på flyplassen. Det var rart å se Bente igjen.

Hun hadde ikke forandret seg. John ga Bente en liten klem og hilste på de to små guttene. Så kjørte de til hotellet.

Bente og barna fikk et stort, pent rom med utsikt til fjellene i sør. Mens John arbeidet, var Bente i svømmehallen med barna. Det var også et stort lekerom. Sue passet barna om kvelden slik at Bente og John fikk tid til å snakke sammen. Sue var flink med barna og de likte å være sammen med henne.

En dag sto John og Bente opp tidlig og kjørte til Saltstraumen. De sto på den store, fine broen og så ned på vannmassene som strømmet under dem. Så kjørte de opp i fjellene og gikk en lang tur. De hadde matpakke og termos med kaffe, og de spiste og pratet sammen. De fikk tid til å kjøre et stykke på den nye kystriksveien før de drog tilbake til Bodø.

Senere på kvelden spiste de en god middag på restauranten. Barna sov og Bente hadde tatt på seg en ny, svart genser og noen smarte, smale bukser. John syntes hun var nydelig. De har spist, og nå sitter de med et glass vin hver.

John	Skål, Bente. Du er enda nydeligere enn før.

Bente blir rød.

Bente	Skål, John. Dette har vært en kjempefin dag. Det er så vakkert her. Og fargene er spesielle nå om høsten.
John	Ja, Norge er et vakkert land. En blir så vant til det at en nesten ikke ser det! Saltstraumen er fantastisk. Tenk på alt det vannet som fosser frem og tilbake hver dag! Det er verdens sterkeste tidevannsstrøm. Jeg fisker der med en av vennene mine. Det er utrolig mye fisk der.
Bente	Jeg tenker du er glad for at vi reiser i morgen! Det er livlig med småbarn!
John	Ja, de er helt umulige! Jeg skal trenge en ukes søvn! Nei, du, fra spøk til alvor: jeg skal savne dere alle tre.
Bente	Jeg er lei for at vi skal reise. Dette har vært en veldig fin uke.

(Contd)

John	Jeg liker barna dine. De likner deg, men de er veldig forskjellige. Per er livlig, men Pål er mer rolig. Det er to fine unger. Ser du Knut ofte?
Bente	Nei, nesten aldri. Han har flyttet til Stavanger med den nye venninnen sin. De har et lite barn. En pike. Han er ikke interessert i guttene sine. Han har en stor gutt fra før også.
John	Hva nå, Bente. Har du planer for fremtiden?
Bente	Jeg vet ikke.
John	Av og til lurer jeg på om du og jeg kan ha en fremtid sammen. Vi er eldre og klokere nå. I hvert fall jeg.
Bente	Det vil tiden vise. Hva med julen? Har du juleferie?
John	Nei, men jeg kunne tenke meg noen dager i Bergen i desember.
Bente	Fint! Jeg gleder meg til du kommer.
John	På en betingelse! At dere kommer hit i juleferien.
Bente	Ja! Skål, John!
John	Skål for oss, Bente!

Insight

John says 'Du er enda nydeligere enn før' meaning *You are even more beautiful than before* (ahhhh). 'Nydelig' means *beautiful*. You can say either 'Du er enda mer nydelig enn før' or 'Du er enda nydeligere enn før'. As in English there are two ways to compare adjectives, either by endings or by using *more* and *most*. Unit 9 will explain it all.

QUICK VOCAB

alvor *seriousness*
av og til *now and then*
betingelse (en) *condition*
drog (å dra) *went*
eldre *older*
forandret seg (å forandre seg) *changed*
forskjellige (forskjellig) *different*
fosser (å fosse) *surge*
frem og tilbake *to and fro*

fremtiden (en) *the future*
i hvert fall *in any case*
klokere (klok) *wiser*
kystriksveien *the coastal main road*
lurer på (å lure på) *wonder/wonders*
nydelig *beautiful*
planer (en plan) *plans*
rart *strange*
riksveien (en) *the main/national road*
spøk (en) *joke*
strømmet (å strømme) *stream*
stykke (et) *bit/piece*
søvn (en) *sleep*
umulige *impossible* (plural)
vannmassene (en vannmasse) *the masses of water*

True or false? 3

a Bente synes at naturen i Nord-Norge er stygg.
b John liker Bentes gutter.
c Bentes gutter heter Per og Pål.
d John skal reise til Amerika i juleferien.

This is how we say it

▶ How to get something to drink:

Hvor er Vinmonopolet?	*Where is the wine monopoly shop?*
Hvor er nærmeste Vinmonopol?	*Where is the nearest wine monopoly shop?*
Hvor mye koster en flaske rødvin?	*How much does a bottle of red wine cost?*
Hva koster en flaske hvitvin?	*What is the price of a bottle of white wine?*
Hvor kan jeg kjøpe øl?	*Where can I buy beer?*

- Some useful expressions:

Jeg trives i Guildford ...	*I am happy in/like to be in ...*
Han trives på hytta.	*He enjoys staying at the cabin.*
Tiden vil vise ...	*Time will show/time will tell.*
Nyt livet!	*Enjoy life!*
Aldri i livet!	*Not on your life!*
Fra spøk til alvor.	*Let us be serious/'from joking to seriousness'/joking apart*
Jeg gleder meg til ...	*I am looking forward to ...*
Jeg ser frem til ...	*I am looking forward to ...*
Jeg er glad i deg.	*I am fond of you/I love you.*

- And the one we haven't used:

Jeg elsker deg! *I love you!*

Language patterns

1 *Hverandre* each other

The reciprocal pronoun in Norwegian is **hverandre** (each other)

De elsket hverandre.	*They loved each other.*
De skriver til hverandre.	*They write to each other.*

The pronoun can take the genitive ending **s**:

De leste hverandres bøker.	*They read each other's books.*
De passet hverandres barn.	*They looked after each other's children.*

Insight

In Norwegian you cannot say 'vi skal møte klokken 12', as you do in English: *we shall meet at 12 o'clock*. You have to say: 'vi skal møte hverandre klokken 12', or 'vi skal møtes klokken tolv', or 'jeg skal møte deg klokken 12'.

2 Prepositions

You have used many of these words in this course already. They are not easy in any language, as they often have more than one meaning.

- av *of*
  part of/made of

et hus av tre	*a house of wood*
en venn av meg	*a friend of mine*

  cause/reason

Jeg dør av sult.	*I'm dying of hunger.*
Hun ropte av glede.	*She shouted for joy.*

- fra *from*

fra morgen til kveld	*from morning to evening*
Han kom fra York.	*He came from York.*

- for *for*

Jeg skal gjøre det for deg.	*I shall do it for you.*
Hva betalte du for kaffen?	*How much did you pay for the coffee?*

- foran *in front of*

Han sto foran hotellet.	*He stood in front of the hotel.*
Hun gikk ut foran ham.	*She went out in front of him.*

- bak *behind*

damen bak disken	*the lady behind the counter*
De satt bak oss.	*They sat behind us.*

- etter *after/for*
  after

De reiste etter frokost	*They went after breakfast.*
Han gikk etter henne.	*He walked after her.*

  for

Jeg ser etter henne.	*I am looking for her.*
Jeg lengter etter våren.	*I am longing for the spring.*

▸ med *with/by*

Vi reiste med fly til Amerika. *We travelled by plane to America.*
Han betalte med kredittkort. *He paid with a credit card.*

▸ ved *by/near/at*

by/at
John satt ved bordet. *John sat by/at the table.*
Huset ligger ved sjøen. *The house is by the sea.*
with the help of
Han kom dit ved egen hjelp. *He got there by his own effort.*
Hun kom dit ved å sykle. *She got there by cycling.*

▸ uten *without*

Jeg kan ikke leve uten deg. *I can't live without you.*
Hun gikk ut uten klær. *She went out without clothes.*

▸ under *under/beneath/below*

Trollet var under broen. *The troll was under the bridge.*
Katten satt under bordet. *The cat sat under the table.*

▸ til *to/till/for*

to
Vi skal reise til Bodø. *We shall go to Bodø.*
Han kom til oss i går. *He came to us yesterday.*
till
Vi skal bli der til fredag. *We shall be there till Friday.*
Vente til sommeren! *Wait until the summer!*
for
Her er et brev til deg. *Here is a letter for you.*
Vi skal ha gjester til middag. *We shall have guests for dinner.*

▸ mellom *between*

Det skal bli mellom oss. *It will be between us.*
Han satt mellom dem. *He sat between them.*

▸ mot/imot *towards/against/to*

towards
Hun kom mot ham. *She came towards him.*

mot slutten av dagen	*towards the end of the day*
against	
Hva er det du har imot meg?	*What it is you have against me?*
Regnet slo mot vinduet.	*The rain hit against the window.*
to	
Du må være snill mot hunden.	*You must be kind to the dog.*
Ikke vær slem mot meg!	*Don't be nasty to me!*

You usually use **mot** in a physical situation, but there is no special rule about when to use **mot** and when to use **imot**.

- gjennom *through*

De gikk gjennom huset.	*They went through the house.*
Vi ble kjent gjennom kurset.	*We got to know each other through the course.*

- før *before*

Han gikk før dem.	*He went before them.*
Hun lærte norsk før ferien.	*She learnt Norwegian before the holiday.*

- hos *in one's company/at one's house* (in French = *chez*)

Min tante bor hos oss.	*My aunt lives with us.*
Det er to katter hos oss.	*There are two cats in our house.*

- i *in/at/into/for*

in	
Vi bor i Oslo.	*We live in Oslo.*
Barna leker i hagen.	*The children play in the garden.*
at	
i samme øyeblikk	*at that moment*
I begynnelsen likte hun ham.	*At the beginning she liked him.*
into	
Hunden falt i vannet.	*The dog fell into the water.*
Gutten løp ut i gaten.	*The boy ran out into the street.*
for	
Vi skal være der i tre uker.	*We shall be there for three weeks.*
De bodde i Norge i seks år.	*They lived in Norway for six years.*

- **om** *about/of/in*

  about/of

Hun fortalte meg om det.	*She told me about it.*
Hva synes du om ham?	*What do you think of him?*

  in

Jeg går på ski om vinteren.	*I go skiing in the winter.*
Om morgenen drikker jeg te.	*In the morning I drink tea.*
Han kommer om ti minutter.	*He will come in ten minutes.*

- **over** *over/across/above/of/more than*

  over, across, above

John gikk over gaten.	*John went across the street.*
Fuglen fløy over treet.	*The bird flew over the tree.*

  of

et kart over Norge	*a map of Norway*
en liste over bøkene	*a list of the books*

  more than

Det er over tre dager siden.	*It is more than three days ago.*

- **på** *on/at* (was dealt with in Unit 12)

3 The *s*-genitive

The genitive is formed by adding **s** to the noun in the singular and plural. There is no apostrophe:

guttens hund	*the boy's dog*
guttenes hund	*the boys' dog*
Johns bil	*John's car*
Bentes bøker	*Bente's books*
en god natts søvn	*a good night's sleep*
husets vinduer	*the windows of the house*

In Norwegian you use the s-genitive for objects as well as for persons.

4 Genitive using prepositions

In formal speech you would often use prepositions:

pikens navn	**navnet til piken**
farmors hus	**huset til farmor**
Johns bok	**boken til John**
byens gater	**gatene i byen**

Notice that what is 'owned' is in the definite form when you use a preposition.

A compound noun can replace the genitive:

en damesko	*a lady's shoe*
en sommerdag	*a summer's day*

5 Indefinite pronouns 1: *man/en* one

The indefinite pronouns are **man** and **en** meaning *one*.

Man is used only as a subject in a sentence:

Man vet ikke hva som kan hende.	*One does not know what may happen.*
Man sier at han er gal.	*They say that he is mad (It is said ...)*

En can replace **man** as a subject:

En vet aldri.	*One never knows.*
En skal ikke være for sikker.	*One shouldn't be too sure.*

En as an object:

Man vet ikke hvem som liker en.	*One doesn't know who likes one.*
Det gjør en glad.	*It makes one happy.*

Ens *one's* (genitive)

Ens egne bøker.	*One's own books.*
Ens pass og penger.	*One's passport and money.*

6 Indefinite pronouns 2: *noen, noe* some, any

Noen means *some* or *any* referring to all nouns in the plural:

Min tykke tante vil kjøpe noen flasker vin.	*My fat aunt will buy some bottles of wine.*
Det er ikke noen bøker her.	*There aren't any books here.*

Noen means *any* or even *a* referring to common gender countable nouns in the singular, in questions and negative sentences:

Har du sett noen gode filmer denne uken?	*Have you seen any good films this week?*
Jeg har ikke noen genser i den fargen.	*I have not got a sweater in that colour.*

Noen means *somebody* or *anybody* when not referring to a noun:

Er det noen der?	*Is there anybody there?*
Jeg hører noen gå opp trappen.	*I hear somebody go up the stairs.*

Noe means *some* or *any* referring to uncountable nouns regardless of gender:

Tom har kjøpt noe mat til kattene.	*Tom has bought some food for the cats.*
Er det noe øl her?	*Is there any beer here?*

Noe means *any* or *a* referring to neuter nouns in the singular, in negative questions and sentences:

Jeg kan ikke se bilen noe sted.	*I cannot see the car any place/anywhere.*

Har han ikke noe hjem? *Hasn't he got a home?*

Noe means *something* or *anything* when not referring to a noun:

John har noe interessant å fortelle oss.	*John has something interesting to tell us.*
Vi kunne ikke gjøre noe mer.	*We could not do any more.*

7 Indefinite pronouns 3: *ingen, ingenting* *no, nobody, nothing*

Ingen (*no*, *nobody*, *nothing*) is the opposite of **noen:**

Det er ikke noen her.	*There is nobody here./There isn't anybody here.*
Det er ingen her.	*There is nobody here./There isn't anybody here.*

Another word for *nothing* is **ingenting:**

Bente vet ikke noe om dette.	*Bente doesn't know anything about this.*
Bente vet ingenting om dette.	*Bente knows nothing about this.*

Intet is the very formal neuter form of **ingen:**

Han var død så det var intet vi kunne gjøre.	*He was dead, so there was nothing we could do.*
Han var død, så det var ingenting vi kunne gjøre.	*He was dead, so there was nothing we could do.*

Exercises

1 Insert prepositions in the gaps. (Look in the **Language patterns** section in this unit):

🔊 **CD2, TR 45**

a Bente er norsk. Hun kommer ___ Norge.
b John reiser ___ Bergen ___ ferie (*to*, *on*).
c Han skal bo ___ Bente.
d De sto ___ hotellet. (*in front of*)
e Hunden gikk ___ mannen. (*behind*)
f Klokken er ti ___ seks. (*to*)
g Du må lære norsk ___ ferien.
h Vi skal være i Norge ___ ti dager. (*for*)
i Dette brevet er ___ deg. (*to*)
j Skal vi gå ___ kino ___ kveld?
k Ja, vi kan gå ___ middag. (*after*)

2 Quiz. How much do you remember?

1	en bil	_____	biler	_____
2	et fly	_____	_____	flyene
3	en mor	moren	_____	_____
4	et barn	_____	_____	_____
5	en lang vei	den _____	_____	_____
6	et gult hus	det _____	_____	_____
7	Klokken er	5.15	_____	
8	Klokken er	7.25	_____	
9	Klokken er	11.50	_____	

10 Hvor mye er sju og ni? ____
11 Hvor mye er fem og fire? _____
12 Det er mandag i dag. Hvilken dag er det i morgen? _____
13 Hvilken dag var det i går? _____
14 I dag er det sekstende juni. Hvilken dato er det i morgen? _____
15 Hvilken dato var det i går? _____
16 I går spiste John frokost klokken åtte. I dag _____ han frokost klokken sju.
17 Han drakk mange store glass øl. I dag vil han ikke _____ øl.
18 Tom og Trond (*play*) _____ med Lego.
19 John og Erik (*play*) _____ poker.
20 (*when*) _____ de kom, spiste de middag.
21 (*when*) _____ det regner, er vi inne.

22 Jeg vil gjerne gå _____ kino.
23 Vi skal reise _____ Norge _____ sommer.
24 Han kjørte (*after*) _____ henne.
25 Er det _____ høyre eller _____ venstre?
26 Han liker _____ i Oslo.
27 Bente ringte til vennen (*her*) _____ .
28 Jeg liker katten (*my*) _____ .
29 John bruker de nye skiene (*his*) _____ .
30 Hva heter du?
31 Hvor kommer du fra?
32 Hva gjør du?
33 Hvorfor vil du lære norsk?
34 Hvordan har du det?
35 Hvilken farge liker du best?
36 Hvor vil du helst reise?
37 Den filmen er god, men denne er (*better*) _____ .
38 Arne er (*older*) _____ enn Tom.
39 Tom er den (*youngest*) _____ .
40 Bente's mother (s-genitive). (Translate!)
41 The reception of the hotel (s-genitive). Translate!
42 The boy's cat (s-genitive). Translate!
43 The Norwegian for these words: Grandparents.
44 Car keys
45 Fourteenth
46 Slowly
47 Write in Norwegian: 368.
48 The Norwegian for these expressions: Wednesday 17 May
49 The time is 25 past three.
50 Forstår du alt?

Buying wine and spirits

Wine and spirits are very expensive in Norway, and can only be purchased from the special state monopoly shops. These are called Vinmonopolet. They can be found in most towns of a certain size, but there are not many of them about.

Each local authority will decide if it wants a wine outlet in its town or not, for whatever reason. This can result in a situation where you may have to travel for miles if you are in need of a bottle of wine. On the west coast, apart from in the big cities, it can be difficult to find a **Vinmonopol**.

The big hotels will sell wine with meals all over Norway – at a price! Beer and lager can be obtained from supermarkets.

Do you understand?

You and your partner have arrived in a small town on the south coast of Norway. You need some information, and you go to the tourist information centre. A smiling lady greets you:

Damen	God dag. Kan jeg hjelpe dere?
Du	*Yes, please. Is there a good hotel in this town? It must not be too expensive.*
Damen	Det beste hotellet er Strandhotellet. Det ligger der nede ved sjøen. Det er dyrt, men rommene er store med balkonger og utsikt over sjøen. Det er også et lite hotell i Storgaten. Det heter Grand Hotel og er meget gammelt. Det er en pen gammel trebygning og det er et hyggelig hotell. Byens beste restaurant er der. Vi har også et lite pensjonat. Det er billig og bra.
Du	*What can we do here in this town? We would like to be here for five days.*
Damen	Det er fint å bade i sjøen. Vannet er varmt nå fordi vi har hatt fint, varmt vær i sommer. Det er et lite museum i den gaten der borte. Vi kan bestille en motorbåt for dere. Dere kan dra ut til holmene og fiske og svømme. Hvis været er dårlig, kan dere bruke svømmehallen ved hotellet. I kveld er det en pop-konsert og på søndag er det kirke-konsert.
Du	*I would like to buy some postcards and stamps and a bottle of wine.*

Damen	Vi har kort og frimerker her. Kortene er alle fra dette stedet. Dere må gå til Vinmonopolet for å kjøpe vin. Vinmonopolet ligger nederst i Parkveien. Det lukker klokken fire, så dere må skynde dere! Klokken er kvart på fire nå.
Du	*Then we shall go to Vinmonopolet first, and come back here afterwards.*
Damen	Vi lukker klokken halv seks. Jeg skal finne noen brosjyrer til dere. På gjensyn!

nederst i *at the bottom of*
pensjonat (et) *guesthouse*
skynde dere (å skynde seg) *hurry*

QV

Saltstraumen

Insight

We have now covered all the essential grammar points. If you didn't get them all the first time round, go back and look them up!

From experience I know that students find adjective/noun combination and the possessive pronouns a bit tricky. The rest is really quite easy!

The *Exercises* and *Quiz* at the end of this unit are actually a comprehensive revision of the whole course. How about doing them? And, for good measure, here is another:

Test yourself

1 Hvor mange barn har Bente?
  a To. **b** Tre. **c** Fire.
2 Hva heter faren deres?
  a John. **b** Knut. **c** Jan.
3 Hvilken farge har Bentes hår?
  a Rødt. **b** Lyst. **c** Mørkt.
4 Hva heter verdens sterkeste tidevannsstrøm?
  a Niagara. **b** Suez-kanalen. **c** Saltstraumen.
5 Når har John ferie?
  a I julen. **b** I januar. **c** I desember.
6 Hvor kan du kjøpe vin i Norge?
  a På apotek. **b** På Vinmonopolet. **c** I butikken
7 Hvor er Bodø?
  a Nord for Polarsirkelen. **b** Sør for Polarsirkelen.
  c I Bergen.
8 Hvor bor tante Maiken?
  a I Leeds. **b** I Trondheim. **c** I Oslo.
9 Hva liker nordmenn å gjøre i påsken?
  a Gå på kino. **b** Arbeide. **c** Gå på ski.
10 Hvilke farger er det i det norske flagget?
  a Rødt, hvitt og blått. **b** Grønt, hvitt og blått.
  c Gult og blått.

Kjære student,

Nå er du kommet til slutten av boken. Gratulerer! Jeg håper du har likt kurset. Det er mange nye ord, og du husker kanskje ikke alle! Det er ikke dumt å lese boken en gang til.

Jeg håper at du gjerne vil lære mer norsk, og at du ikke glemmer det du har lært! Jeg har likt å arbeide med denne boken. Hvis det er noe mer du synes at jeg skulle ha tatt med, vil jeg gjerne høre fra deg!

Ha det!
Margaretha Danbolt Simons

Taking it further

The best way to learn more Norwegian is to go to Norway. There is a variety of Norwegian classes at different levels at the International Summer School, University of Oslo, from late June to August. Contact:

International Summer School
University of Oslo
PO Box 1082 Blindern
0317 Oslo
Norway
E-mail: iss@admin.uio.no

The University of Bergen also runs summer courses for students of Norwegian. These are not for beginners, as all the teaching is in Norwegian. The students are divided into groups according to level, and to have completed a course, like this book, is an absolute minimum requirement. The course lasts for three weeks in July. Students can apply for grants to cover expenses. Contact:

Sommerkurs
Nordisk institutt
Sydnesplassen 7
5007 Bergen
Norway
Tel: +47 55 58 24 07; Fax: +47 55 58 96 60
E-mail: sommerkurs@nor.uib.no

A great institution in the Scandinavian countries is the **Folkehøyskole**. These are residential adult educational colleges with a one-year course from August to May. The teaching is free, but students must pay the boarding cost. There are many of these colleges dotted about the country. Sporting facilities are excellent, and most students find it a very rewarding year. Many of the colleges are especially interested in attracting students from abroad and offer intensive Norwegian tuition. Pastoral care is exceptionally good. No entry qualifications needed. Contact:

Informasjonskontoret for folkehøyskolen
Karl Johansgate 12
0154 Oslo
Norway
E-mail: if@folkehogskole.no
Web: www.folkehogskole.no

Books

If you would like to get hold of Norwegian books and dictionaries, the best way is to contact the Norwegian bookshop **Norli**. They can supply every book published in Norway, provided it is in print. Try them at www.norli.no. You can also write to them, telephone or fax:

Norlis Bokhandel
Universitetsgaten 20–24
0162 Oslo
Norway
Tel: +47 22 00 43 00; Fax: +47 22 42 26 57

Another possibility is the Norwegian mail-order site www.bokkilden.no, who accept credit card payment.

In the UK you can order books from the **Anglo-Norse Society**. The address is:

The Anglo-Norse Society
25 Belgrave Square
London SW1X 8QD
Tel/fax: +44 (0) 20 7235 9529
E-mail: anglonorse@yahoo.co.uk

The **Anglo-Norse Book Scheme** has several dictionaries to suit various needs and pockets, as well as text-books for different levels. There is a comprehensive list of titles of Norwegian classics as well as more contemporary literature.

For travel information there are several excellent guide-books on the market. Some include a lot of cultural information about Norway.

Norway, The Rough Guide, Phil Lee, 2003 (ISBN: 1843530546)
Lonely Planet Norway, Deanna Swaney, Andrew Bender, Graeme Cornwallis, 2002 (ISBN: 174059200X)

For further reading, try the *Dørene Åpnes* series, edited by Elisabeth Borgen *et al.* and available from www.norli.no. The series includes books, workbooks and video, and contains well-reproduced art and a wealth of short stories, poetry, and insight into Norwegian life and culture.

Another course, a good follow-on from *Complete Norwegian*, is *Troll i ord*, by Anne Bjørnebek, again available from www.norli.no. This is a spy thriller, taking the reader all over Norway. Grammatical notes and explanations are all in Norwegian. There are exercises and a comprehensive glossary from Norwegian into French, English and German, and four CDs.

Organizations

The Anglo-Norse Society welcomes new members. Contact them at the address given above for information on membership and of events, lectures, etc. in the London area.

H.M. King Harald of Norway is patron of **Normannsforbundet/ The Norse Federation.** Their goal is to strengthen cultural and personal bonds between Norway and Norwegian speakers abroad, particularly in the USA and Canada. For information on membership and benefits contact:

Normannsforbundet
Rådhusgaten 23 B
0158 Oslo
Norway
Tel: +47 23 35 71 70; Fax: +47 23 35 71 75
E-mail: membership@norseman.no

Many American universities teach Norwegian in their linguistics departments. You can contact **NorTANA** (Norwegian Researchers and Teachers Association of North America) for information at http://www.stolaf.edu/depts/norwegian/nortana/nortana.html

You can also try

Norge-Amerika Foreningen
Rådhusgaten 23 B
0158 Oslo
Norway
Tel: +47 22 35 71 60
Web: www.noram.no

Another helpful organization is the **Norwegian Seamen's Church Abroad:**

Sjømannskirken
Postboks 2007 Nordnes
5817 Bergen
Norway
Tel: +47 55 55 22 55; Fax: +47 55 55 22 50
E-mail: info@sjomannskirken.no
http://www.sjomannskirken.no/

The Norwegian Seamen's Church provides a link between Norway and Norwegians living abroad and offers useful contact and friendship to people in their host towns. The Church has branches in a vast number of major cities across the world. These are listed on its website (which is available in English).

Another organization in the USA is **Sons of Norway,** www.sofn.com. This is mainly a social organization, and arranges Lutefisk suppers, etc. Every year a big autumn festival is arranged in North Dakota, with Norwegians and Americans from most of the USA taking part.

Newspapers and websites

The Internet has various websites for national newspapers. The paper which is read by most people is **Aftenposten** (www.aftenposten.no). The two biggest national tabloids are **Dagbladet** (www.dagbladet.no) and **Verdens Gang** (www.vg.no). Don't get disheartened if you find newspapers a bit difficult. Journalists often use a rather racy style. The tabloids are easier to read than **Aftenposten.**

Also on the Internet, try searching for Norge Aviser. At 'Finn din norske avis' you will be able to get most Norwegian newspapers. Try also **News Index Norge.**

Radio

If you live in the UK and tune your radio to 1314 kHz medium wave, you will get Norwegian radio. Reception is variable, but better in the evening than during the day. There is a wide variety of programmes, and the presenters speak very clearly. For more information contact the **Norwegian Broadcasting Corporation:**

NRK (Norsk Rikskringkasting)
Bjørnstjerne Bjørnsons plass 1
0340 Oslo
Norway
Tel: +47 23 04 70 00; Fax: +47 75 12 27 77

You can get Norwegian radio and TV on broadband internet: www.nrk.no.

Embassies

The **Norwegian Embassies** are very useful. They will provide addresses and information about travelling and working in Norway. Here are some addresses:

Royal Norwegian Embassy
25 Belgrave Square
London SW1X 8QD

Royal Norwegian Embassy
2720 34th Street NW
Washington DC
20008 – 2714 USA

Royal Norwegian Consulate General
825 Third Avenue, 38th Floor
New York
NY 10033 – 7584 USA

Royal Norwegian Embassy
17 Hunter Street
Yarralumla
Canberra ACT 2600
Australia

Good luck with your further studies!

Key to the exercises

Unit 1

True or false? **1 a** F, **b** T, **c** T. **2 a** T, **b** F, **c** F. **3 a** F, **b** T, **c** F.

Exercises **1 a** Jeg heter ..., **b** Jeg kommer fra ..., **c** Bare bra, takk, **d** Nei, jeg er ikke norsk, **e** Jeg bor i .... **2 a** Hei, **b** Adjø, **c** God dag, **d** God natt, **e** Ha det! **3 a** Nei, John er ikke norsk. **b** Nei, jeg vil ikke ha en kopp kaffe. **c** Nei, Bente kommer ikke fra York. **d** Nei, jeg bor ikke i Wales. **e** Nei, Bente har ikke bil. **4 a** Er John norsk? **b** Kommer han fra York? **c** Bor du i London? **d** Har hun bil? **e** Lærer Bente engelsk? **5 a** Hva heter han? **b** Hvor bor du? **c** Hvordan har du det? **d** Hvor kommer han fra? **e** Hva studerer han? **6 a** reiser, **b** bor, **c** har, **d** har, **e** kommer. **7** Wordsearch: fly, reise, norsk, bil, ferie, motorsykkel, tog. Do you understand? **1** Er du norsk? **2** Nei, jeg er engelsk. Jeg lærer norsk. **3** (Name) Hva heter du? **4** Jeg kommer fra ... Og du? **5** Er du student? **6** Jeg skal reise til Norge i sommer. **7** Nei, jeg har motorsykkel.

Test yourself 1,a 2,c 3,b 4,c 5,c 6,a 7,b 8,a 9,b 10,c

Unit 2

True or false? **1 a** T, **b** F, **c** F, **d** T. **2 a** F, **b** T, **c** T, **d** T. **3 a** F, **b** T, **c** T, **d** T.

Exercises **1 a** på mandag, **b** til Bergen, **c** norsk, **d** en kopp kaffe. **2 a** skolen, **b** studenten, **c** hotellet, **d** damen, **e** fergen, **f** kartet, **g** veien, **h** passet. **3 a** reise, **b** ha, **c** ha, **d** lære, **e** kjøre, **f** bestille. **4 a** en student, **b** en direktør, **c** en dame, **d** et hotell, **e** en lærer, **f** en kveld, **g** et glass, **h** en kopp. **5 a** stort, **b** gammelt, **c** kjedelig, **d** engelsk. **6 a** tirsdag, **b** fredag, **c** fem, **d** ti, **e** ni, **f** ti. **7 a** en, **b** fem, **c** ett. **8** Wordsearch: møte, jeg, med, kjedelig, de, han, hun, stor, og, lærer, dame. Do you understand? **1** Hei! Er du norsk? **2** Nei, jeg er engelsk. Jeg lærer norsk. **3** Ja, jeg går på norsk-kurs, men det er kjedelig! **4** Fordi læreren er en kjedelig, gammel dame.

5 (Name) Og du? **6** Hei, Kari! Hyggelig å møte deg. Vil du ha en kopp kaffe? **7** Ha det!

Test yourself 1,c 2,a 3,a 4,b 5,b 6,c 7,b 8,a 9,c 10,b

Unit 3

True or false? **1 a** F, **b** T, **c** T, **d** T. **2 a** T, **b** T, **c** T, **d** T. **3 a** T, **b** F, **c** F, **d** F.

Exercises **1 a** en kopp, koppen, kopper, **b** et glass, glasset, glass, **c** en ferge, fergen, ferger, **d** et bord, bordet, bord, **e** en time, timen, timer, **f** en middag, middagen, middager. **2 a** en tørst student, den tørste studenten, tørste studenter, **b** en sulten dame, den sultne damen, sultne damer, **c** et norsk pass, det norske passet, norske pass, **d** et engelsk sertifikat, det engelske sertifikatet, engelske sertifikater, **e** en liten bil, den lille bilen, små biler, **f** et lite glass, det lille glasset, små glass. **3** skal/vil/kan/må **a** spise, **b** lære, **c** reise, **d** kjøre. **4 a** S, **b** Q, **c** Q, **d** S, **e** Q, **f** Q. **5 a** Bente kommer ikke fra Bergen. **b** Fergen har ikke mange passasjerer. **c** Studenten lærer ikke engelsk. **d** Kari er ikke sulten. **e** Hun spiser ikke en god middag. **6** Wordsearch: reker, kaffe, salat, øl, marmelade, kjøtt, fisk, brød, sild, rødvin. Do you understand? **1** Hvor skal du reise? **2** Er du norsk? **3** Hvor er Trondheim? **4** Jeg skal reise til Oslo også. Jeg skal være i Oslo fra tirsdag til lørdag. **5** Jeg skal reise over fjellet til Bergen. Neste onsdag skal jeg reise til Amerika. **6** Og du?

Test yourself 1,b 2,b 3,a 4,c 5,c 6,a 7,c 8,a 9,b 10,a

Unit 4

True or false? **1 a** F, **b** F, **c** F, **d** T. **2 a** T, **b** F, **c** T, **d** F. **3 a** T, **b** F, **c** T, **d** T.

Exercises **1 a** bussen, busser, bussene, **b** trikken, trikker, trikkene, **c** flyet, fly, flyene, **d** toget, tog, togene, **e** lastebilen, lastebiler, lastebilene, **f** fergen, ferger, fergene. **2 a** den store bussen, store busser, de store bussene, **b** den gule trikken, gule trikker, de gule trikkene, **c** det store flyet, store fly, de store flyene, **d** det fine toget, fine tog, de fine togene, **e** den grønne lastebilen, grønne lastebiler, de grønne lastebilene, **f** den gode fergen, gode ferger, de gode fergene. **3 a** damen, damene, **b** en student, studentene, **c** skolen, skoler, skolene, **d** et hus, huset, hus, **e** kurset, kurs, kursene, **f** en kopp, koppen, koppene, **g** en flaske, flasker, flaskene. **4 a** Det er et stort hus som ligger i en grønn park. **b** De tar trikken som går til Frognerparken. **c** Solen skinner på sjøen som er blå. **d** Bente spiser mange reker som er gode. **5 a** Nå kommer vi til Frognerparken. **b** Nå skal vi spise reker. **c** Nå går John og Bente til Aker Brygge. **d** Til venstre kan du se den britiske ambassaden. **e** Til venstre ser vi Slottet. **f** Til venstre ser John en restaurant. **6 a** hit / dit, **b** her / der, **c** her / der, **d** hit / dit. **7 a** stor, **b** store, **c** store, stor, **d** store, store. (You can of course use other adjectives!) **8 a** Akershus er til høyre for Rådhuset. **b** Frognerparken er på venstre side av kartet. **c** Nei, Slottet er i en stor park. **9 a** Kongen og dronningen bor på Slottet. **b** Nei. Slottet er en stor gul bygning. **c** Trikkene i Oslo er blå. Do you understand? **1** Er dette Slottet? **2** Det er en fin bygning. Er kongen her nå? **3** Jeg kommer fra … **4** Ja, jeg liker den norske maten. Hva heter den lange gaten der? **5** Jeg vil gjerne gå til Frognerparken. **6** Takk. Jeg synes at Oslo er en pen/vakker by. **7** Ja, jeg har et godt kart. Her er det. **8** Takk. Nå går jeg. Adjø.

Test yourself 1,a 2,b 3,b 4,c 5,b 6,c 7,a 8,b 9,b 10,a

Unit 5

True or false? **1 a** F, **b** F, **c** F, **d** F. **2 a** T, **b** F, **c** T, **d** F. **3 a** F, **b** F, **c** F, **d** T.

Exercises **1 a** den, **b** den, **c** dette, **d** de, **e** de, **f** dette. **2 a** kjør!, **b** sitt! **c** gå! **d** kjøp! **3 a** ferien, feriene, **b** en by, byene, **c** veien, veier, **d** et hotell, hotellet, hotellene, **e** en park, parker, parkene, **f** kortet, kort, kortene, **g** et frimerke, frimerker, frimerkene. **4 a** stor, **b** kjedelige, **c** gamle, **d** blå, **e** norske, **f** grønne, **g** pene. **6** Bente is in a bad mood. The weather is bad. It is not fine (good) weather. It is not sunny. It rains. John is in Oslo alone. He is in a good mood. He buys many pretty cards and some stamps. Then he goes to the tourist information and to a bank. He has no money, and he would like to change some travellers' cheques. Do you understand? **1** Jeg vet ikke. Jeg kommer fra England. **2** Jeg har et kart. Vi kan se på det. **3** (Name) **4** Ja, jeg studerer i England. Er du student? **5** Nei, jeg skal reise til Bergen på mandag. **6** Nei, jeg skal reise med fly. **7** Jeg vil gå med deg. **8** Jeg vil gjerne ha en kopp kaffe, men jeg vil heller snakke norsk! **9** Ja, men jeg vil heller reise til Amerika!

Test yourself 1,b 2,a 3,c 4,c 5,a 6,b 7,c 8,a 9,b 10,a

Unit 6

True or false? **1 a** F, **b** F, **c** F. **2 a** T, **b** T, **c** F, **d** F. **3 a** F, **b** F, **c** F, **d** T.

Exercises **1 a** reiste, **b** spiste, **c** drakk, **d** hadde, **e** gikk. **2 a** hjemme, **b** der, **c** inn, **d** ute, **e** hjem. **3 a** Liker John øl? **b** Kommer han fra York? **c** Vil Bente reise til Bergen? **d** Heter Bentes bror Tom? **4 a** Jo, jeg liker kaffe. **b** Ja, jeg vil komme med deg til Bodø. **c** Jo, han vil ringe til Bente. **d** Jo, han heter Per. **5 a** blå, blå, blå, **b** store, store, store, **c** lange, lange, lange, **d** fine, fine, fine. **6 a** 16, **b** 25, **c** 59, **d** 74, **e** 202. **7 a** sju, **b** sytten, **c** atten, **d** åtti, **e** sekshundreogtrettito. **8 a** fire pluss/og fem er ni, **b** femten minus sju er åtte, **c** tre ganger seks er atten, **d** tjueåtte delt på/dividert med sju er fire, **e** tolv pluss/og to er fjorten. Do you understand? **1** Jeg heter ... Jeg vil gjerne bestille time. **2** Nei, jeg kommer fra England. Jeg er på ferie her. **3** Kan jeg komme litt senere? Jeg kommer tilbake fra Hamar den dagen. **4** Det er fint/bra. Dere er i Storgaten. Hvordan kommer jeg dit fra Oslo S? **5** Takk. Jeg skal være der på fredag. **6** Adjø.

Test yourself 1,c 2,a 3,c 4,b 5,b 6,b 7,a 8,b 9,c 10,c

Unit 7

True or false? **1 a** F, **b** F, **c** F, **d** F. **2 a** F, **b** F, **c** T, **d** T. **3 a** T, **b** F, **c** F, **d** T.

Exercises **1 a** søsteren, søstre, søstrene, **b** en far, fedre, fedrene, **c** et barn, barnet, barn, **d** en mann, mannen, mennene, **e** læreren, lærere, lærerne. **2 a** den gode vennen, gode venner, de gode vennene, **b** det store huset, store hus, de store husene, **c** det lille barnet, små barn, de små barna, **d** den kjedelige filmen, kjedelige filmer, de kjedelige filmene. **3 a** min, **b** hennes, **c** min, **d** sin, **e** hennes. **4 a** farfar, **b** nieser, **c** svoger, **d** foreldre, **e** sønnen /

broren. Do you understand? **1** Ja, jeg liker å være alene. **2** Hva heter du? **3** Andrew er ikke et norsk navn. **4** Og din søster, har hun et amerikansk og et fransk navn også? **5** Er ikke din far her? **6** Hvorfor er du ikke med ham?

Test yourself 1,c 2,a 3,b 4,c 5,b 6,b 7,a 8,c 9,b 10,a

Unit 8

True or false? **1 a** F, **b** F, **c** F, **d** F. **2 a** T, **b** T, **c** T, **d** T. **3 a** F, **b** T, **c** F, **d** F.

Exercises **1 a** spiste, **b** drakk, **c** reiste, **d** tok. **2 a** bodd, **b** trodd, **c** stoppet, **d** brukket. **3** hode, øyne, ører, nese, munn, armer, ben, fingre, tær, hodet, magen. **4 a** brune, **b** blå, **c** stort, **d** rødt, stor. **5 a** sitt, **b** sine, **c** hans, **d** hans. **6** våkner, er, har, sier, vil, har, er, er, er, ser, må, sier, har, heter. **7** Jan woke up in a hospital bed. He was at a big hospital. He had pains everywhere. The doctor said that he would get some scars on his feet. He had many stitches in his head and on his arms and legs, but he was lucky not to have been killed. Sue was also at the hospital. She saw her face in the mirror. Then she had to vomit (throw up). The nurse said she had a brother called Arne. Do you understand? **1** (Name) **2** Jeg har vondt i magen! **3** Ja, og jeg har kastet opp mange ganger. **4** Jeg har vondt i hele magen. Au! **5** Vi gikk til en restaurant og hadde reker og majones og hvitvin, så kjøttkaker i brun saus med poteter og salat og rødvin. Etterpå hadde vi is. Så gikk vi i gatene og hadde to varme pølser med sennep, og senere hadde vi noen øl i en pub. Vi hadde en varm pølse til og pommes frites.

Test yourself 1,c 2,b 3,c 4,a 5,c 6,a 7,c 8,b 9,c 10,a

Unit 9

True or false? **1 a** T, **b** F, **c** F, **d** F. **2 a** F, **b** F, **c** F, **d** F. **3 a** F, **b** F, **c** T, **d** F.

Exercises **1 a** grønne, grønne, grønne; **b** blått, blå, blå; **c** stripet, stripete, stripete; **d** pen, pene, pene. **2 a** fælere, fælest; **b** finere, finest; **c** smartere, smartest; **d** blekere, blekest. **3 a** større, **b** mindre, **c** minst, **d** størst. **4 a** brødre; **b** en far, fedrene; **c** en søster, søsteren, søstrene; **d** moren, mødre, mødrene; **e** en mann, menn, mennene. **5 a** Dem, **b** De, **c** Dem, **d** Deres. **6 a** synes, **b** tror, **c** tror, **d** synes.

Test yourself 1,c 2,a 3,a 4,c 5,b 6,b 7,c 8,c 9,b 10,a

Unit 10

True or false? **1 a** F, **b** T, **c** T, d F. **2 a** T, **b** F, **c** T, **d** F. **3 a** F, **b** F, **c** F, **d** F.

Exercises **1 a** til, **b** på, **c** til, **d** over, **e** i. **2 a** i dag, **b** i går, **c** i morges, **d** om morgenen, **e** på. **3 a** fjerde, **b** sekstende, **c** tjuesjette, **d** første, **e** niende. **4 a** fem, **b** tolv, **c** fjorten, **d** førtisju, **e** sekstini. **5 a** Gratulerer med dagen, **b** Velkommen (til oss), **c** Vil du ha litt mer?, **d** Nei takk, jeg er forsynt, **e** Takk for maten. **6 a** den sinte naboen, **b** det spesielle selskapet, **c** den koselige kvelden, **d** den deilige bløtkaken, **e** det store smilet. **7 a** en god venn, **b** en kjedelig gjest, **c** en stor kake, **d** en snill søster, **e** en dårlig bror. **8 a** setter, **b** satt, **c** ligger, **d** lå, **e** sitter. **9 a** smiler, har smilt, **b** tenker, tenkte, **c** å kaste, kastet, **d** drikker, drakk, har drukket, **e** ser, har sett. Do you understand? **1** Jeg håper du kan finne hvor vennene dine bor! Du kjente ikke Oslo godt i juli! **2** Martin spurte meg om å komme. Jeg håper det er i orden. **3** Takk for meg!

Test yourself 1,b 2,c 3,a 4,c 5,a 6,a 7,c 8,b 9,a 10,b

Unit 11

True or false? **1 a** F, **b** T, **c** F, **d** F. **2 a** F, **b** T, **c** T, **d** F. **3 a** F, **b** F, **c** T, **d** F.

Exercises **1 a** 6.10, **b** 10.15, **c** 10.55, **d** 7.30, **e** 1.40. **2 a** fem over tre, **b** halv fem, **c** kvart på sju, **d** ti på åtte, **e** fem på halv ti. **3 a** 23rd April, **b** 7th January, **c** 10th October, **d** 11th May, **e** 18th August. **4 a** femte februar, **b** tolvte mars, **c** fjortende juni, **d** sekstende juli, **e** tjuesjette September. **5 a** Gratulerer med dagen, **b** God jul, farmor, **c** Godt nyttår, **d** Takk for maten, **e** Takk, det samme / takk i like måte. **6 a** legger, **b** sitter/setter seg **c** legger seg, **d** sitter/setter seg **e** legger meg. **7 a** satt, **b** la seg, **c** satte oss, **d** la, **e** lå. Do you understand? **1** Jo, litt. Men jeg liker å være her i Norge i julen. **2** Ja, men ikke julaften. Juledag, tjuefemte desember, er vår jul. **3** Jeg liker å feire julaften. Jeg liker den norske maten og tradisjonene. **4** Nei, og jeg vil ikke spise den! Jeg tror ikke at jeg vil like den. **5** Jeg vil gjerne ha en dram, men ikke lutefisk. **6** Julen er fin alle steder, hvis du er sammen med dem du liker. Det var hyggelig å snakke med deg/Dem, men nå må jeg gå. **7** Adjø!

Test yourself 1,a 2,b 3,a 4,a 5,c 6,c 7,c 8,b 9,c 10,a

Unit 12

True or false? **1 a** T, **b** T, **c** F, **d** T. **2 a** T, **b** T, **c** T, **d** F. **3 a** T, **b** F, **c** F. **4 a** F, **b** T, **c** F.

Exercises **1 a** ja, **b** helt, **c** kjedelig, **d** liten, **e** pen, **f** lys, **g** regn. **2 a** hjem, **b** inne, **c** bort, **d** dit, **e** hit. **3 a** meg, **b** seg, **c** seg, **d** seg. **4 a** mange hilsener fra / hjertelig hilsen, **b** klem fra, **c** ærbødigst / med hilsen, **d** kjærlig hilsen / klem fra/kyss fra. **5 a** drikker, **b** stopper, **c** bor, **d** ligger, **e** smiler. **6 a** god, **b** rødt, **c** lille, **d** stygge, **e** blå, **f** vonde. Do you understand? Tjueto – sekstifire – trettifem – nittiåtte **1** Kan jeg få snakke med Bente? **2** Nei, jeg er ikke John. Jeg heter ... Jeg er en av Bentes venner fra Amerika. **3** Hei, Nina! Bente sa at jeg kunne være en uke eller to. Er det i orden? **4** Hvorfor det? **5** Hvem er John? **6** Jeg gleder meg til å treffe deg, Nina. Ha det!

Test youself 1,c 2,c 3,b 4,c 5,a 6,b 7,a 8,b 9,c 10,a

Unit 13

True or false? **1 a** F, **b** T, **c** F, **d** T. **2 a** F, **b** F, **c** T, **d** T. **3 a** T, **b** F, **c** F, **d** F.

Exercises **1 a** Det er sol, men / og det er kaldt. **b** Den ene stolen er blå, og / men den andre stolen er rød. **c** De ringte på døren, men han var ikke hjemme. **2 a** Nå er Kari på ferie. **b** Her kan vi gå på ski. **c** Der kommer Hilde og Erik. **d** Nå vil jeg gjerne ha en kopp kaffe. **e** Snart skal hun studere i London. **3 a** hadde invitert, **b** hadde snødd, **c** hadde vært, **d** hadde hatt. **4 a** John bruker piggdekk bare om vinteren. **b** Det var ikke elektrisitet i hytten, så de brukte parafinlamper. **c** Om vinteren smeltet de snø for å få vann. **d** Toalettet var utenfor. **5 a** har, **b** går, **c** kjører, **d** står. **6 a** lite, ikke; **b** meget; **c** etterpå; **d** veldig. **7 a** Bøy! **b** Kjør! **c** Sitt!

d vær! Do you understand? **1** Jeg liker det! Jeg er med noen venner i en hytte. Den er litt primitiv. Doen er utenfor og det er ikke bad. **2** Jeg liker å gå på ski. Jeg liker slalom best. I begynnelsen var jeg redd, men nå kjører jeg fort ned bakken. Jeg faller ikke ofte. **3** Vil dere ha en kopp sjokolade på hotellet når vi kommer ned? Jeg vil gjerne høre mer om norske hytter.

Test yourself 1,b 2,b 3,a 4,a 5,c 6,b 7,c 8,c 9,a 10,a

Unit 14

True or false? **1 a** T, **b** T, **c** F, **d** T. **2 a** T, **b** F, **c** T, **d** F. **3 a** T, **b** F, **c** F, **d** T.

Exercises **1 a** da, **b** når, **c** når, **d** når, **e** da. **2 a** gå, **b** reise, **c** går, **d** gå, **e** reise. **3 a** skal kjøpe, **b** skal reise, **c** vil sende, **d** vil spise, **e** vil drikke. **4 a** nitten, **b** tretti, **c** tjueseks, **d** tretti, **e** trettifire. **5 a** den store gutten, store gutter, de store guttene; **b** det gule bordet, gule bord, de gule bordene; **c** det lange toget, lange tog, de lange togene; **d** den gode klemmen, gode klemmer, de gode klemmene; **e** den sinte damen, sinte damer, de sinte damene. **6 a** den dårlige faren, dårlige fedre, de dårlige fedrene; **b** den lille søsteren, små søstre, de små søstrene; **c** den tykke mannen, tykke menn, de tykke mennene; **d** det snille barnet, snille barn, de snille barna. **7 a** jeg er lei meg; **b** unnskyld!/om forlatelse!; **c** ikke vær sint på meg!; **d** unnskyld, **e** kan du tilgi meg?/om forlatelse. **8 a** ofte, **b** fortere, **c** styggere, styggest, **d** heller, **e** bedre. Do you understand? **1** Det har vært en veldig fin dag. Jeg er så trett! Vi må ha gått mange kilometer. **2** Har du hørt fra Knut? **3** Vil du gjerne se Knut igjen? **4** Du vil snart møte en hyggelig ung mann. Skål for deg, Silje, og Skål for Norge!

Test yourself 1,c 2,b 3,a 4,c 5,a 6,a 7,a 8,c 9,b 10,b

Unit 15

True or false? **1 a** F, **b** T, **c** F, **d** F. **2 a** F, **b** T, **c** F, **d** T. **3 a** T, **b** T, **c** T, **d** T.

Exercises **1 a** et, **b** en, **c** et, **d** en. **2 a** Bussen blir kjørt av John. **b** Kari blir likt av Per. **c** Genseren blir kjøpt av Bente. **d** Frokosten ble spist av mannen. **e** Brevet ble lest av Hilde. **3 a** stoppet, **b** arbeidet, **c** ventet, **d** ryddet, **e** bråket. **4 a** reiste, **b** kjørte, **c** spiste, **d** hørte, **e** likte. **5 a** hvilken, **b** hvilket, **c** hvilke, **d** hvilket, **e** hvilken. **6 a** Hva heter han? **b** Hvor kommer de fra? **c** Hvordan har hun det? **d** Hvem er det som sitter der? **e** Hvorfor smiler hun? **7 a** Jeg vil gjerne bestille et rom for to personer. **b** Er frokost inkludert? **c** Er det svømmehall her? **d** Kan jeg få regningen? **e** Jeg vil gjerne snakke med direktøren. Do you understand? **1** Jeg vil gjerne bestille et rom for i morgen natt, for en natt. **2** Jeg vil gjerne ha et dobbelt rom med bad. **3** Jeg tar rommet med utsikt over sjøen. Kan jeg ta med hunden min? **4** Vi ankommer klokken ni og vi vil gjerne ha middag. **5** Fint. Vi kommer i morgen.

Test yourself 1,a 2,b 3,c 4,a 5,b 6,c 7,a 8,a 9,a 10,b

Unit 16

True or false? **1 a** T, **b** F, **c** F, **d** F. **2 a** F, **b** F, **c** F, **d** T. **3 a** F, **b** T, **c** T, **d** F.

Exercises **1 a** fra; **b** til, på; **c** hos; **d** foran; **e** bak; **f** på; **g** før; **h** i; **i** til; **j** på, i; **k** etter. Quiz **1** bilen, bilene; **2** flyet, fly; **3** mødre, mødrene; **4** barnet, barn, barna; **5** den lange veien, lange veier, de lange veiene; **6** det gule huset, gule hus, de gule husene; **7** kvart over fem; **8** fem på halv åtte; **9** ti på tolv; **10** seksten; **11** ni; **12** tirsdag; **13** søndag; **14** syttende juni; **15** femtende juni; **16** spiser; **17** drikke; **18** leker; **19** spiller; **20** Da; **21** Når; **22** på; **23** til, i **24** etter; **25** til, til; **26** seg; **27** sin; **28** min; **29** sine; **30** Jeg heter … **31** Jeg kommer fra …; **32** Jeg er …; **33** Jeg vil gjerne lære norsk fordi …; **34** Takk, bare bra; **35** ?, **36** Jeg vil gjerne / helst reise til …; **37** bedre; **38** eldre; **39** yngste; **40** Bentes mor; **41** hotellets resepsjon; **42** guttens katt; **43** besteforeldre; **44** bilnøkler; **45** fjortende; **46** sakte; **47** trehundreogsekstiåtte; **48** onsdag syttende mai; **49** klokken er fem på halv fire; **50** ? Do you understand? **1** Ja takk. Er det et godt hotell i denne byen? Det må ikke være for dyrt. **2** Hva kan vi gjøre i denne byen? Vi vil gjerne være her i fem dager. **3** Jeg vil gjerne kjøpe noen kort og frimerker og en flaske vin. **4** Da skal vi gå til Vinmonopolet først og komme tilbake hit etterpå.

Test yourself 1,a 2,b 3,b 4,c 5,c 6,b 7,a 8,c 9,c 10,a

Grammar

Irregular nouns

barn	barnet	barn	barna	(et)	(*child*)
begynner	begynneren	begynnere	begynnerne	(en)	(*beginner*)
ben	benet	ben	bena	(et)	(*leg/bone*)
		beste foreldre	beste foreldrene		*(grand parents)*
bok	boken	bøker	bøkene	(en)	(*book*)
bror	broren	brødre	brødrene	(en)	(*brother*)
engel	engelen	engler	englene	(en)	(*angel*)
far	faren	fedre	fedrene	(en)	(*father*)
farfar	farfaren	farfedre	farfedrene	(en)	(*father's father*)
farmor	farmoren	farmødre	farmødrene	(en)	(*father's mother*)
finger	fingeren	fingre	fingrene	(en)	(*finger*)
fot	foten	føtter	føttene	(en)	(*foot*)
genser	genseren	gensere	genserne	(en)	(*sweater*)
hybel	hybelen	hybler	hyblene	(en)	(*bedsit*)
juletre	juletreet	juletrær	juletrærne	(et)	(*Christmas tree*)
kafé	kaféen	kaféer	kaféene	(en)	(*café*)
kne	kneet	knær	knærne	(et)	(*knee*)
lærer	læreren	lærere	lærerne	(en)	(*teacher*)
mann	mannen	menn	mennene	(en)	(*man*)
mor	moren/mora	mødre	mødrene	(en/ei)	(*mother*)
morfar	morfaren	morfedre	morfedrene	(en)	(*mother's father*)
mormor	mormoren/ mormora	mormødre	mormødrene	(en/ei)	(*mother's mother*)
museum	museet	museer	museene	(et)	(*museum*)
natt	natten	netter	nettene	(en)	(*night*)
rom	rommet	rom	rommene	(et)	(*room*)
seddel	seddelen	sedler	sedlene	(en)	(*note, banknote*)
ski	skien	ski	skiene	(en)	(*ski*)
sko	skoen	sko	skoene	(en)	(*shoe*)
skulder	skulderen	skuldre	skuldrene	(en)	(*shoulder*)
sommer	sommeren	somre	somrene	(en)	(*summer*)
studium	studiet	studier	studiene	(et)	(*university course*)

støvel	støvelen	støvler	støvlene	(en)	(*boot*)
svoger	svogeren	svogre	svogrene	(en)	(*brother-in-law*)
sykkel	sykkelen	sykler	syklene	(en)	(*bike*)
søster	søsteren/ søstera	søstre	søstrene	(en/ei)	(*sister*)
tre	treet	trær	trærne	(et)	(*tree*)
tå	tåen	tær	tærne	(en)	(*toe*)
vinter	vinteren	vintre	vintrene	(en)	(*winter*)
øye	øyet	øyne	øynene	(et)	(*eye*)

Irregular verbs

Infinitive	Present	Past	Past participle	
bli	blir	ble	blitt	(*become*)
brekke	brekker	brakk	brukket	(*break*)
brenne	brenner	brant	brent	(*burn*)
delta	deltar	deltok	deltatt	(*take part in*)
dra	drar	drog	dradd	(*go, travel*)
drikke	drikker	drakk	drukket	(*drink*)
falle	faller	falt	falt	(*fall*)
fare	farer	for	fart	(*travel*)
finne	finner	fant	funnet	(*find*)
finnes	finnes	fantes	funnes	(*be found*)
fly	flyr	fløy	fløyet	(*fly, rush*)
foreslå	foreslår	foreslo	foreslått	(*suggest*)
forstå	forstår	forstod	forstått	(*understand*)
fortelle	forteller	fortalte	fortalt	(*tell*)
fortsette	fortsetter	fortsatte	fortsatt	(*continue*)
fryse	fryser	frøs	frosset	(*freeze*)
føles	føles	føltes	føltes	(*feels*)
følge	følger	fulgte	fulgt	(*follow*)
få	får	fikk	fått	(*get, receive*)
gi	gir	ga	gitt	(*give*)
gjøre	gjør	gjorde	gjort	(*do*)
gli	glir	gled	glidd	(*slide, slip*)
gå	går	gikk	gått	(*go, travel*)
ha	har	hadde	hatt	(*have*)
hete	heter	het	hett	(*be called, named*)
hjelpe	hjelper	hjalp	hjulpet	(*help*)
holde	holder	holdt	holdt	(*hold*)
komme	kommer	kom	kommet	(*come*)
la	lar	lot	latt	(*let*)

(Contd)

le	ler	lo	ledd	(*laugh*)
legge	legger	la	lagt	(*lay, put*)
ligge	ligger	lå	ligget	(*lie*)
løpe	løper	løp	løpt	(*run*)
møte	møter	møtte	møtt	(*meet*)
nyse	nyser	nøs	nyst	(*sneeze*)
nyte	nyter	nøt	nytt	(*enjoy*)
se	ser	så	sett	(*see*)
selge	selger	solgte	solgt	(*sell*)
sette	setter	satte	satt	(*set, put*)
sitte	sitter	satt	sittet	(*sit*)
si	sier	sa	sagt	(*say*)
skilles	skilles	skiltes	skilt	(*separate*)
skrike	skriker	skrek	skreket	(*cry, scream*)
skrive	skriver	skrev	skrevet	(*write*)
slå	slår	slo	slått	(*hit, tap*)
sove	sover	sov	sovet	(*sleep*)
spørre	spør	spurte	spurt	(*ask*)
stå	står	sto	stått	(*stand*)
synes	synes	syntes	synes	(*think, be of the opinion*)
synge	synger	sang	sunget	(*sing*)
ta	tar	tok	tatt	(*take*)
tilby	tilbyr	tilbød	tilbudt	(*offer*)
tilgi	tilgir	tilga	tilgitt	(*forgive*)
treffe	treffer	traff	truffet	(*meet*)
trives	trives	trivdes	trives	(*thrive, flourish*)
vite	vet	visste	visst	(*know*)
være	er	var	vært	(*be*)
ødelegge	ødelegger	ødela	ødelagt	(*spoil, break*)

Modal verbs

Infinitive	Present	Past	Perfect	
burde	bør	burde	burdet	(*ought to*)
kunne	kan	kunne	kunnet	(*can*)
måtte	må	måtte	måttet	(*must, have to*)
skulle	skal	skulle	skullet	(*shall*)
tore	tør	torde	tort	(*dare*)
ville	vil	ville	villet	(*will*)

Modal verbs in Norwegian are conjugated in the same way as other verbs.

Grammar glossary

adjectives Adjectives give us more information about the nouns. See **nouns.** They tell us about colours and shapes and whether somebody or something is good, bad, interesting or boring. **Jeg har en bil** *I have a car*, doesn't tell anything about the noun, **bil**. By adding a few descriptive adjectives, **Jeg har en liten, gammel, rød bil** *I have a small, old, red car*, one can imagine what the car looks like. **En kjedelig lærer** *a boring teacher* is quite different from **en hyggelig lærer** *a nice teacher.*

adverbs An adverb provides more information about a verb and how something happens. **Han kjørte fort**. *He drove fast*. Some adjectives convert to adverbs by adding **-t: god godt**, *good well*. This is similar to the English *-ly* ending: *slow slowly*. All sorts of words fall into the 'bag' of adverbs, like **ikke** *not*, **alltid** *always*, **aldri** *never* and so on. If you cannot find a sensible grammatical group for a word, it is very likely to be an adverb!

articles In English the indefinite article is *a/an*, which in Norwegian is **en/(ei)/et**. Whereas in English the definite article is *the*, the definite of nouns in Norwegian is formed by adding the indefinite article to the word itself: **en bil** *a car* **bilen** *the car*. **Et hus** *a house* **huset** *the house*. When there is an adjective in front of the noun, and only then, one uses a definite article as well as the ending. This article is **den/det**. More about this in Units 1–4. See **gender**.

clause A clause can be either main or subordinate. A main clause must have at least one subject and one verb, and can end with a full stop. A subordinate clause will also have a subject and a verb, but is formed in such a way that it must be attached to a main clause. See **main clause** and **subordinate clause**.

comparative When we make comparisons, we use the comparative form of the adjective. In English this usually means adding *-er* to the adjective, or putting *more* in front, and adding *than* to make the comparison. In Norwegian one usually adds **-ere** to the adjective, or **mer** *more* in front, and **enn** *than*: **Richard er flinkere enn Robert.** *Richard is cleverer than Robert.* **Richard er mer flink enn Robert.** *Richard is more clever than Robert.* See also **superlative.**

conjunctions Conjunctions are words used to link two phrases together. **Ingen liker Robert.** *Nobody likes Robert.* **Alle liker Richard.** *Everybody likes Richard.* These two phrases can be linked together with the help of a conjunction: **Ingen liker Robert og alle liker Richard** (**og** *and*). Or: **Ingen liker Robert, men alle liker Richard** (**men** *but*).

demonstratives In English the demonstratives are *this/these* and *that/those*. In Norwegian the demonstratives are, according to gender, **denne/dette** (*this*) **disse** (*these*) and **den/det** (*that*) **de** (*those*).

gender In English one usually thinks of *gender* in connection with male and female people or animals, and we refer to them as *he* or *she*. Objects are usually referred to as *it* and are of *neuter* gender. We refer to a *car* or *house* as *it*. In Norwegian every single noun has a gender, either masculine, feminine or neuter, indicated by **en**, **ei**, or **et**, the indefinite articles. Sometimes the gender follows common sense, but very often it does not. As the gender of the noun affects other words it is important to try to learn the gender with each noun. We have **en bil** *a car*, but **et tog** *a train*, and **en kopp** *a cup*, but **et glass** *a glass*. It is perfectly acceptable to use just one gender for masculine and feminine nouns, called the common gender, indicated by **en**. Neuter is indicated by **et**. In this book we use the common gender and neuter only, but where one could use feminine if one so wishes, this is indicated in the Vocabulary at the back of the book. See **articles**.

genitive Genitive is a way of expressing ownership. In English *Robert's money* means that the money belongs to Robert. In Norwegian this is done in a similar way, but with no apostrophe: **Roberts penger**.

imperative The imperative is the form of the verb used to give instructions, orders, directions or commands. In Norwegian one strips the verb down to its shortest possible form to make it sound really snappy. **Smil!** *Smile!* The verb is **å smile** *to smile*. If the verb is very short, the imperative will be the same: **Gå!** *Go!* The verb is **å gå** *to go*. See **infinitive**.

infinitive The traditional way of listing verbs in a dictionary is in what we call the infinitive, **å sove** *to sleep*.

irregular verbs Many verbs follow a set pattern for the different tenses, present, past and perfect, but unfortunately many do not! In Norwegian these irregular verbs are called strong verbs.

main clause A main clause is a complete sentence, containing at least one subject and one verb and after which we can put a full stop if we so wish. **Odd sover**. *Odd sleeps*. Usually, however, a main clause will offer a little more information. See **clause** and **subordinate clause**.

nouns A noun is a word that means a person, a thing, an animal or a place. **Student** *student*, **bil** *car*, **katt** *cat* and **by** *town* are examples of nouns. Proper nouns are names of people and places, such as Tim and Guildford, and are spelt with a capital letter in Norwegian as in English.

object See also **subject**. The term 'object' refers to the person or thing on the 'receiving end' of a verb. **Robert drikker øl.** *Robert drinks beer*. Here, *Robert* is the subject, as he is the one who is doing something. *Drinks* is the verb, expressing the action. What is he drinking? *Beer* is the object, as it is what Robert is drinking.

personal pronouns The personal pronouns are *I*, *you*, *he*, *she*, *it*, *we*, *you*, *they*. In Norwegian they are **jeg**, **du**, **han**, **hun** **den/det**, **vi**, **dere**, **de**. Proper nouns and other nouns can be replaced by a personal pronoun. Instead of **Richard spiser** *Richard eats*, we can say **han spiser** *he eats*. We can replace **bil** *car* with **den** *it* and **mor** *mother* with **hun** *she*.

plural The plural of a noun means that we are concerned with more than one person or object. See **singular**.

possessives Possessive pronouns define ownership of something or somebody. **Min katt** *my cat*, **hans tante** *his aunt* are examples. Ownership can also be expressed in this way: **katten min** *the cat of mine*, **tanten hans** *the aunt of his*.

prepositions Prepositions are rather tricky words in any language. They are used in time expressions, such as **på fredag** *on Friday*, and for defining places, **katten sitter på/under/ved bordet** *the cat sits on/under/by the table*. A difficulty with Norwegian prepositions is that they sometimes have more than one meaning.

pronouns We have mentioned personal and possessive pronouns. There are other groups of pronouns, such as the reflexive and indefinite pronouns, which are explained in the book.

singular The term 'singular' is used when we are concerned with only one person or object. See **plural**.

subject The subject of a sentence is who is doing whatever. In the sentence **Robert drikker øl** *Robert drinks beer*, it is Robert who is doing something, and so he is the subject. In **Andrew og Martin snakker norsk** *Andrew and Martin speak Norwegian* there are two subjects. They both speak Norwegian. See **object**.

subordinate clause A main clause can stand on its own. A subordinate clause will also have a subject and a verb, but it needs to be attached to a main clause. **Når jeg er sulten** *When I am hungry* has a subject and a verb, but when it's on its own it cannot end with a full stop. We add a main clause: **Når jeg er sulten, spiser jeg**. *When I am hungry, I eat.* Or: **Jeg spiser når jeg er sulten**. *I eat when I am hungry.* A subordinate clause needs the support of a main clause. See **clause** and **main clause.**

superlative The superlative form of the adjective is used for the most extreme version of comparison. **Jeg er den beste** *I am the best*, and **katten min er den dummeste av alle** *my cat is the stupidest of all*, are examples. One can also use **mest** *most* to express superlative: **katten min er den mest dumme av alle**, *my cat is the most stupid of all.* See **comparative.**

tense The tenses of the verb tell us about when things happened or are going to happen, as they express the past, the future or right now, by their endings. Some verbs, called strong verbs, are irregular. See **irregular verbs.** Others follow a regular pattern and fall into four categories. They are called weak verbs. See **verbs.**

verbs A verb is a word which states what someone or something is doing. **Reise** *travel*, **drikke** *drink* and **se** *see* are examples of verbs.

word order In Norwegian the order in which we put words, mainly the subject and the verb, varies in different situations. This is explained as we get to it, quite early in the book.

Norwegian–English vocabulary

n	noun	adv	adverb
(en) (en/ei) (et)	gender	pre	preposition
v	verb	p	pronoun
(s)	strong/irregular verb	c	conjunction
(1) (2) (3) (4)	weak verb group	pl	plural
a	adjective		

The unit in which the word is first used is indicated by a number.

adresse *n* **(en) 6** *address*
aftens *n* **(en) 10** *supper*
akevitt *n* **(en) 11** *aquavit*
akseptere *v* **(2) 14** *accept*
aldri *adv* **11** *never*
alene *adv* **5** *alone*
alkohol *n* **(en) 3** *alcohol*
alle *p* **4** *all (pl)*
allerede *adv* **12** *already*
allergi *n* **(en) 9** *allergy*
allergisk *a* **9** *allergic*
alltid *adv* **3** *always*
alt *p* **5** *everything*
alt *adv* **10** *already*
altfor *adv* **5** *much too*
altså *adv* **6** *consequently*
alvor *n* **(et) 16** *seriousness*
alvorsord *n* **(et) 7** *telling off*
ambassade *n* **(en) 4** *embassy*
ambulanse *n* **(en) 8** *ambulance*
Amerika 3 *America*
amerikansk *a* **4** *American*
andre *p* **6** *others*
andre *a* **5** *second, other*
angre *v* **(1) 16** *regret*
ankomme *v* **(s) 15** *arrive*
anlegg *n* **(et) 10** *installation*
annonse *n* **(en) 12** *advert*
anorakk *n* **(en) 13** *anorak*
ansikt *n* **(et) 8** *face*
apotek *n* **(et) 9** *pharmacy*
april 10 *April*
arbeide *v* **(1) 4** *work*
arbeidsdag *n* **(en) 10** *working day*
arm *n* **(en) 8** *arm*
arr *n* **(et) 8** *scar*
at *p* **3** *that*
atten 5 *eighteen*
attende 10 *eighteenth*
attest *n* **(en) 12** *reference*
au! 8 *ouch!*
au pair *n* **(en) 1** *au pair*
august 10 *August*
av *pre* **3** *of, by*
av og til 16 *now and then*
avgang *n* **(en) 6** *departure*
avis *n* **(en) 11** *newspaper*

bad *n* **(et) 15** *bathroom*
bade *v* **(1) 8** *bathe, swim*
badstue *n* **(en) 13** *sauna*
bak *pre* **5** *behind*
bake *v* **(2) 10** *bake*
bakke *n* **(en) 13** *slope, hill*
balkong *n* **(en) 11** *balcony*
bank *n* **(en) 5** *bank*
bankdirektør *n* **(en) 12** *bank manager*
bar *n* **(en) 3** *bar*
bare *adv* **1** *only*
barn *n* **(et) 7** *child*
barndomshjem *n* **(et) 10** *childhood home*
barnebarn *n* **(et) 7** *grandchild*
barnegudstjeneste *n* **(en) 11** *children's service*
barnetog *n* **(et) 14** *children's parade*
bedre *a, adv* **2** *better*
befolkning *n* **(en) 14** *population*
begge *p* **5** *both*
begynne *v* **(2) 9** *begin, start*
begynnelse *n* **(en) 13** *beginning*
begynner *n* **(en) 13** *beginner*
beklage *v* **(1) 15** *be sorry*
belte *n* **(et) 9** *belt*
ben *n* **(et) 12** *leg, bone*
besette *v* **(s) 12** *take, occupy*
best *a, adv* **3** *best*
besteforeldre *n* **(pl) 7** *grandparents*
bestemt *a* **13** *certain*
bestille *v* **(2) 2** *book, order*
besøk *n* **(et) 7** *visit*
besøke *v* **(2) 7** *visit*
betale *v* **(2) 3** *pay*
betingelse *n* **(en) 16** *condition*
beundre *v* **(1) 10** *admire*
bh *n* **(en) 9** *bra*
bil *n* **(en) 1** *car*
bilde *n* **(et) 11** *picture*
bilist *n* **(en) 13** *driver*
billett *n* **(en) 2** *ticket*
billig *a* **6** *cheap*
bilnøkkel *n* **(en) 7** *car key*
biltur *n* **(en) 16** *car trip*
biologisk *a* **13** *biological*
bitteliten *a* **12** *tiny*
bleie *n* **(en) 7** *nappy, diaper*
blek *a* **9** *pale*
bli *v* **(s) 2** *become*
bli kjent med 10 *get to know*
bluse *n* **(en) 9** *blouse*
bløtkake *n* **(en) 10** *gateau, cake*
blå *a* **4** *blue*
blåse *v* **(2) 16** *blow*
bo *v* **(4) 1** *live, reside*
bok *n* **(en) 11** *book*
bokhylle *n* **(en) 13** *bookshelf*
bolle *n* **(en) 7** *bun*
bomull *n* **(en) 9** *cotton*
bord *n* **(et) 3** *table*
borte *adv* **4** *away*
bra *adv* **1** *well*
bratt *a* **13** *steep*
brekke *v* **(s) 8** *break*
brenne *v* **(s) 15** *burn*
brev *n* **(et) 12** *letter*
britisk *a* **4** *British*
bro *n* **(en) 4** *bridge*
bronse *n* **(en) 4** *bronze*
bror *n* **(en) 7** *brother*
brosjyre *n* **(en) 5** *brochure*
bruke *v* **(2) 9** *use, wear*

brun *a* **4** *brown*
brun saus *n* **(en) 8** *gravy*
bry *n* **(et) 12** *trouble*
brygge *n* **(en) 4** *quay, jetty*
bryst *n* **(et) 14** *breast, chest*
brød *n* **(et) 3** *bread, loaf*
brønn *n* **(en) 13** *well*
brøytekant *n* **(en) 13** *bank of snow*
bråke *v* **(2) 11** *make a noise*
bukse *n* **(en) 9** *trousers*
buss *n* **(en) 3** *bus*
butikk *n* **(en) 9** *shop*
by *n* **(en) 3** *town, city*
bygning *n* **(en) 4** *building*
bøtte *n* **(en) 13** *bucket*
bøye *v* **(1) 13** *bend*
både *c* **6** *both*
bål *n* **(et) 15** *fire, bonfire*
bånd *n* **(et) 14** *ribbon, tie*
båt *n* **(en) 15** *boat*

campingplass *n* **(en) 8** *campsite*

da *c* **7** *when, since*
da *adv* **5** *then*
dag *n* **(en) 2** *day*
Dagsnytt 11 *news on TV*
dame *n* **(en/ei) 2** *lady*
Danmark 14 *Denmark*
dans *n* **(en) 10** *dance*
danse *v* **(1) 10** *dance*
dansk *a* **14** *Danish*
dato *n* **(en)** *date*
de *p* **3** *they*
De *p* **9** *you (formal)*
deg *p* **1** *you*
deilig *a* **10** *delicious, lovely*
dekk *n* **(et) 13** *tyre*
del *n* **(en) 14** *part*
dele *v* **(2) 11** *share*
delta *v* **(s) 13** *take part*
dem *p* **5** *them*
Dem *p* **9** *you (formal)*
dempe *v* **(1) 10** *quieten*
den *p* **4** *it, that*
denne *p* **5** *this*
der *adv* **4** *there*
der borte 4 *over there*
dere *p* **6** *you (plural)*
Deres *p* **9** *yours*
derfor *adv* **13** *therefore*
desember 10 *December*
dessert *n* **(en) 10** *sweet, pudding*
dessverre *adv* **12** *unfortunately*
det *p* **1** *it, that*
dette *p* **3** *this*
diaré *n* **(en) 8** *diarrhoea*
din *p* **5** *your, yours*
direktør *n* **(en) 2** *director, manager*
disk *n* **(en) 5** *counter*
disse *p* **4** *these*
dit *adv* **4** *there*
dividere *v* **(2) 6** *divide*
divisjon *n* **(en) 6** *division*
do *n* **(en) 13** *loo*
dobbel *a* **15** *double*
dra *v* **(s) 15** *go, travel*
dram *n* **(en) 11** *tot of aquavit*
drepe *v* **(2) 7** *kill*
dress *n* **(en) 9** *suit*
drikke *v* **(s) 3** *drink*
drink *n* **(en) 10** *drink*
drittunge *n* **(en) 7** *brat*
dronning *n* **(en/ei) 4** *queen*

du *p* **1** *you*
dum *a* **10** *stupid*
dusj *n* **(en) 15** *shower*
dyp *a* **13** *deep*
dyr *a* **9** *expensive*
dør *n* **(en/ei) 5** *door*
dørklokke *n* **(en/ei) 10** *doorbell*
dårlig *a, adv* **5** *bad*

egen *a* **11** *own*
egentlig *a, adv* **14** *really*
egg *n* **(et) 3** *egg*
eggerøre *n* **(en) 10** *scrambled eggs*
ei *(ind art)* **1** *a, an*
eie *v* **(3) 13** *own*
ekkel *a, adv* **13** *awful*
ekstra *a, adv* **15** *additional, extra*
eldre *a* **16** *older*
eldst *a* **7** *oldest*
elegant *a* **9** *elegant*
elektrisitet *n* **(en) 13** *electricity*
eller *c* **2** *or*
elleve **5** *eleven*
ellevte **10** *eleventh*
elske *v* **(1) 10** *love*
en **1** *a, an*
enda *adv* **9** *even*
ende *n* **(en) 5** *end*
engel *n* **(en) 7** *angel*
engelsk *a* **1** *English*
England **1** *England*
enn *c* **7** *than*
ensom *a* **14** *lonely*
eplesaft *n* **(en) 10** *apple juice*
erfaring *n* **(en) 12** *experience*
erme *n* **(et) 9** *sleeve*
eske *n* **(en) 9** *box*
et **1** *a, an*
etasje *n* **(en) 8** *floor, level*
etter *adv, pre* **2** *after*
etternavn *n* **(et) 7** *surname*
etterpå *adv* **4** *afterwards*
Europa **2** *Europe*

falle *v* **(s) 13** *fall*
familie *n* **(en) 6** *family*
familieselskap *n* **(et) 10** *family party*
fantastisk *a* **8** *fantastic*
far *n* **(en) 6** *father*
fare *v* **(s) 11** *travel*
farfar *n* **(en) 7** *grandfather*
farge *n* **(en) 9** *colour*
farge *v* **(1) 11** *colour*
farlig *a* **13** *dangerous*
farmasøyt *n* **(en) 9** *chemist*
farmor *n* **(en) 7** *grandmother*
fart *n* **(en) 13** *speed*
fartsgrense *n* **(en) 3** *speed limit*
fat *n* **(et) 13** *serving dish*
feber *n* **(en) 9** *temperature*
februar **10** *February*
feire *v* **(1) 11** *celebrate*
felles *a* **7** *common*
fem **2** *five*
femte **10** *fifth*
femten **5** *fifteen*
femtende **10** *fifteenth*
femti **5** *fifty*
femtiende **10** *fiftieth*
ferdig *a* **12** *ready, finished*
ferge *n* **(en) 2** *ferry*
ferie *n* **(en) 2** *holiday*
festlig *a* **10** *festive, fun*
festning *n* **(en) 4** *castle*

fetter *n* **(en) 7** *cousin (male)*
film *n* **(en) 2** *film*
fin *a* **3** *fine*
finger *n* **(en) 8** *finger*
finne *v* **(s) 5** *find*
finnes *v* **(s) 15** *can be found*
fint *adv* **1** *fine*
fire 2 *four*
firma *n* **(et) 10** *firm, company*
fisk *n* **(en) 3** *fish*
fiske *v* **(1) 16** *fish*
fjell *n* **(et) 3** *mountain*
fjerde 10 *fourth*
fjord *n* **(en) 15** *fjord*
fjorten 5 *fourteen*
fjortende 10 *fourteenth*
flagg *n* **(et) 11** *flag*
flaske *n* **(en/ei) 3** *bottle*
flere *a, p* **8** *several, more*
flink *a* **10** *clever*
fly *n* **(et) 1** *aeroplane*
fly *v* **(s) 13** *rush, fly*
flyplass *n* **(en) 3** *airport*
flytte *v* **(1) 12** *move*
folk *n* **(pl) 8** *people*
fontene *n* **(en) 4** *fountain*
for *pre* **5** *for*
for *adv* **8** *too*
for ... siden *pre* **7** *ago*
for seg selv 14 *by oneself*
for tiden 12 *at the moment*
foran *adv, pre* **13** *in front of*
forandre *v* **(1) 16** *change*
forbause *v* **(1) 10** *surprise*
forbi *pre* **4** *past*
forbudt *a* **3** *not allowed, forbidden*
fordi *c* **2** *because*
foreldre *n* **(pl) 7** *parents*
forelsket *a* **14** *in love*
foreslå *v* **(s) 12** *suggest*
forkjølet *a* **9** *suffering from a cold*
forklare *v* **(2) 5** *explain*
forme *v* **(1) 11** *form, shape*
fornøyd *a* **15** *satisfied*
forover *adv* **13** *forward*
forretning *n* **(en) 12** *business*
forrett *n* **(en) 10** *starter*
forsiktig *a, adv* **13** *careful*
forskjellig *a, adv* **16** *different*
forstoppelse *n* **(en) 9** *constipation*
forstå *v* **(s) 6** *understand*
forsyne seg *v* **(2) 10** *help oneself*
fort *a* **13** *fast*
fortelle *v* **(s) 7** *tell*
fortøye *v* **(1) 15** *tie up (a boat)*
fosse *v* **(1) 16** *surge*
fot *n* **(en) 8** *foot*
fotball *n* **(en) 12** *football*
fotografere *v* **(2) 16** *take photos*
fra *pre* **1** *from*
frakk *n* **(en) 9** *overcoat*
fransk *a* **7** *French*
fredag 2 *Friday*
frem *adv* **11** *forward, forth*
fremdeles *adv* **10** *still*
fremtid *n* **(en) 16** *future*
fri *a, adv* **15** *free*
frimerke *n* **(et) 5** *stamp*
frisk *a* **8** *healthy, well*
frisør *n* **(en) 6** *hairdresser*
frokost *n* **(en) 3** *breakfast*
fru 12 *Mrs*
frukt *n* **(en) 10** *fruit*
fryktelig *a, adv* **14** *terrible, terribly*

fryse *v* **(s) 13** *freeze*
frøken 12 *Miss*
full *a* **6** *full*
fylle ut *v* **(2) 15** *fill in*
fyrverkeri *n* **(et) 11** *fireworks*
fæl *a* **9** *gruesome*
føde *v* **(2) 15** *give birth, be born*
fødselsdag *n* **(en) 10** *birthday*
føle seg *v* **(2) 9** *feel*
følge *v* **(s) 10** *follow*
før *pre, adv* **6** *before*
først *adv* **4** *first*
førti 5 *forty*
førtiende 10 *fortieth*
få *v* **(s) 3** *get, receive*
få lov til 5 *be allowed to*
få tak i 7 *get hold of*

galt *adv* **13** *wrong*
gammel *a* **2** *old*
gang *n* **(en) 5** *time*
gang *n* **(en) 13** *passage*
ganger *v* **(1)** *times (multiplication)*
ganske *adv* **12** *quite*
gardin *n* **(en) 13** *curtain*
gate *n* **(en/ei) 4** *street*
geitost *n* **(en) 4** *goat cheese*
gelé *n* **(en) 3** *jelly*
genser *n* **(en) 9** *sweater*
gi *v* **(s) 7** *give*
gi opp 16 *give in*
gift med 7 *married to*
gifte seg *v* **(1) 7** *marry*
gitar *n* **(en) 15** *guitar*
gjennom *pre* **13** *through*
gjerne *adv* **1** *with pleasure*
gjest *n* **(en) 10** *guest*
gjøre *v* **(s) 5** *do*
glad *a, adv* **7** *happy, pleased*
glad for at 6 *pleased, happy that*
glad *i* **7** *fond of*
glass *n* **(et) 1** *glass*
glatt *a* **13** *slippery*
glede *v* **(1) 13** *please*
glede seg til 2 *look forward to*
glemme *v* **(2) 3** *forget*
gli *v* **(s) 16** *slide*
glitter *n* **(et) 11** *tinsel*
god *a* **2** *good*
god bedring 8 *get well soon*
godt *adv* **3** *well*
grad *n* **(en) 8** *degree*
granitt *n* **(en) 4** *granite*
gratulere *v* **(2) 10** *congratulate*
gravlaks *n* **(en) 3** *cured salmon*
gressløk *n* **(en) 10** *chives*
grille *v* **(1) 15** *grill, barbecue*
gris *n* **(en) 11** *pig*
grunnlov *n* **(en) 14** *constitution*
gryterett *n* **(en) 10** *casserole*
grønn *a* **4** *green*
grønnsak *n* **(en) 10** *vegetable*
grå *a* **9** *grey*
gudstjeneste *n* **(en) 11** *church service*
gul *a* **4** *yellow*
gutt *n* **(en) 4** *boy*
Gøteborg 2 *Gothenburg*
gøy *n* **(et) 13** *fun*
gå *v* **(s) 1** *go, travel*

ha *v* **(s) 1** *have*
hage *n* **(en) 7** *garden*
hals *n* **(en) 9** *neck*
halv 11 *half*

ham *p* **7** *him*
han *p* **1** *he*
hard *a* **2** *hard*
hatt *n* **(en) 9** *hat*
hav *n* **(et) 8** *sea*
hei 1 *hi/hello*
heis *n* **(en) 15** *lift*
hel *a* **2** *whole*
heldig *a* **6** *lucky*
heldigvis *adv* **9** *luckily*
heller *adv* **2** *rather, either*
helt *adv* **8** *completely*
hende *v* **(2) 12** *happen*
henge *v* **(2) 9** *hang*
henne *p* **2** *her*
hennes *p* **6** *her, hers*
hente *v* **(1) 6** *collect, gather*
her *adv* **3** *here*
herfra *adv* **14** *from here*
herr 12 *Mr*
hest *n* **(en) 14** *horse*
hete *v* **(s) 1** *be called*
hilse *v* **(2) 6** *greet*
hilsen *n* **(en) 11** *greeting*
himmel *n* **(en) 11** *sky, heaven*
historie *n* **(en) 14** *history, story*
hjelp *n* **(en) 5** *help*
hjelpe *v* **(s) 5** *to help*
hjem *adv* **6** *home*
hjemme *adv* **6** *at home*
hjernerystelse *n* **(en) 8** *concussion*
hode *n* **(et) 8** *head*
hodepine *n* **(en) 9** *headache*
hodepinetablett *n* **(en) 9** *headache pill*
holde *v* **(s) 6** *keep, hold*
holme *n* **(en) 15** *small island*
hos *pre* **2** *by, with, at the house of*
hoste *v* **(1) 9** *cough*
hostesaft *n* **(en) 9** *cough medicine*
hotell *n* **(et) 2** *hotel*
hotellbransje *n* **(en) 12** *hotel business*
hoved- 11 *main*
hovedgate *n* **(en) 4** *main street*
humør *n* **(et) 5** *mood, humour*
hun *p* **1** *she*
hund *n* **(en) 15** *dog*
hundre 5 *hundred*
hus *n* **(et) 4** *house*
huske *v* **(1) 3** *remember*
hva *p* **1** *what*
hva slags 5 *what kind of*
hvem *p* **4** *who*
hver *a, p* **2** *each, every*
hverandre *p* **5** *each other*
hvilken *a, p* **5** *which*
hvis *c* **2** *if*
hvit *a* **7** *white*
hvitvin *n* **(en) 3** *white wine*
hvor *adv* **1** *where*
hvor *adv* **8** *how*
hvordan *adv* **1** *how*
hvorfor *adv* **2** *why*
hybel *n* **(en) 14** *bedsit*
hygge seg *v* **(1) 8** *have a good time*
hyggelig *a* **2** *nice, pleasant*
hytte *n* **(en/ei) 13** *cottage, cabin*
høre *v* **(2) 6** *hear*
høres bra ut 15 *sounds good*
høst *n* **(en) 9** *autumn*
høy *a* **8** *tall, high*

høyfjell *n* **(et) 13** *mountain, above the tree line*
høyre *a* **3** *right*
hånd *n* **(en/ei) 8** *hand*
håpe *v* **(1) 10** *hope*

i *pre* **1** *in*
i aften 10 *this evening*
i dag 7 *today*
i en uke 7 *for a week*
i fjor 12 *last year*
i går 6 *yesterday*
i hvert fall 16 *in any case*
i kveld 2 *this evening*
i morgen 2 *tomorrow*
i morges 14 *this morning*
i orden 7 *in order*
i sommer 1 *this summer*
i tur og orden 11 *one by one*
i uken 12 *per week*
idé *n* **(en) 14** *idea*
idiot *n* **(en) 13** *idiot*
igjen *adv* **4** *again, left*
ikke *adv* **1** *not*
ikke sant 10 *isn't that so*
ikke så verst 6 *not too bad*
ingen *a, p* **5** *nobody, no, none*
ingeniør *n* **(en) 10** *engineer*
ingenting *p* **16** *nothing*
inkludere *v* **(2) 15** *include*
inn *i* **3** *into*
inne *adv* **7** *inside*
innen *adv, c* **12** *before, within*
interessant *a* **11** *interesting*
interessert *a* **9** *interested*
invitere *v* **(2) 10** *invite*
is *n* **(en) 7** *ice-cream*
ivrig *a* **13** *eager*

ja 1 *yes*
jada 14 *yes, all right!*
jakke *n* **(en) 7** *coat, jacket*
januar 10 *January*
jeg *p* **1** *I*
jente *n* **(en/ei) 13** *girl*
jo 6 *yes (after negative)*
jobb *n* **(en) 7** *job, position*
jobbe *v* **(1) 12** *work*
jord *n* **(en) 13** *earth*
jul *n* **(en) 10** *Christmas*
julaften *n* **(en) 11** *Christmas Eve*
juledag *n* **(en) 11** *Christmas Day*
juleferie *n* **(en) 16** *Christmas holiday*
julegris *n* **(en) 11** *Christmas pig*
julekake *n* **(en) 11** *Christmas cake*
julekveld *n* **(en) 11** *Christmas Eve*
julesang *n* **(en) 11** *Christmas carol*
juleskikk *n* **(en) 11** *Christmas tradition*
juletre *n* **(et) 11** *Christmas tree*
juli 2 *July*
juling *n* **(en) 7** *beating, hiding*
juni 10 *June*

kafé *n* **(en) 4** *café*
kafeteria *n* **(en) 3** *cafeteria*
kaffe *n* **(en) 1** *coffee*
kake *n* **(en/ei) 10** *cake*
kald *a* **8** *cold*
kalle *v* **(2) 7** *call*
kamera *n* **(et) 16** *camera*
kanskje *adv* **5** *perhaps*
karamellpudding *n* **(en) 10** *crème caramel*

kart *n* **(et) 2** *map*
kasse *n* **(en) 5** *till*
kaste *v* **(1) 8** *throw*
kaste opp 8 *vomit*
katt *n* **(en) 15** *cat*
kino *n* **(en) 2** *cinema*
kiosk *n* **(en) 5** *kiosk*
kirke *n* **(en) 11** *church*
kirkeklokke *n* **(en/ei) 11** *church bell*
kjedelig *a* **2** *boring*
kjempe- 12 *very, 'mega-'*
kjempefin *a* **12** *very fine, superb*
kjempekjekk *a* **12** *very hunky*
kjenne *v* **(2) 10** *know, be acquainted with*
kjole *n* **(en) 9** *dress*
kjære 10 *dear*
kjøkken *n* **(et) 10** *kitchen*
kjøkkenhjelp *n* **(en) 12** *kitchen hand*
kjøpe *v* **(2) 5** *buy*
kjøre *v* **(2) 2** *drive*
kjøtt *n* **(et) 3** *meat*
kjøttkake *n* **(en/ei) 8** *meat ball*
klage *v* **(1) 15** *complain*
kle *v* **(4) 9** *suit*
kle på *v* **(4) 9** *to dress*
klem *n* **(en) 7** *hug*
klemme *v* **(2) 11** *hug*
klippe *v* **(1) 8** *cut (with scissors)*
klok *a* **16** *wise*
klokke *n* **(en/ei)** *6 clock, time*
klær *n* **(pl) 9** *clothes*
klø *v* **(4) 9** *itch*
kne *n* **(et) 8** *knee*
koke *v* **(2) 3** *boil*
koldtbord *n* **(et) 3** *cold buffet*
kollega *n* **(en) 9** *colleague*
komme *v* **(s) 1** *come*
kone *n* **(en/ei) 10** *wife*
konge *n* **(en) 4** *king*
kongefamilie *n* **(en) 14** *royal family*
kongelig høyhet *n* **(en) 12** *royal highness*
konsert *n* **(en) 5** *concert*
kontakt *n* **(en) 9** *contact*
kontor *n* **(et) 12** *office*
kopp *n* **(en) 1** *cup*
korallrød *a* **9** *coral-red*
kort *a* **9** *short*
kort *n* **(et) 5** *card, postcard*
kos *a* **10** *pleasant (slang)*
kose seg *v* **(2) 13** *enjoy oneself*
koselig *a* **10** *pleasant, lovely*
koste *v* **(1) 5** *cost*
kraftig *a* **8** *strong*
krangle *v* **(1) 6** *argue, quarrel*
kredittkort *n* **(et) 15** *credit card*
krem *n* **(en) 11** *cream*
krig *n* **(en) 14** *war*
krone *n* **(en) 5** *unit of Norwegian currency*
kronprins *n* **(en) 14** *crown prince*
kropp *n* **(en) 8** *body*
kul *a* **14** *fun (slang)*
kuldegrad *n* **(en) 13** *minus degree*
kunde *n* **(en) 9** *customer*
kunne *v* **(modal) 2** *can*
kunstmaler *n* **(en) 12** *artist*
kurs *n* **(et) 2** *course*
kusine *n* **(en) 7** *cousin (female)*
kvalifisere *v* **(2) 12** *qualify*
kvalm *a* **8** *nauseous*

kvart på 11 *quarter to*
kveld *n* **(en) 2** *evening*
kvittering *n* **(en) 5** *receipt*
kyss *n* **(et) 11** *kiss*
kysse *v* **(1) 11** *kiss*
kyst *n* **(en) 16** *coast*
køye *n* **(en/ei) 3** *bunk*
kåpe *n* **(en/ei) 9** *overcoat*

la *v* **(s) 15** *let*
lage *v* **(1) 4** *make*
laks *n* **(en) 3** *salmon*
lammestek *n* **(en) 10** *roast lamb*
lammeull *n* **(en) 9** *lambswool*
land *n* **(et) 14** *country*
lang *a* **3** *long*
langs *pre* **13** *along*
langsom *a* **13** *slow*
langt *adv* **4** *far*
lastebil *n* **(en) 3** *lorry*
latter *n* **(en) 15** *laughter*
le *v* **(s) 10** *laugh*
ledig *a* **6** *free, vacant*
lege *n* **(en) 8** *doctor*
legekontor *n* **(et) 7** *surgery*
legge *v* **(s) 11** *put*
legge seg *v* **(s) 11** *go to bed*
lei av 9 *tired of*
lei meg 14 *sorry*
leie *v* **(1) 12** *rent*
leilighet *n* **(en) 7** *flat*
leke *v* **(2) 7** *play (with toys)*
lekerom *n* **(et) 15** *playroom*
lekker *a* **9** *super*
lenge *adv* **5** *a long time*
lese *v* **(2) 11** *read*
lett *a* **5** *easy*
ligge *v* **(s) 4** *lie*
lik *a* **5** *like*
like *v* **(2) 2** *like*
like *adv* **12** *just*
likevel *adv* **12** *after all*
likne *v* **(1) 4** *look like*
lillebror *n* **(en) 6** *little brother*
lite *adv* **13** *not much*
liten *a* **3** *small*
litt *adv* **3** *a little*
liv *n* **(et) 12** *life*
livlig *a* **13** *lively*
livredd *a* **13** *frightened to death*
lue *n* **(en/ei) 9** *cap*
luft *n* **(en) 11** *air*
lugar *n* **(en) 3** *cabin*
lukke *v* **(1) 11** *shut*
lunsj *n* **(en) 15** *lunch*
lure på *v* **(2) 16** *wonder*
lys *n* **(et) 3** *light*
lys *n* **(et) 10** *candle*
lys *a* **15** *light*
lyse *v* **(2) 11** *shine*
lære *v* **(2) 1** *learn*
lærer *n* **(en) 2** *teacher*
løfte *v* **(1) 10** *lift*
løpe *v* **(s) 14** *run*
lørdag 2 *Saturday*
låne *v* **(2) 7** *borrow*

mai 10 *May*
majestet *n* **(en) 12** *majesty*
majones *n* **(en) 8** *mayonnaise*
mandag 2 *Monday*
mange *p, a* **3** *many*
mann *n* **(en) 5** *man*
marmelade *n* **(en) 3** *marmalade*
mars 10 *March*
marsipan *n* **(en) 11** *marzipan*

marsipankake *n* **(en/ei) 10** *marzipan cake*
marsj *n* **(en) 14** *march*
mase *v* **(2) 14** *nag*
mat *n* **(en) 3** *food*
matpakke *n* **(en) 15** *packed meal*
matpapir *n* **(et) 15** *greaseproof paper*
med *pre* **1** *with*
med en gang 6 *at once*
meddele *v* **(2) 12** *inform*
medisin *n* **(en) 1** *medicine*
meg *p* **2** *me*
meget *adv* **3** *much, very*
melk *n* **(en) 3** *milk*
melodi *n* **(en) 14** *tune*
men *c* **1** *but*
mene *v* **(2) 5** *think, mean*
menneske *n* **(et) 14** *person*
mens *c* **7** *while*
mer *a, adv* **3** *more*
merkelig *a* **16** *strange, peculiar*
middag *n* **(en) 3** *dinner*
midnatt *n* **(en) 15** *midnight*
min *p* **2** *my, mine*
mindre *a, adv* **9** *smaller, less*
mineralvann *n* **(et) 10** *mineral water*
minst *a, adv* **9** *smallest*
minutt *n* **(et) 5** *minute*
misfornøyd *a* **15** *dissatisfied*
miste *v* **(1) 16** *lose*
monolitt *n* **(en) 4** *monolith*
mor *n* **(en/ei) 6** *mother*
morfar *n* **(en) 7** *grandfather*
morgen *n* **(en) 9** *morning*
mormor *n* **(en) 7** *grandmother*
morn 1 *hi/hello*
moro *n* **(ei, en) 10** *fun*
morsom *a* **10** *funny, amusing*
mot *pre* **8** *towards*
mote *n* **(en) 9** *fashion*
motorbåt *n* **(en) 15** *motor boat*
motorsykkel *n* **(en) 1** *motorbike*
mulighet *n* **(en) 12** *possibility*
multe *n* **(en) 11** *cloudberry*
munn *n* **(en) 8** *mouth*
museum *n* **(et) 5** *museum*
musikk *n* **(en) 10** *music*
musikk-korps *n* **(et) 14** *band*
musserende *a* **11** *sparkling (of wine)*
mye *adv* **3** *much, a lot of*
mynt *n* **(en) 5** *coin*
mønster *n* **(et) 9** *pattern*
mønstret *a* **9** *patterned*
mørk *a* **8** *dark*
møte *v* **(s) 1** *meet*
måltid *n* **(et) 11** *meal*
måned *n* **(en) 7** *month*
måtte *v* **(modal) 2** *must, have to*

nabo *n* **(en) 10** *neighbour*
nasjonaldag *n* **(en) 14** *national day*
Nationalteatret 5 *The National Theatre*
natt *n* **(en) 15** *night*
natur *n* **(en) 8** *nature*
navn *n* **(et) 5** *name*
ned *pre* **5** *down*
nederst i 16 *at the bottom of*
nei 1 *no*
nese *n* **(en) 8** *nose*
neste *a* **3** *next*
nesten *adv* **5** *nearly, almost*

nettopp *adv* **9** *just*
nevø *n* **(en) 7** *nephew*
ni 2 *nine*
niende 10 *ninth*
niese *n* **(en) 7** *niece*
niste *n* **(en) 15** *packed meal*
nitten 5 *nineteen*
nittende 10 *nineteenth*
nitti 5 *ninety*
nittiende 10 *ninetieth*
noe *p* **5** *some/any, something*
noen *p* **5** *somebody, some, any*
nok *adv* **3** *enough*
nokså *adv* **16** *fairly*
Nord-Norge 1 *north Norway*
nord 3 *north*
nordmann *n* **(en) 12** *Norwegian*
Norge 1 *Norway*
norsk *a* **1** *Norwegian*
november 10 *November*
nummer *n* **(et) 6** *number*
ny *a* **7** *new*
nydelig *a* **16** *lovely*
nyse *v* **(s) 9** *sneeze*
nyte *v* **(s) 16** *enjoy*
nyttår *n* **(et) 11** *New Year*
nyttårsaften *n* **(en) 11** *New Year's Eve*
nærmere *adv* **14** *nearer*
nøkkel *n* **(en) 15** *key*
nå *adv* **1** *now*
nå *v* **(4) 7** *reach*
nå og da 12 *now and then*
når *adv* **1** *when*
når som helst 12 *any time*

ofte *adv* **7** *often*
og *c* **1** *and*
også *adv* **2** *also*
oktober 10 *October*
ola-bukser *n* **(pl) 8** *jeans*
om *pre* **4** *in, about*
om *c* **12** *whether*
om et par uker 6 *in a couple of weeks*
om forlatelse 13 *sorry*
ombord *adv* **3** *on board*
omegn *n* **(en) 14** *neighbourhood*
onkel (en) 7 *uncle*
onsdag 2 *Wednesday*
operasanger *n* **(en) 12** *opera singer*
opp *pre* **6** *up*
oppleve *v* **(3) 11** *experience*
opplysninger *n* **(pl) 12** *information*
ordliste *n* **(en)** *word list*
organisasjon *n* **(en) 12** *organization*
oss *p* **6** *us*
ost *n* **(en) 3** *cheese*
over *pre, adv* **2** *over, more than*
overnatte *v* **(1) 10** *stay overnight*
ovn *n* **(en) 13** *stove, oven*

pakke *v* **(1) 6** *pack*
papir *n* **(et) 5** *paper*
par *n* **(et) 6** *couple*
parafinlampe *n* **(en) 13** *paraffin lamp*
park *n* **(en) 4** *park*
parkeringsplass *n* **(en) 13** *parking place*
pasient *n* **(en) 6** *patient*
pass *n* **(et) 2** *passport*
passasjer *n* **(en) 3** *passenger*
passe *v* **(1) 3** *mind, look after*

passe *v* **(1) 9** *fit*
passe til 9 *go with*
peis *n* **(en) 13** *fireplace*
pen *a* **4** *pretty*
penere *a* **9** *prettier*
penger *n* **(pl) 5** *money*
pensjonat *n* **(en) 16** *guesthouse*
person *n* **(en) 15** *person*
personalsjef *n* **(en) 12** *personnel director*
piggdekk *n* **(et) 13** *studded tyre*
pike *n* **(en) 4** *girl*
pille *n* **(en) 9** *pill*
pinnekjøtt *n* **(et) 11** *mutton dish*
plan *n* **(en) 16** *plan*
plass *n* **(en) 3** *space, place*
plassbillett *n* **(en) 6** *booked seat*
plaster *n* **(et) 8** *plaster*
plikt *n* **(en) 10** *duty*
ploge *v* **(1) 13** *plough*
plutselig *a, adv* **6** *suddenly*
Polarsirkelen 5 *the Arctic Circle*
politimann *n* **(en) 14** *policeman*
pommes frites *n* **(pl) 8** *chips*
pop-konsert *n* **(en) 5** *pop concert*
porsjon *n* **(en) 3** *portion*
port *n* **(en) 4** *gate*
poste *v* **(1) 11** *post*
potet *n* **(en) 8** *potato*
prate *v* **(1) 10** *chatter*
presang *n* **(en) 11** *present*
primitiv *a* **13** *primitive*
prins *n* **(en) 14** *prince*
program *n* **(et) 11** *programme*
prosesjon *n* **(en) 14** *procession*
provins *n* **(en) 14** *province*
prøve *v* **(3) 9** *try*
prøverom *n* **(et) 9** *changing room*
pub *n* **(en) 2** *pub*
pynt *n* **(en) 11** *decoration*
pynte *v* **(1) 11** *decorate*
pølse *n* **(en) 3** *sausage*
på *pre* **2** *on, at*
på gjensyn! 1 *See you (soon)!*
på vegne av 10 *on behalf of*
påkjørt *a* **8** *run over*
påske *n* **(en) 12** *Easter*

rakett *n* **(en) 11** *rocket, fireworks*
rart *adv* **16** *strange*
redd *a* **13** *frightened*
reddhare *n* **(en) 13** *coward*
redningsvest *n* **(en) 15** *life jacket*
regne *v* **(1) 5** *rain*
regning *n* **(en) 15** *bill*
reise *v* **(2) 1** *travel*
reise *n* **(en) 6** *journey*
reisesjekk *n* **(en) 5** *traveller's cheque*
reisesykemiddel *n* **(et) 9** *travelsickness remedy*
reke *n* **(en/ei) 3** *prawn*
rekved *n* **(en) 15** *driftwood*
ren *a* **13** *clean*
resepsjon *n* **(en) 12** *reception*
respekt *n* **(en) 15** *respect*
rest *n* **(en) 5** *rest*
restaurant *n* **(en) 3** *restaurant*
returbillett *n* **(en) 6** *return ticket*
riksvei *n* **(en) 6** *main road*
ringe *v* **(2) 6** *ring*
riste *v* **(1) 3** *toast, shake*
rom *n* **(et) 8** *room*
rope *v* **(2) 14** *shout*
rundstykke *n* **(et) 3** *bread roll*
rundt *pre, adv* **4** *around*

russisk *a* **7** *Russian*
rutet *a* **9** *checked*
rydde *v* **(1) 7** *tidy*
ryggsekk *n* **(en) 13** *rucksack*
rød *a* **8** *red*
rødvin *n* **(en) 3** *red wine*
røkelaks *n* **(en) 10** *smoked salmon*
røre *v* **(2) 8** *touch*
røre seg *v* **(2) 8** *move*
rørt *a* **10** *touched, moved*
rådhus *n* **(et) 4** *city/town hall*

saft *n* **(en) 7** *juice, squash*
sak *n* **(en) 15** *matter, case*
sakte *a* **11** *slow*
salat *n* **(en) 3** *salad*
samboer *n* **(en) 16** *live-in partner*
samme *a* **9** *same*
sammen *adv* **2** *together*
samtale *n* **(en) 12** *dialogue*
sann *a* **5** *true*
saus *n* **(en) 10** *sauce, gravy*
savne *v* **(1) 9** *miss*
se *v* **(s) 1** *see, look*
se frem til 12 *look forward to*
seddel *n* **(en) 5** *note*
seks 2 *six*
seksten 5 *sixteen*
sekstende 10 *sixteenth*
seksti 5 *sixty*
sekstiende 10 *sixtieth*
selge *v* **(s) 5** *sell*
selskap *n* **(et) 9** *party*
selv *p* **7** *-self*
selv om *c* **3** *even if*
selvfølgelig *a, adv* **11** *of course*
selvstendig *a* **14** *independent*
semester *n* **(et) 9** *term, semester*
sen *a* **6** *late*
sende *v* **(2) 5** *send*
senere *adv* **6** *later*
seng *n* **(en/ei) 8** *bed*
sennep *n* **(en) 8** *mustard*
sent *adv* **2** *late*
september 10 *September*
sertifikat *n* **(et) 3** *driving licence*
servere *v* **(2) 15** *serve*
servitør *n* **(en) 15** *waiter*
sette *v* **(s) 11** *place, put*
sette i gang 13 *start*
sette opp *v* **(s) 8** *set up*
sette seg 10 *sit down*
si *v* **(s) 5** *say*
side *n* **(en) 3** *side*
siden *c* **6** *since*
sikker *a* **12** *sure*
sikkert 4 *certainly*
sild *n* **(en/ei) 3** *herring*
sin *p* **5** *his, her(s)*
sint *a* **4** *cross, angry*
sist *a* **9** *last*
situasjon *n* **(en) 13** *situation*
sjalu *a* **14** *jealous*
sjef *n* **(en) 12** *boss*
sjette 10 *sixth*
sjokolade *n* **(en) 13** *chocolate*
sju 2 *seven*
sjuende 10 *seventh*
sjø *n* **(en) 4** *sea*
skandinavisk *a* **3** *Scandinavian*
ski *n* **(en/ei) 13** *ski*
skifte *v* **(1) 7** *change*
skikk *n* **(en) 11** *custom, tradition*
skilles *v* **(2) 15** *get divorced*
skilt *a* **16** *separated*

saus *n* **(en) 8** *sauce*
skinne *v* **(2) 4** *shine*
skitten *a* **15** *dirty*
skitur *n* **(en) 13** *skiing trip*
skje *n* **(en) 9** *spoon*
skjev *a* **8** *crooked*
skjorte *n* **(en/ei) 9** *shirt*
skjørt *n* **(et) 7** *skirt*
sko *n* **(en) 9** *shoe*
skole *n* **(en) 2** *school*
skolebarn *n* **(et) 14** *pupil, school child*
skoletid *n* **(en) 10** *school time*
skrike *v* **(s) 7** *cry, scream*
skrive *v* **(s) 5** *write*
skrå *a* **13** *crooked*
skulder *n* **(en) 8** *shoulder*
skulle *v* **(modal) 1** *shall*
skulptur *n* **(en) 1** *statue, sculpture*
skynde seg *v* **(2) 16** *hurry*
skål! 3 *cheers!*
skåle *v* **(2) 10** *say* **'skål'**
slik *a, adv* **15** *like this*
slik at *c* **13** *so that*
slott *n* **(et) 4** *palace*
slutt *n* **(en) 12** *end*
slå *v* **(s) 6** *hit, dial*
smak *n* **(en) 9** *taste*
smake *v* **(2) 11** *taste*
smal *a* **9** *narrow*
smart *a* **9** *smart*
smelle *v* **(2) 11** *bang*
smelte *v* **(1) 13** *melt*
smil *n* **(et) 10** *smile*
smile *v* **(2) 5** *smile*
smilende *a* **10** *smiling*
smør *n* **(et) 4** *butter*
småbåt *n* **(en) 15** *small boat*
snakke *v* **(1) 3** *talk*
snart *adv* **6** *soon*
snekker *n* **(en) 12** *carpenter*
snill *a* **7** *good, kind*
snø *n* **(en) 11** *snow*
snø *v* **(4) 11** *snow*
snødekt *a* **16** *snow-covered*
snøfnugg *n* **(et) 9** *snow flake*
sokk *n* **(en) 9** *sock*
sol *n* **(en) 3** *sun*
solbriller *n* **(pl) 13** *sun glasses*
solbrun *a* **16** *sun-tanned*
solkrem *n* **(en) 13** *suntan lotion*
som *p* **2** *who, which, that*
som *c* **8** *like, as*
som om *c* **16** *as if*
sommer *n* **(en) 1** *summer*
sommerklær *n* **(pl) 14** *summer clothes*
sove *v* **(s) 7** *sleep*
soverom *n* **(et) 13** *bedroom*
spa *v* **(4) 13** *dig*
speil *n* **(et) 8** *mirror*
spennende *a* **12** *exciting*
spesielt *adv* **9** *especially*
spille *v* **(2) 14** *play*
spise *v* **(2) 3** *eat*
spøk *n* **(en) 16** *joke*
spørre *v* **(s) 7** *ask*
stadig *adv* **12** *often, steadily*
stakkars *a* **8** *poor*
starte *v* **(1) 15** *start, begin*
stasjon *n* **(en) 5** *station*
stativ *n* **(et) 5** *stand*
sted *n* **(et) 8** *place*
stemme *n* **(en) 16** *voice*
sterk *a* **13** *strong*
stil *n* **(en) 9** *style*

stille *adv* **8** *still*
stilling *n* **(en) 12** *position*
sting *n* **(et) 8** *stitch*
stol *n* **(en) 13** *chair*
stoppe *v* **(1) 4** *stop*
stor *a* **2** *big*
Stortinget 5 *the Norwegian Parliament*
strengt *adv* **3** *strictly*
strømme *v* **(1) 16** *stream*
strømpe *n* **(en) 9** *stocking*
strømpebukse *n* **(en) 9** *tights*
student *n* **(en) 1** *student*
studere *v* **(2) 1** *study*
studielån *n* **(et) 16** *study loan*
studium *n* **(et) 12** *study course*
stue *n* **(en/ei) 10** *living room*
stund *n* **(en) 6** *time, while*
stygg *a* **9** *ugly*
stykke *n* **(et) 16** *bit*
størrelse *n* **(en) 9** *size*
støttebandasje *n* **(en) 9** *support bandage*
støvel *n* **(en) 9** *boot*
stå *v* **(s) 8** *stand*
sulten *a* **3** *hungry*
svak *a* **7** *weak*
svare *v* **(2) 6** *answer*
svart *a* **8** *black*
svensk *a* **14** *Swedish*
Sverige 2 *Sweden*
svinge *v* **(2) 13** *turn*
svoger *n* **(en) 7** *brother-in-law*
svømmehall *n* **(en) 13** *swimming-pool*
sykehus *n* **(et) 8** *hospital*
sykepleier *n* **(en) 8** *nurse*
sykeseng *n* **(en/ei) 8** *hospital bed*
sykkel *n* **(en) 1** *bicycle*
synd *n* **(en) 14** *pity*
synes *v* **(s) 4** *think, find*
synge *v* **(s) 11** *sing*
sytten 5 *seventeen*
syttende 10 *seventeenth*
sytti 5 *seventy*
syttiende 10 *seventieth*
særlig *adv* **14** *especially*
søker *n* **(en) 12** *applicant*
søndag 2 *Sunday*
sør 16 *south*
sørover 8 *southwards*
søsken *n* **7** *siblings*
søster *n* **(en/ei) 7** *sister*
søt *a* **4** *sweet*
søvn *n* **(en) 16** *sleep*
så *c, adv* **2** *so, subsequently*
så ... som *c* **8** *as ... as*
så vidt 11 *hardly*
sånn *a* **13** *such*
sår *n* **(et) 8** *wound*
såre *v* **(1) 14** *hurt, wound*

ta *v* **(s) 2** *take*
ta seg *av* **7** *take care of*
takk 1 *thank you*
takk i like måte 11 *thank you, the same*
takke *v* **(1) 10** *thank*
tale *n* **(en) 10** *speech*
tale *v* **(2) 10** *speak*
tankeløs *a* **12** *thoughtless*
tannlege *n* **(en) 6** *dentist*
tante *n* **(en) 2** *aunt*
te *n* **(en) 3** *tea*
teater *n* **(et) 5** *theatre*
teaterstykke *n* **(et) 5** *play*

telefon *n* **(en) 6** *telephone*
telefonkatalog *n* **(en) 6** *directory*
televisjon *n* **(en) 10** *television*
telt *n* **(et) 6** *tent*
tenke *v* **(2) 8** *think*
tenke seg *v* **(2) 16** *imagine*
tenne *v* **(2) 11** *light*
termos *n* **(en) 15** *Thermos*
ti 2 *ten*
ti over 11 *ten past*
ti på 11 *ten to*
tid *n* **(en/ei) 2** *time*
tidevannsstrøm *n* **(en) 16** *tidal flow*
tidlig *a, adv* **10** *early*
tiende 10 *tenth*
til *pre* **1** *to, till*
til felles 7 *in common*
til slutt 10 *at the end*
tilbake *adv* **3** *back*
tilbud *n* **(et) 13** *offer*
tilby *v* **(s) 16** *offer*
tilgi *v* **(s) 14** *forgive*
time *n* **(en) 3** *hour*
tirsdag 2 *Tuesday*
tjue 5 *twenty*
tjueen 5 *twenty-one*
tjueførste 10 *twenty-first*
tjuende 10 *twentieth*
to 2 *two*
toalett *n* **(et) 15** *toilet*
tog *n* **(et) 1** *train*
tog *n* **(et) 14** *parade*
tolv 5 *twelve*
tolvte 10 *twelfth*
topp *n* **(en) 8** *peak*
tore *v* **(modal) 13** *dare*
torsdag 2 *Thursday*
tradisjon *n* **(en) 11** *tradition*
trafikk *n* **(en) 15** *traffic*
travel *a* **12** *busy*
tre 2 *three*
tre *n* **(et) 11** *tree*
trebygning *n* **(en) 16** *wooden building*
tredje 8 *third*
treffe *v* **(s) 8** *meet*
trenge *v* **(2) 5** *need*
trepanel *n* **(en) 13** *wood panelling*
trett *a* **13** *tired*
tretten 5 *thirteen*
trettende 10 *thirteenth*
tretti 5 *thirty*
trettiende 10 *thirtieth*
trikk *n* **(en) 4** *tram*
trimrom *n* **(et) 15** *gym*
trives *v* **(s) 16** *thrive*
tro *v* **(4) 3** *believe*
troll *n* **(et) 9** *troll, ogre*
truse *n* **(en) 9** *pants*
trøye *n* **(en) 9** *vest*
tulling *n* **(en) 13** *idiot*
tung *a* **13** *heavy*
tur *n* **(en) 7** *trip*
tur *n* **(en) 10** *turn*
turisme *n* **(en) 12** *tourism*
turistinformasjon *n* **(en) 5** *tourist information*
turkis *a* **9** *turquoise*
tusen 5 *thousand*
tusenvis 5 *thousands*
tykk *a* **4** *thick, fat*
tynn *a* **15** *thin*
typisk *a* **3** *typical*
tømmerhytte *n* **(en/ei) 13** *timber cabin*

tørke *v* **(1) 10** *dry*
tørr *a* **7** *dry*
tørst *a* **3** *thirsty*
tå *n* **(en/ei) 8** *toe*
tålmodig *a* **14** *patient*
tåre *n* **(en) 10** *tear*
tårn *n* **(et) 4** *tower*

uke *n* **(en/ei) 5** *week*
ull *n* **(en) 9** *wool*
ulykke *n* **(en) 8** *accident*
under *pre* **11** *under*
underbukse *n* **(en/ei) 9** *underpants*
undersøke *v* **(2) 8** *examine*
ung *a* **9** *young*
unge *n* **(en) 14** *child, kid*
union *n* **(en) 14** *union*
universitet *n* **(et) 9** *university*
unnskyld 5 *excuse me*
urmaker *n* **(en) 12** *watch-maker*
ut *adv* **4** *out*
ute *adv* **4** *out*
uten *pre* **8** *without*
utenfor *adv, pre* **13** *outside*
utkjørt *a* **14** *exhausted*
utland *n* **(et) 16** *abroad*
utrolig *a* **16** *unbelievable*
utsikt *n* **(en) 8** *view*
utstilling *n* **(en) 5** *exhibition*
utålmodig *a* **11** *impatient*

vaffel *n* **(en) 10** *waffle*
vakker *a* **4** *beautiful*
vaktmester *n* **(en) 12** *caretaker*
vaniljesaus *n* **(en) 3** *custard*
vanlig *a* **13** *usual*
vann *n* **(et) 4** *water*
vannmasse *n* **(en) 16** *mass of water*
vanskelig *a* **6** *difficult*
vant til 13 *used to*
vare *v* **(2) 14** *last*
varm *a* **8** *warm*
vaske *v* **(1) 7** *wash*
vaske opp *v* **(1) 7** *do the dishes*
vaske seg *v* **(1) 13** *wash oneself*
vaskerom *n* **(et) 13** *washroom*
ved pre 5 *by, at, near*
ved siden *av* **13** *next to*
vedlegge *v* **(s) 12** *enclose*
vegg *n* **(en) 13** *wall*
vei *n* **(en) 2** *road*
vekk *adv* **13** *away*
veksle *v* **(1) 5** *change (money)*
veldig *a, adv* **3** *very*
velkommen *a* **10** *welcome*
venn *n* **(en) 3** *friend*
venninne *n* **(en/ei) 10** *female friend*
venstre *a* **4** *left*
vente *v* **(1) 6** *wait*
verden *n* **(en) 14** *world*
verken ... eller *c* **13** *neither ... nor*
verst *a* **6** *worst*
vest 12 *west*
Vestlandet 2 *west Norway*
veterinær *n* **(en) 12** *veterinary surgeon*
vi *p* **2** *we*
videre *adv* **2** *further*
vikingskip *n* **(et) 6** *Viking ship*
viktig *a* **6** *important*
ville *v* **(modal) 1** *will, want*
vin *n* **(en) 3** *wine*

vindu *n* **(et) 11** *window*
vindusplass *n* **(en) 6** *window seat*
vinke *v* **(1) 14** *wave*
vinter *n* **(en) 12** *winter*
virkelig *adv* **8** *really*
vise *v* **(2) 16** *show*
visst *adv* **10** *certainly*
vite *v* **(s) 5** *know*
voksende *a* **12** *growing*
vond *a* **8** *painful, bad*
vær *n* **(et) 6** *weather*
vær så god 6 *can I help you?, do help yourself*
være *v* **(s) 2** *be*
våkne *v* **(1) 8** *wake up*
vår *n* **(en) 12** *spring*
vår *p* **7** *our*
våt *a* **8** *wet*

WC *n* **(et)** *WC, toilet*

yngste *a* **7** *youngest*

ærbødigst 12 *yours faithfully*
æsj! 7 *yuk!*

ødelegge *v* **(s) 13** *ruin, spoil*
økonomi *n* **(en) 12** *economics*
øl *n* **(et) 1** *beer, ale*
ønske *v* **(1) 10** *wish*
ønske *n* **(et) 11** *wish*
øre *n* **(en) 5** *1/100th of a krone*
øre *n* **(et) 8** *ear*
øye *n* **(et) 8** *eye*
øyeblikk *n* **(et) 6** *moment*

åpen *a* **4** *open*
åpne *v* **(1) 10** *open*
åpningstid *n* **(en) 5** *opening time*
år *n* **(et) 7** *year*
årsak *n* **(en) 5** *reason*
årstid *n* **(en) 12** *season*
åtte 2 *eight*
åttende 10 *eighth*
åtti 5 *eighty*
åttiende 10 *eightieth*

English–Norwegian vocabulary

n	noun	adv	adverb
(en) (en/ei) (et)	gender	pre	preposition
v	verb	p	pronoun
(s)	strong/irregular verb	c	conjunction
(1) (2) (3) (4)	weak verb group	pl	plural
a	adjective		

The unit in which the word is first used is indicated by a number.

a little **litt** *adv* **3**
accept **akseptere** *v* **(2) 14**
accident **ulykke** *n* **(en) 8**
additional **ekstra** *a, adv* **6**
address **adresse** *n* **(en) 6**
admire **beundre** *v* **(1) 10**
advert **annonse** *n* **(en) 12**
aeroplane **fly** *n* **(et) 1**
after **etter** *adv, pre* **2**
after **all likevel** *adv* **12**
afterwards **etterpå** *adv* **4**
again **igjen** *adv* **4**
ago **for ... siden** *pre* **7**
air **luft** *n* **(en)**
airport **flyplass** *n* **(en) 3**
alcohol **alkohol** *n* **(en) 3**
all (pl) **alle** *p* **4**
allergic **allergisk** *a* **9**
allergy **allergi** *n* **(en) 9**
allowed to, be **få lov til 5**
almost **nesten** *adv* **5**
alone **alene** *adv* **5**
along **langs** *pre* **13**
already **allerede** *adv* **12, alt** *adv* **10**
also **også** *adv* **2**
always **alltid** *adv* **3**
ambulance **ambulanse** *n* **(en) 8**
America **Amerika**
American **amerikansk** *a* **4**
amusing **morsom** *a* **10**
and **og** *c* **1**
angel **engel** *n* **(en) 7**
anorak **anorakk** *n* **(en) 13**
answer **svare** *v* **(2) 6**
apple juice **eplesaft** *n* **(en) 10**
applicant **søker** *n* **(en) 12**
april **april 10**
aquavit **akevitt** *n* **(en) 11**
Arctic Circle, the **Polarsirkelen 16**
argue **krangle** *v* **(1) 6**
arm **arm** *n* **(en) 8**
around **rundt** *pre, adv* **4**
arrive **ankomme** *v* **(s) 15**
artist **kunstmaler** *n* **(en) 12**
ask **spørre** *v* **(s) 7**

at **på** *pre* **2**
at the house of **hos** *pre* **2**
at home **hjemme** *adv* **6**
au pair **au pair** *n* **(en) 1**
august **august 10**
aunt **tante** *n* **(en/ei) 2**
autumn **høst** *n* **(en) 9**
away **borte** *adv* **4, vekk** *adv* **13**
awful **ekkel** *a, adv* **13**

back **tilbake** *adv* **3**
bad **dårlig** *a, adv* **5**
bake **bake** *v* **(2) 10**
balcony **balkong** *n* **(en) 11**
bang **smelle** *v* **(2) 11**
bank **bank** *n* **(en) 5**
bank of snow **brøytekant** *n* **(en) 13**
bank manager **bankdirektør** *n* **(en) 12**
bar **bar** *n* **(en) 3**
barbecue **grille** *v* **(1) 15**
bathe, swim **bade** *v* **(1) 8**
bathroom **bad** *n* **(et) 15**
be **være** *v* **(s) 2**
beating **juling** *n* **(en) 7**
beautiful **vakker** *a* **4**
because **fordi** *c* **2**
become **bli** *v* **(s) 2**
bed **seng** *n* **(en/ei) 8**
bedroom **soverom** *n* **(et) 13**
bedsit **hybel** *n* **(en) 14**
beer **øl** *n* **(et) 1**
before **før** *pre, adv* **6, innen** *adv* **12**
begin **begynne** *v* **(2) 9**
beginner **begynner** *n* **(en) 13**
beginning **begynnelse** *n* **(en) 13**
behind **bak** *pre* **5**
believe **tro** *v* **(4) 3**
bell **klokke** *n* **(en/ei) 6**
belt **belte** *n* **(et) 9**
bend **bøye** *v* **(1) 13**
best **best** *a, adv* **3**
better **bedre** *a, adv* **2**
bicycle **sykkel** *n* **(en) 1**
big **stor** *a* **2**
bill **regning** *n* **(en) 15**
biological **biologisk** *a* **13**
birth, give **føde** *v* **(2) 15**
birthday **fødselsdag** *n* **(en) 10**
bit **stykke** *n* **(et) 16**
black **svart** *a* **8**
blouse **bluse** *n* **(en) 9**
blow **blåse** *v* **(2) 16**
blue **blå** *a* **4**
board, on **ombord 3**
boat **båt** *n* **(en) 15**
body **kropp** *n* **(en) 8**
boil **koke** *v* **(2) 3**
bone **ben** *n* **(et) 9**
bonfire **bål** *n* **(et) 15**
book **bestille** *v* **(2) 2, bok** *n* **(en) 11**
booked seat **plassbillett** *n* **(en) 6**
bookshelf **bokhylle** *n* **(en) 13**
boot **støvel** *n* **(en) 9**
boring **kjedelig** *a* **2**
borrow **låne** *v* **(2) 7**
boss **sjef** *n* **(en) 12**
both **begge** *p* **5, både** *c* **6**
bottle **flaske** *n* **(en/ei) 3**
bowl **fat** *n* **(et) 13**
box **eske** *n* **(en) 9**
boy **gutt** *n* **(en) 4**
bra **bh** *n* **(en) 9**

brass band **musikk-korps** *n* **(et) 14**
brat **drittunge** *n* **(en) 7**
bread roll **rundstykke** *n* **(et) 3**
bread **brød** *n* **(et) 3**
break **brekke** *v* **(s) 8**
breakfast **frokost** *n* **(en) 3**
breast **bryst** *n* **(et) 14**
bridge **bro** *n* **(en) 4**
british **britisk** *a* **4**
brochure **brosjyre** *n* **(en) 5**
bronze **bronse** *n* **(en) 4**
brother **bror** *n* **(en) 7**
brother-in-law **svoger** *n* **(en) 7**
brown **brun** *a* **4**
bucket **bøtte** *n* **(en) 13**
building **bygning** *n* **(en) 4**
bun **bolle** *n* **(en) 7**
bunk **køye** *n* **(en/ei) 3**
burn **brenne** *v* **(s) 15**
bus **buss** *n* **(en) 3**
business **forretning** *n* **(en) 12**
busy **travel** *a* **13**
but **men** *c* **1**
butter **smør** *n* **(et) 4**
buy **kjøpe** *v* **(2) 5**
by **av** *pre* **3, ved** *pre* **5**
by, with **hos** *pre* **2**

cabin **lugar** *n* **(en) 3**
café **kafé** *n* **(en) 12**
cafeteria **kafeteria** *n* **(en) 3**
cake **kake** *n* **(en/ei) 10**
called, be **hete** *v* **(s) 1**
camera **kamera** *n* **(et) 16**
campsite **campingplass** *n* **(en) 8**
candle **lys** *n* **(et) 10**
cap **lue** *n* **(en/ei) 9**
car **bil** *n* **(en) 1**
car key **bilnøkkel** *n* **(en) 7**
car trip **biltur** *n* **(en) 16**
card **kort** *n* **(et) 5**
careful **forsiktig** *a, adv* **13**
caretaker **vaktmester** *n* **(en) 12**
carpenter **snekker** *n* **(en) 12**
casserole **gryterett** *n* **(en) 10**
castle **festning** *n* **(en) 4**
cat **katt** *n* **(en/ei) 15**
celebrate **feire** *v* **(1) 11**
certain **bestemt** *a* **13**
certainly **sikkert** *adv* **16, visst** *adv* **10**
chair **stol** *n* **(en)**
change **forandre** *v* **(1) 4, skifte** *v* **(1) 7**
change (money) **veksle** *v* **(1) 5**
changing room **prøverom** *n* **(et) 9**
chatter **prate** *v* **(1) 10**
cheap **billig** *a* **6**
checked **rutet** *a* **9**
cheers **skål 3**
cheese **ost** *n* **(en) 3**
chemist **farmasøyt** *n* **(en) 9**
child **barn** *n* **(et) 7**
child **unge** *n* **(en) 14**
childhood **barndom** *n* **(en) 10**
childhood home **barndomshjem** *n* **(et) 10**
chips **pommes frites** *n (pl)* **8**
chives **gressløk** *n* **(en) 10**
chocolate **sjokolade** *n* **(en) 13**
Christmas **jul** *n* **(en/ei) 10**
church **kirke** *n* **(en) 11**
church bell **kirkeklokke** *n* **(en/ei) 11**
church service **gudstjeneste** *n* **(en) 11**

cinema **kino** *n* **(en) 2**
clean **ren** *a* **13**
clever **flink** *a* **10**
clock **klokke** *n* **(en/ei) 6**
clothes **klær** *n* **(pl) 9**
cloudberry **multe** *n* **(en) 11**
coast **kyst** *n* **(en) 16**
coat (lady's) **kåpe** *n* **(en/ei) 9**
coat **jakke** *n* **(en/ei) 7**
coffee **kaffe** *n* **(en) 1**
coin **mynt** *n* **(en) 5**
cold **kald** *a* **8**
cold, suffering from a **forkjølet** *a* **9**
cold buffet **koldtbord** *n* **(et) 3**
colleague **kollega** *n* **(en) 9**
collect **hente** *v* **(1) 6**
colour **farge** *n* **(en) 9, farge** *v* **(1) 11**
come **komme** *v* **(s) 1**
common **felles** *a* **7**
complain **klage** *v* **(1) 15**
completely **helt** *adv* **8**
concert **konsert** *n* **(en) 5**
concussion **hjernerystelse** *n* **(en) 8**
condition **betingelse** *n* **(en) 16**
congratulate **gratulere** *v* **(2) 10**
consequently **altså** *adv* **6**
constipation **forstoppelse** *n* **(en) 9**
constitution **grunnlov** *n* **(en) 14**
contact **kontakt** *n* **(en) 9**
coral red **korallrød** *a* **9**
cost **koste** *v* **(1) 5**
cosy, pleasant **koselig** *a* **10**
cottage **hytte** *n* **(en/ei) 13**
cotton **bomull** *n* **(en) 9**
cough **hoste** *v* **(1) 9**
cough medicine **hostesaft** *n* **(en) 9**
counter **disk** *n* **(en) 5**
country **land** *n* **(et) 14**
couple **par** *n* **(et) 6**
course **kurs** *n* **(et) 2**
cousin (f) **kusine** *n* **(en) 7**
cousin (m) **fetter** *n* **(en) 7**
coward **reddhare** *n* **(en) 13**
cream **krem** *n* **(en) 11**
credit card **kredittkort** *n* **(et) 15**
crème caramel **karamellpudding** *n* **(en) 10**
crooked **skjev** *a* *8*
cross **sint** *a* *4*
crown prince **kronprins** *n* **(en) 14**
cry **skrike** *v* **(s) 7**
cup **kopp** *n* **(en) 1**
cured salmon **gravlaks** *n* **(en) 3**
curtain **gardin** *n* **(en) 13**
custard **vaniljesaus** *n* **(en) 3**
custom **skikk** *n* **(en) 11**
customer **kunde** *n* **(en) 9**
cut **klippe** *v* **(1) 8**

dance **dans** *n* **(en) 10, danse** *v* **(1) 10**
dangerous **farlig** *a* **13**
Danish **dansk** *a* **14**
dare **tore** *v* **(modal) 13**
dark **mørk** *a* **8**
date **dato** *n* **(en)**
day **dag** *n* **(en) 2**
dear **kjære 10**
December **desember 10**
decorate **pynte** *v* **(1) 11**
decoration **pynt** *n* **(en) 11**
deep **dyp** *a* **13**
delicious **deilig** *a* **10**
Denmark **Danmark 14**
dentist **tannlege** *n* **(en) 6**

departure **avgang** *n* **(en) 6**
dial **slå** *v* **(s) 6**
diaper **bleie** *n* **(en) 7**
diarrhoea **diaré** *n* **(en) 8**
different **forskjellig** *a, adv* **16**
difficult **vanskelig** *a* **6**
dig **spa** *v* **(4) 13**
dinner **middag** *n* **(en) 3**
director **direktør** *n* **(en) 2**
directory **telefonkatalog** *n* **(en) 6**
dirty **skitten** *a* **15**
dissatisfied **misfornøyd** *a* **15**
divide **dividere** *v* **(2) 6**
division **divisjon** *n* **(en) 6**
divorced, get **skilles** *v* **(2) 15**
do **gjøre** *v* **(s) 5**
doctor **lege** *n* **(en) 8**
dog **hund** *n* **(en) 15**
door **dør** *n* **(en/ei) 5**
doorbell **dørklokke** *n* **(en/ei) 10**
double **dobbel** *a* **15**
down **ned** *pre* **5**
dress **kjole** *n* **(en) 9**
driftwood **rekved** *n* **(en) 15**
drink **drikke** *v* **(s) 3, drink** *n* **(en) 10**
drive **kjøre** *v* **(2) 2**
driver **bilist** *n* **(en) 13**
driving licence **sertifikat** *n* **(et) 3**
dry **tørke** *v* **(1) 10, tørr** *a* **7**
duty **plikt** *n* **(en) 10**

each **hver** *p* **2**
each other **hverandre** *p* **5**
eager **ivrig** *a* **13**
ear **øre** *n* **(et) 8**
early **tidlig** *a, adv* **10**
earth **jord** *n* **(en) 13**
Easter **påske** *n* **(en) 12**
easy **lett** *a* **5**
eat **spise** *v* **(2) 3**
economics **økonomi** *n* **(en) 12**
egg **egg** *n* **(et) 3**
eight **åtte 2**
eighteen **atten 5**
eighty **åtti 5**
electricity **elektrisitet** *n* **(en) 13**
elegant **elegant** *a* **9**
eleven **elleve 5**
eleventh **ellevte 10**
embassy **ambassade** *n* **(en) 4**
enclose **vedlegge** *v* **(s) 12**
end **ende** *n* **(en) 5, slutt** *n* **(en) 12**
engineer **ingeniør** *n* **(en) 10**
English **engelsk** *a* **1**
enjoy **nyte** *v* **(s) 16**
enough **nok** *adv* **3**
especially **spesielt** *adv* **9, særlig** *adv* **14**
Europe **Europa** *n* **2**
evening **kveld** *n* **(en) 2**
everything **alt** *p* **5**
examine **undersøke** *v* **(2) 8**
exciting **spennende** *a* **12**
excuse me **unnskyld 5**
exhausted **utkjørt** *a* **14**
exhibition **utstilling** *n* **(en) 5**
expensive **dyr** *a* **9**
experience **erfaring** *n* **(en) 12, oppleve** *v* **(3) 11**
explain **forklare** *v* **(2) 5**
eye **øye** *n* **(et) 8**

face **ansikt** *n* **(et) 8**
fairly **nokså**
faithfully, yours **ærbødigst 12**

fall **falle** *v* **(s) 13**
family **familie** *n* **(en) 6**
family party **familieselskap** *n* **(et) 10**
fantastic **fantastisk** *a* **8**
far **langt** *adv* **4**
fashion **mote** *n* **(en) 9**
fast **fort** *a, adv* **12**
fat **tykk** *a* **4**
father **far** *n* **(en) 6**
February **februar 10**
fed up with **lei av 9**
feel **føle seg** *v* **(2) 9**
ferry **ferge** *n* **(en) 2**
festive **festlig** *a* **10**
fever **feber** *n* **(en) 9**
fifteen **femten 5**
fifth **femte 10**
fifty **femti 5**
fill in **fylle ut** *v* **(2) 15**
film **film** *n* **(en) 2**
find **finne** *v* **(s) 5**
fine **fin** *a* **3**
finger **finger** *n* **(en) 8**
fireplace **peis** *n* **(en) 13**
fireworks **fyrverkeri** *n* **(et) 11**
firm **firma** *n* **(et) 10**
first **først** *adv* **4**
fish n **fisk** *n* **(en) 3, fiske** *v* **(1) 16**
fit **passe** *v* **(1) 9**
five **fem 2**
fjord **fjord** *n* **(en) 15**
flag **flagg** *n* **(et) 11**
flat **leilighet** *n* **(en) 7**
floor **etasje** *n* **(en) 8**
follow **følge** *v* **(s) 10**
fond of **glad i 7**
food **mat** *n* **(en) 3**
foot **fot** *n* **(en) 8**
football **fotball** *n* **(en) 12**
for **for** *pre* **5**
forbidden **forbudt** *a* **3**
forget **glemme** *v* **(2) 3**
forgive **tilgi** *v* **(s) 14**
form **forme** *v* **(1) 11**
forty **førti 5**
forward **forover** *adv* **13**
forward **frem** *adv* **11**
found, can be **finnes** *v* **(s) 15**
fountain **fontene** *n* **(en) 4**
four **fire 2**
fourteen **fjorten 5**
fourth **fjerde 10**
free **fri** *a, adv* **15**
freeze **fryse** *v* **(s) 13**
French **fransk** *a* **7**
Friday **fredag 2**
friend **venn** *n* **(en) 3**
friend (female) **venninne** *n* **(en) 10**
frightened **redd** *a* **13**
from **fra** *pre* **1**
from here **herfra** *adv* **14**
fruit **frukt** *n* **(en) 10**
full **full** *a* **6**
fun **gøy** *adv* **13, kul** *(slang) a* **14**
funtime **moro** *n* **(en/ei) 10**
further **videre** *adv* **2**
future **fremtid** *n* **(en) 16**

garden **hage** *n* **(en) 7**
gate **port** *n* **(en) 4**
gateau **bløtkake** *n* **(en) 10**
get **få** *v* **(s) 3**
get hold of **få tak i 7**
get to know **bli kjent med 10**

get well soon **god bedring 8**
girl **jente** *n* **(en/ei) 13, pike** *n* **(en) 4**
give **gi** *v* **(s) 7**
give birth **føde** *v* **(2) 15**
give in **gi opp 16**
gladly **gjerne** *adv* **1**
glass **glass** *n* **(et) 1**
go **gå** *v* **(s) 1**
go **dra** *v* **(s) 15**
goat cheese **geitost** *n* **(en) 4**
good **god** *a* **2**
Gothenburg **Gøteborg 3**
grandchild **barnebarn** *n* **(et) 7**
grandfather (paternal) **farfar** *n* **(en) 7**
grandfather (maternal) **morfar,** *n* **(en) 7**
grandmother (paternal) **farmor,** *n* **(en) 7**
grandmother (maternal) **mormor,** *n* **(en) 7**
grandparents **besteforeldre** *n* **7**
granite **granitt** *n* **(en) 4**
gravy **brun saus, saus** *n* **(en) 8**
green **grønn** *a* **4**
greet **hilse** *v* **(2) 6**
greeting **hilsen** *n* **(en) 11**
grey **grå** *a* **9**
growing **voksende** *a* **12**
gruesome **fæl a 9**
guest **gjest** *n* **(en) 10**
guesthouse **pensjonat** *n* **(et) 16**
guitar **gitar** *n* **(en) 15**
gym **trimrom** *n* **(et) 15**

hairdresser **frisør** *n* **(en) 6**
half **halv 11**
hand **hånd** *n* **(en/ei) 8**
hang **henge** *v* **(2) 9**
happen **hende** *v* **(2) 12**
happy **glad** *a, adv* **7**
hard **hard** *a* **2**
hat **hatt** *n* **(en) 9**
have **ha** *v* **(s) 1**
he **han** *p* **1**
head **hode** *n* **(et) 8**
headache **hodepine** *n* **(en) 9**
headache pill **hodepinetablett** *n* **(en) 9**
healthy, well **frisk** *a* **8**
hear **høre** *v* **(2) 6**
heavy **tung** *a* **13**
help **hjelp** *n* **(en), hjelpe** *v* **(s) 5**
help oneself **forsyne seg** *v* **(2) 10**
her **henne** *p* **2**
here **her** *adv* **3**
herring **sild** *n* **(en) 3**
hers **hennes** *p* **6**
hi **hei 1**
high **høy** *a* **8**
him **ham** *p* **7**
history **historie** *n* **(en) 14**
hit **slå** *v* **(s) 6**
hold **holde** *v* **(s) 6**
holiday **ferie** *n* **(en) 2**
home **hjem** *adv* **6**
hope **håpe** *v* **(1) 10**
horse **hest** *n* **(en) 14**
hospital **sykehus** *n* **(et) 8**
hotel **hotell** *n* **(et) 2**
hotel business **hotellbransje** *n* **(en) 12**
hour **time** *n* **(en) 3**
house **hus** *n* **(et) 4**
how **hvordan** *adv* **1, hvor** *adv* **8**

hug **klem** *n* **(en) 7, klemme** *v* **(2) 11**
humour **humør** *n* **(et) 5**
hundred **hundre 5**
hungry **sulten** *a* **3**
hurry **skynde seg** *v* **(2) 16**
hurt **såre** *v* **(1) 14**

I **jeg** *p* **1**
ice cream **is** *n* **(en) 7**
idea **idé** *n* **(en) 14**
idiot **idiot** *n* **(en), tulling** *n* **(en) 13**
if **hvis** *c* **2**
imagine **tenke seg 16**
impatient **utålmodig** *a* **11**
important **viktig** *a* **6**
in **i** *pre* **1**
in, about **om** *pre* **4**
in front of **foran** *adv, pre* **13**
in love **forelsket** *a* **14**
include **inkludere** *v* **(2) 15**
independent **selvstendig** *a* **14**
inform **meddele** *v* **(2) 12**
inside **inne** *adv* **7**
installation **anlegg** *n* **(et) 10**
interested **interessert** *a* **9**
interesting **interessant** *a* **11**
into **inn** *i* **3**
invite **invitere** *v* **(2) 10**
islet **holme** *n* **(en) 15**
it **den, det** *p* **4**
itch **klø** *v* **(4) 9**

jacket **jakke** *n* **(en/ei) 7**
January **januar 10**
jealous **sjalu** *a* **14**
jeans **ola-bukser** *n* **(en) 8**
jelly **gelé** *n* **(en) 3**
job **jobb** *n* **(en) 7**
joke **spøk** *n* **(en) 16**
juice **saft** *n* **(en) 7**
July **juli 2**
June **juni 10**
just **nettopp** *adv* **9, like** *adv* **12**

key **nøkkel** *n* **(en) 15**
kill **drepe** *v* **(2) 7**
kind **snill** *a* **7**
king **konge** *n* **(en) 4**
kiosk **kiosk** *n* **(en) 5**
kiss **kyss** *n* **(et), kysse** *v* **(1) 11**
kitchen **kjøkken** *n* **(et) 10**
knee **kne** *n* **(et) 8**
know (somebody) **kjenne** *v* **(2) 10**
know (as of knowledge) **vite** *v* **(s) 5**

lady **dame** *n* **(en/ei) 2**
lamb **lam** *n* **(et) 10**
lambswool **lammeull** *n* **(en) 9**
last **sist** *adv* **9, vare** *v* **(2) 14**
last year **i fjor 12**
late **sen** *a* **6, sent** *adv* **2**
later **senere** *adv* **6**
laugh **le** *v* **(s) 10**
laughter **latter** *n* **(en) 15**
learn **lære** *v* **(2) 1**
left **venstre** *a* **4**
leg **ben** *n* **(et) 9**
less **mindre** *adv* **9**
letter **brev** *n* **(et) 12**
lie **ligge** *v* **(s) 4**
life **liv** *n* **(et) 12**
life jacket **redningsvest** *n* **(en) 15**
lift **heis** *n* **(en) 15, løfte** *v* **(1) 10**
light **lys** *n* **(et) 10, lys** *a* **15, tenne** *v* **(2) 11**

like **like** *v* **(2) 2, som** *c* **8**
live **bo** *v* **(4) 1**
lively **livlig** *a* **13**
living room **stue** *n* **(en/ei) 10**
log cabin **tømmerhytte** *n* **(en/ei) 13**
lonely **ensom** *a* **14**
long **lang** *a* **3**
long time **lenge** *adv* **5**
loo **do** *n* **(en) 13**
look **se** *v* **(s)** *s* **1**
look forward to **glede seg til 2**
look like **likne** *v* **(1) 4**
lorry **lastebil** *n* **(en) 3**
love **elske** *v* **(1) 10**
lovely **nydelig** *a* **16**
luckily **heldigvis** *adv* **9**
lucky **heldig** *a* **6**
lunch **lunsj** *n* **(en) 15**

main **hoved- 11**
main road **riksvei** *n* **(en) 6**
main street **hovedgate** *n* **(en) 4**
majesty **majestet** *n* **(en) 12**
make **lage** *v* **(1) 4**
man **mann** *n* **(en) 5**
manager **direktør** *n* **(en) 2**
many **mange** *p,a* **3**
map **kart** *n* **(et) 2**
March **mars 10**
march **marsj** *n* **(en) 14**
married to **gift med 7**
marry **gifte seg** *v* **(1) 7**
marzipan **marsipan** *n* **(en) 11**
mayonnaise **majones** *n* **(en) 8**
me **meg** *p* **2**
meal **måltid** *n* **(et) 11**
mean **mene** *v* **(2) 5**
meat **kjøtt** *n* **(et) 3**
meat ball **kjøttkake** *n* **(en/ei) 8**
medicine **medisin** *n* **(en) 9**
meet **møte** *v* **(s) 1, treffe** *v* **(s) 8**
melt **smelte** *v* **(1) 13**
milk **melk** *n* **(en) 3**
mind **passe** *v* **(1) 3**
mineral water **mineralvann** *n* **(et) 10**
minus degree **kuldegrad** *n* **(en) 13**
minute **minutt** *n* **(et) 5**
mirror **speil** *n* **(et) 8**
miss **savne** *v* **(1) 9**
Miss **frøken** *n* **(en) 12**
moment **øyeblikk** *n* **(et) 6**
Monday **mandag 2**
money **penger** *n* **(pl) 5**
monolith **monolitt** *n* **(en) 4**
month **måned** *n* **(en) 7**
more **mer** *a, adv* **3, flere** *a, p* **8**
morning **morgen** *n* **(en) 9**
mother **mor** *n* **(en/ei) 6**
motorbike **motorsykkel** *n* **(en) 1**
motor boat **motorbåt** *n* **(en) 15**
mountain **fjell** *n* **(et) 3**
mountain, high **høyfjell** *n* **(et) 13**
move **flytte** *v* **(1) 12**
move (limbs) **røre seg 8**
Mr **herr 12**
Mrs **fru 12**
much **mye** *adv* **3**
much **meget** *adv* **3**
much too **altfor** *adv* **5**
music **musikk** *n* **(en) 10**
mustard **sennep** *n* **(en) 8**
mutton dish **pinnekjøtt** *n* **(et) 11**
my, mine **min** *p* **2**

nag **mase** *v* **(2) 14**
name **navn** *n* **(et) 5**
nappy **bleie** *n* **(en) 7**
narrow **smal** *a* **9**
national day **nasjonaldag** *n* **(en) 14**
nature **natur** *n* **(en) 8**
nauseous **kvalm** *a* **8**
neck **hals** *n* **(en) 9**
need **trenge** *v* **(2) 5**
neighbour **nabo** *n* **(en) 10**
neighbourhood **omegn** *n* **(en) 14**
nephew **nevø** *n* **(en) 7**
never **aldri** *adv* **11**
new **ny** *a* **7**
New Year **nyttår** *n* **(et) 11**
news on TV **Dagsnytt 11**
newspaper **avis** *n* **(en) 11**
next **neste** *s* **3**
nice, pleasant **hyggelig** *a* **2**
niece **niese** *n* **(en) 7**
night **natt** *n* **(en/ei) 15**
nine **ni 2**
nineteen **nitten 5**
ninety **nitti 5**
no **nei 1**
nobody **ingen** *p* **5**
noise, make a **bråke** *v* **(2) 11**
north **nord 3**
Norway **Norge 1**
Norwegian **nordmann** *n* **(en) 12, norsk** *a* **1**
nose **nese** *n* **(en/ei) 8**
not **ikke** *adv* **1**
note **seddel** *n* **(en) 5**
nothing **ingenting** *p* **16**
now **nå** *adv* **1**
now and then **av og til 16**
nuisance **bry** *n* **(et) 12**
number **nummer** *n* **(et) 6**
nurse **sykepleier** *n* **(en) 8**

occupy **besette** *v* **(s) 12**
ocean **hav** *n* **(et) 8**
October **oktober 10**
of **av** *pre* **3**
of course **selvfølgelig** *adv* **11**
offer **tilbud** *n* **(et) 13, tilby** *v* **(s) 16**
office **kontor** *n* **(et) 12**
often **ofte** *adv* **7, stadig** *adv* **12**
old **gammel** *a* **2**
older **eldre** *a* **16**
oldest **eldst** *a* **7**
on **på** *pre* **2**
on board **ombord 3**
only **bare** *adv* **1**
open **åpen** *a* **4, åpne** *v* **(1) 10**
opening time **åpningstid** *n* **(en) 5**
or **eller** *c* **2**
order **bestille** *v* **(2) 2**
organization **organisasjon** *n* **(en) 12**
others **andre** *p* **6**
ouch! **au! 8**
out **ut** *adv* **4**
outside **ute** *adv* **4**
overcoat **frakk** *n* **(en) 9**
own **egen** *a* **11, eie** *v* **(3) 13**

pack **pakke** *v* **(1) 6**
packed meal **matpakke** *n* **(en), niste** *n* **(en) 15**
painful **vond** *a* **8**
palace **slott** *n* **(et) 4**
pale **blek** *a* **9**
pants **truse** *n* **(en) 9**

paper **papir** *n* **(et) 5**
parade **tog** *n* **(et) 14**
paraffin lamp **parafinlampe** *n* **(en) 13**
parents **foreldre** *n* **(pl) 7**
park **park** *n* **(en) 4**
parking place **parkeringsplass** *n* **(en) 13**
partner, live-in **samboer** *n* **(en) 10**
party **selskap** *n* **(et) 9**
passage **gang** *n* **(en) 13**
passenger **passasjer** *n* **(en) 3**
passport **pass** *n* **(et) 2**
past **forbi** *pre* **4**
patient **pasient** *n* **(en) 6, tålmodig** *a* **14**
pattern **mønster** *n* **(et) 9**
pay **betale** *v* **(2) 3**
peak **topp** *n* **(en) 8**
perhaps **kanskje** *adv* **5**
person **menneske** *n* **(et) 14**
pharmacy **apotek** *n* **(et) 9**
photograph **fotografere** *v* **(2) 16**
picture **bilde** *n* **(et) 11**
pig **gris** *n* **(en) 11**
pill **pille** *n* **(en) 9**
place **sted** *n* **(et) 8**
plan **plan** *n* **(et) 16**
plaster **plaster** *n* **(et) 8**
play **spille** *v* **(2) 14**
play (with toys) **leke** *v* **(2) 7**
playroom **lekerom** *n* **(et) 15**
plough **ploge** *v* **(1) 13**
policeman **politiman** *n* **(en) 14**
poor **stakkars** *a* **8**
population **befolkning** *n* **(en) 14**
portion **porsjon** *n* **(en) 3**
position **stilling** *n* **(en) 12**
possibility **mulighet** *n* **(en) 12**
post **poste** *v* **(1) 11**
potato **potet** *n* **(en) 8**
prawn **reke** *n* **(en/ei) 3**
present **presang** *n* **(en) 11**
pretty **pen** *a* **4**
prince **prins** *n* **(en) 14**
procession **prosesjon** *n* **(en) 14**
programme **program** *n* **(et) 11**
province **provins** *n* **(en) 14**
pub **pub** *n* **(en) 2**
pupil **skolebarn** *n* **(et) 14**
put **legge** *v* **(s) 11**
put **sette** *v* **(s) 10**

qualify **kvalifisere** *v* **(2) 12**
quay **brygge** *n* **(en) 4**
queen **dronning** *n* **(en, ei) 4**
quieten **dempe** *v* **(1) 10**
quite **ganske** *adv* **12**

rain **regne** *v* **(1) 5**
rather **heller** *adv* **2**
reach **nå** *v* **(4) 7**
read **lese** *v* **(2) 11**
ready **ferdig** *a* **12**
really **egentlig** *adv* **14, virkelig** *adv* **8**
reason **årsak** *n* **(en) 5**
receipt **kvittering** *n* **(en) 5**
receive **få** *v* **(s) 3**
red **rød** *a* **9**
red wine **rødvin** *n* **(en) 3**
reference **attest** *n* **(en) 12**
regret **angre** *v* **(1) 16**
remember **huske** *v* **(1) 3**
rent **leie** *v* **(1) 12**
respect **respekt** *n* **(en) 15**

return ticket **returbillett** *n* **(en) 6**
ribbon **bånd** *n* **(et) 14**
right **høyre** *a* **3**
ring **ringe** *v* **(2) 6**
road **vei** *n* **(en) 2**
rocket **rakett** *n* **(en) 11**
room **rom** *n* **(et) 8**
roughly **omtrent 5**
royal family **kongefamilie** *n* **(en) 14**
rucksack **ryggsekk** *n* **(en) 13**
ruin **ødelegge** *v* **(s) 13**
run **løpe** *v* **(2) 14**
run over **påkjørt** *a* **8**
rush **fly** *v* **(s) 13**
Russian **russisk** *a* **7**

salad **salat** *n* **(en) 3**
salmon **laks** *n* **(en) 3**
satisfied **fornøyd** *a* **15**
Saturday **lørdag 2**
sauce **saus** *n* **(en) 10**
sauna **badstue** *n* **(en) 13**
sausage **pølse** *n* **(en) 3**
say **si** *v* **(s) 5**
Scandinavian **skandinavisk** *a* **3**
scar **arr** *n* **(et) 8**
scared (very) **livredd** *a* **13**
school **skole** *n* **(en) 2**
scrambled eggs **eggerøre** *n* **(en) 10**
sculpture **skulptur** *n* **(en) 4**
sea **sjø** *n* **(en) 4**
season **årstid** *n* **(en) 12**
second **andre** *a* **5**
see **se** *v* **(s) 1**
See you (soon) **På gjensyn!! 1**
sell **selge** *v* **(s) 5**
send **sende** *v* **(2) 5**
seriousness **alvor** *n* **(et) 16**
serve **servere** *v* **(2) 15**
seven **sju 2**
seventeen **sytten 5**
seventy **sytti 5**
several **flere** *a* **p 8**
share **dele** *v* **(2) 11**
she **hun** *p* **1**
shine **lyse** *v* **(2) 11, skinne** *v* **(2) 4**
shirt **skjorte** *n* **(en/ei) 9**
shoe **sko** *n* **(en) 9**
shop **butikk** *n* **(en) 9**
short **kort** *a* **9**
shoulder **skulder** *n* **(en) 8**
shout **rope** *v* **(2) 14**
show **vise** *v* **(2) 16**
shower **dusj** *n* **(en) 15**
shut **lukke** *v* **(1) 11**
siblings **søsken** *n* **(pl) 7**
side **side** *n* **(en) 3**
since **siden** *c* **6**
sing **synge** *v* **(s) 11**
sister **søster** *n* **(en/ei) 7**
six **seks 2**
sixteen **seksten 5**
sixty **seksti 5**
size **størrelse** *n* **(en) 9**
ski **ski** *n* **(en/ei) 13**
skiing trip **skitur** *n* **(en) 13**
skirt **skjørt** *n* **(et) 7**
sky **himmel** *n* **(en) 11**
sleep **sove** *v* **(s) 7**
sleeve **erme** *n* **(et) 9**
slide **gli** *v* **(s) 16**
slippery **glatt** *a* **13**
slope **bakke** *n* **(en) 13**
slow **langsom** *a* **13**

slowly **sakte** *adv* **11**
small **liten** *a* **3**
smaller **mindre** *adv* **9**
smile **smil** *n* **(et) 10, smile** *v* **(2) 5**
smiling **smilende** *a* **10**
smoked salmon **røkelaks** *n* **(en) 10**
sneeze **nyse** *v* **(s) 9**
snøfnugg **snowflake** *n* **(et) 9**
snow **snø** *n* **(en) 11, snø** *v* **(4) 11**
sock **sokk** *n* **(en) 9**
somebody **noen** *p* **5**
something **noe** *p* **5**
soon **snart** *adv* **6**
sorry **om forlatelse 13**
sorry, be **beklage** *v* **(1) 15**
sounds good **høres bra ut 15**
south **sør 16**
southwards **sørover 8**
space **plass** *n* **(en) 3**
sparkling (wine) **musserende** *a* **11**
speech **tale** *n* **(en) 10**
speed **fart** *n* **(en) 13**
speed limit **fartsgrense** *n* **(en) 3**
spoon **skje** *n* **(en) 9**
spring **vår** *n* **(en) 12**
stamp **frimerke** *n* **(et) 5**
stand **stativ** *n* **(et) 5, stå** *v* **(s) 8**
start **begynne** *v* **(2) 9**
start **starte** *v* **(1) 15**
starter **forrett** *n* **(en) 10**
station **stasjon** *n* **(en) 5**
stay overnight **overnatte** *v* **(1) 10**
steep **bratt** *a* **13**
still **fremdeles** *adv* **11, stille** *adv* **8**
stitch **sting** *n* **(et) 8**
stocking **strømpe** *n* **(en) 9**
stop **stoppe** *v* **(1) 4**
stove **ovn** *n* **(en) 13**
strange **rart** *adv* **16; merkelig** *a* **16**
stream **strømme** *v* **(1) 16**
street **gate** *n* **(en/ei) 4**
strictly **strengt** *adv* **3**
strong **kraftig** *a* **8, sterk** *a* **13**
studded tyre **piggdekk** *n* **(et) 13**
study **studere** *v* **(2) 1**
study loan **studielån** *n* **(et) 16**
stupid **dum** *a* **10**
style **stil** *n* **(en) 9**
subsequently **så** *adv* **2**
suddenly **plutselig** *a, adv* **6**
suggest **foreslå** *v* **(s) 12**
suit **dress** *n* **(en) 9, kle** *v* **(4) 9**
summer **sommer** *n* **(en) 1**
sun **sol** *n* **(en/ei) 3**
Sunday **søndag 2**
sunglasses **solbriller** *n* **(pl)**
super **lekker** *a* **9**
supper **aftens** *n* **(en) 10**
sure **sikker** *a* **12**
surge **fosse** *v* **(1) 16**
surgery **legekontor** *n* **(et) 7**
surname **etternavn** *n* **(et) 7**
surprise **forbause** *v* **(1) 10**
sweater **genser** *n* **(en) 9**
Sweden **Sverige 2**
Swedish **svensk** *a* **14**
sweet **søt** *a* **4**
sweet (pudding) **dessert** *n* **(en) 10**

table **bord** *n* **(et) 3**
take **ta** *v* **(s) 2, besette** *v* **(s) 12**
take **part delta** *v* **(s) 11**
talk **snakke** *v* **(1) 3**
tall **høy** *a* **8**
taste **smak** *n* **(en) 9, smake** *v* **(2) 11**

tea **te** *n* **(en) 3**
teacher **lærer** *n* **(en) 2**
tear **tåre** *n* **(en) 10**
telephone **telefon** *n* **(en) 6**
television **televisjon (TV)** *n* **(en) 10**
tell **fortelle** *v* **(s) 7**
telling off **alvorsord** *n* **(et) 7**
ten **ti 2**
tent **telt** *n* **(et) 6**
terrible **fryktelig** *a* **14**
terribly **fryktelig** *adv* **14**
than **enn** *c* **7**
thank **takke** *v* **(1) 10**
thank you **takk 1**
that **som** *p* **2, at** *p* **3, den** *p* **5**
theatre **teater** *n* **(et) 5**
them **dem** *p* **5**
then **da** *adv* **5**
there **der** *adv*, **dit** *adv* **4**
therefore **derfor** *adv* **13**
thermos **termos** *n* **(en) 15**
these **disse** *p* **4**
they **de** *p* **3**
thick **tykk** *a* **4**
thin **tynn** *a* **15**
think **tenke** *v* **(2) 8, synes** *v* **(s) 4, mene** *v* **(2) 5**
thirsty **tørst** *a* **3**
thirteen **tretten 5**
thirty **tretti 5**
this **denne, dette** *p* **5**
this evening **i aften 10**
this morning **i morges 14**
thoughtless **tankeløs** *a* **12**
thousand **tusen 5**
thousands **tusenvis 5**
three **tre 2**
thrive **trives** *v* **(s) 16**
through **gjennom** *pre* **13**
throw **kaste** *v* **(1) 8**
Thursday **torsdag 2**
thus **slik** *a, adv* **1**
ticket **billett** *n* **(en) 2**
tidal flow **tidevannsstrøm** *n* **(en) 16**
tidy **rydde** *v* **(1) 7**
tie up (a boat) **fortøye** *v* **(1) 15**
tights **strømpebukse** *n* **(en) 9**
till **kasse** *n* **(en/ei) 5**
time **gang** *n* **(en) 5, tid** *n* **(en) 2**
tinsel **glitter** *n* **(et) 11**
tiny **bitteliten** *a* **12**
tired **trett** *a* **13**
to **til** *pre* **1**
toast **riste** *v* **(1) 3**
today **i dag 7**
together **sammen** *adv* **2**
toilet **toalett** *n* **(et) 15**
tomorrow **i morgen 2**
too **for** *adv* **8**
tot (drink) **dram** *n* **(en) 11**
touch **røre** *v* **(2) 8**
tourism **turisme** *n* **(en) 12**
towards **mot** *pre* **8**
tower **tårn** *n* **(et) 4**
town hall **rådhus** *n* **(et) 4**
town **by** *n* **(en) 3**
tradition **tradisjon** *n* **(en) 11**
traffic **trafikk** *n* **(en) 15**
train **tog** *n* **(et) 1**
tram **trikk** *n* **(en) 4**
travel **fare** *v* **(s) 11, reise** *v* **(2) 1**
tree **tre** *n* **(et) 11**
trip **tur** *n* **(en) 7**
troll **troll** *n* **(et) 9**

trouble **bry** *n* **(et) 12**
trousers **bukse** *n* **(en) 9**
true **sann** *a* **5**
try **prøve** *v* **(3) 8**
Tuesday **tirsdag 2**
tune **melodi** *n* **(en) 14**
turn **svinge** *v* **(2) 13; tur** *n* **(en) 10**
turquoise **turkis** *a* **9**
twelve **tolv 5**
twenty **tjue 5**
two **to 2**
typical **typisk** *adv* **3**
tyre **dekk** *n* **(et) 13**

ugly **stygg** *a* **9**
unbelievable **utrolig** *a* **16**
uncle **onkel** *m* **(en) 7**
under **under** *pre* **11**
underpants **underbukse** *n* **(en/ei) 9**
understand **forstå** *v* **(s) 6**
unfortunately **dessverre** *adv* **12**
up **opp** *pre* **6**
us **oss** *p* **6**
use **bruke** *v* **(2) 9**
usual **vanlig** *a* **13**

vacant **ledig** *a* **6**
vegetable **grønnsak** *n* **(en) 10**
very **veldig** *adv* **3, meget** *adv* **3**
vest **trøye** *n* **(en) 9**
view **utsikt** *n* **(en) 8**
Viking ship **vikingskip** *n* **(et) 6**
visit **besøke** *v* **(2) 7, besøk** *n* **(et) 7**
voice **stemme** *n* **(en) 16**

waffle **vaffel** *n* **(en) 10**
wait **vente** *v* **(1) 6**
waiter **servitør** *n* **(en) 15**
wake up **våkne** *v* **(1) 8**
war **krig** *n* **(en) 14**
warm **varm** *a* **8**
wash **vaske** *v* **(1) 7**
washroom **vaskerom** *n* **(et) 13**
watch-maker **urmaker** *n* **(en) 12**
water **vann** *n* **(et) 4**
wave **vinke** *v* **(1) 14**
we **vi** *p* **2**
weak **svak** *a* **7**
wear **bruke** *v* **(2) 9**
weather **vær** *n* **(et) 5**
Wednesday **onsdag 2**
week **uke** *n* **(en/ei) 5**
welcome **velkommen** *a* **10**
well **bra** *adv* **1, brønn** *n* **(en) 13, godt** *adv* **3**
west **vest 12**
wet **våt** *a* **8**
what **hva** *p* **1**
what kind of **hva slags 5**
when **da** *c* **7, når** *adv* **1**
where **hvor** *adv* **1**
whether **om** *c* **12**
which **hvilken** *p* **5, som** *p* **2**
while **mens** *c* **7, stund** *n* **(en) 6**
white **hvit** *a* **7**
white wine **hvitvin** *n* **(en) 3**
who **hvem** *p* **4**
who **som** *p* **2**
whole **hel** *a* **2**
why **hvorfor** *adv* **2**
wife **kone** *n* **(en/ei) 10**
window **vindu** *n* **(et) 11**
window seat **vindusplass** *n* **(en) 6**
wine **vin** *n* **(en) 3**
winter **vinter** *n* **(en) 12**

wise **klok** *a* **16**
wish **ønske** *v* **(1) 10, ønske** *n* **(et) 11**
with **med** *pre* **1**
without **uten** *pre* **8**
wonder **lure på** *v* **(2) 16**
wood panelling **trepanel** *n* **(et) 13**
wool **ull** *n* **(en) 9**
work **arbeide** *v* **(1) 4, jobbe** *v* **(1) 12**
working day **arbeidsdag** *n* **(en) 10**
world **verden** *n* **(en) 14**
worst **verst** *a* **6**
wound **sår** *n* **(et) 8**
write **skrive** *v* **(s) 8**
wrong **galt** *adv* **13**

year **år** *n* **(et) 7**
yellow **gul** *a* **4**
yes **ja 1, jo 6**
yesterday **i går 6**
you **du** *(subject) p* **1, deg** *(object) p* **1, dere** *pl* **6**
you (formal) **De** *p* **9**
young **ung** *a* **9**
your, yours **din** *p* **5; deres** *p* **9**
yuk! **Æsj! 7**

Index

Bold numbers refer to units.